Inventing Leonardo

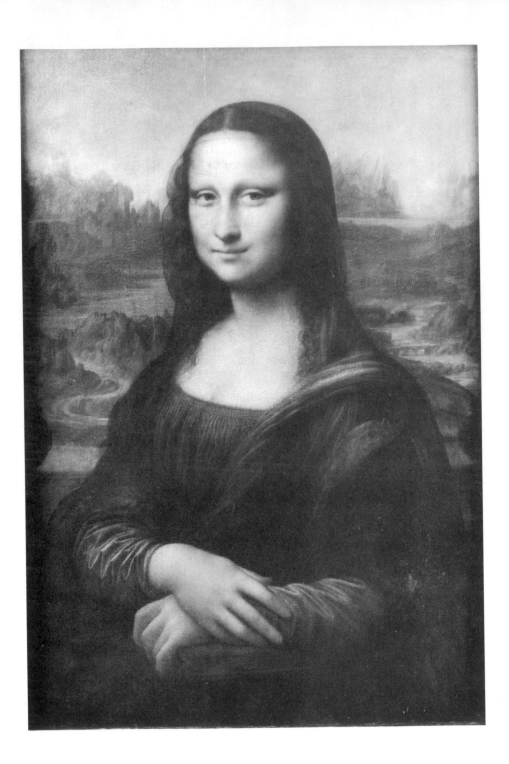

INVENTING LEONARDO

A. Richard Turner

UNIVERSITY OF CALIFORNIA PRESS

Berkeley   Los Angeles

University of California Press
Berkeley and Los Angeles

First Paperback Printing 1994

Library of Congress Cataloging-in-Publication Data

Turner, Richard, 1932–
    Inventing Leonardo / A. Richard Turner.
        p.   cm.
    Includes bibliographical references and index.
    ISBN 0-520-08938-3 (pbk. : alk. paper)
    1. Leonardo, da Vinci, 1452–1519—Criticism and interpretation.
I. Leonardo, da Vinci, 1452–1519.   II. Title.
N6923.L33T87   1994
709'.2—dc20   94-11338
                                                             CIP

Manufactured in the United States of America

        1   2   3   4   5   6   7   8   9

Frontispiece (fig. 1): Leonardo, *Lady on a Balcony* (or *Mona Lisa*).
Louvre, Paris

The paper used in this publication meets the minimum
requirements of American National Standard for Information
Sciences—Permanence of Paper for Printed Library Materials,
ANSI Z39.48–1984. ♾

FOR JANE AND SUSAN,
AND IN MEMORY OF
RENS

In love and friendship,
". . . as new as the foam, as old as the rock."

Contents

PART III
LEONARDO NOW

Acknowledgments

GIVEN TWO CENTURIES of study on Leonardo da Vinci on the part
of scores of distinguished students, at this point any new general book
on him incurs enormous debts, and at worst is an act of benign plagiarism. I warmly if inadequately acknowledge those debts in my Bibliography, and hope that this synthesis based on the work of many others
will shed some new light on understanding the presence of the idea of
Leonardo among us.

This book originated in conversations with Rensselaer W. Lee some
twenty years ago, and my first serious reading and looking at art related
to this project were done in the 1970s in Florence, where I enjoyed the
hospitality of the Harvard Center for Italian Renaissance Studies and the
Kunsthistorisches Institut.

I returned to America to become a full-time college administrator,
and the project was shelved for more than a decade. I resumed work on
it in the mid-eighties, and am grateful to New York University for a
paid leave of absence, and to the Institute for Advanced Study in Princeton for residency at a critical juncture.

As is usually the case, so in mine wittingly and unwittingly many
colleagues, students, and friends have assisted in various ways, particularly those at New York University in the Department of Fine Arts,
the Institute of Fine Arts, and the New York Institute for the Humanities. I would like to especially thank Luisa Coliati Arano, Leonor Gon-
zalez, Constance Herndon, Irving and Marilyn Lavin, and Craig Smyth.

What more generous gift is there than that of colleagues, friends, and
relatives who read a manuscript in progress and evaluate it candidly?
This book is better than it would have been because of the comments
of Denis Donoghue, Isabelle Hyman, Susan Resneck Pierce, and Jane
Turner.

As for my editor, Susan Ralston, what higher praise can I give than to say working with her was fun from beginning to end? No amount of thanks is sufficient.

The transition from a mess to IBM disk was patiently and ably done by Christine Mitchell.

Thanks to Carol Kerlinger for several line drawings, and to David A. Brown for assistance with illustrations.

Translations from Leonardo, save the very last, are by Richter, McMahon, or O'Malley and Saunders (see the bibliography, page 242). Translations from other writers, where not my own, are credited in the bibliographies to individual chapters.

Finally, there are those few who manage to keep one whole—the late Rens Lee, who always wore his erudition lightly; my friend and fellow veteran in the administrative wars, Susan Pierce; and my partner of nearly forty years, Jane Turner. To these boon companions on the road this book is dedicated.

A. RICHARD TURNER
Cape May, New Jersey
January 1992

Inventing Leonardo

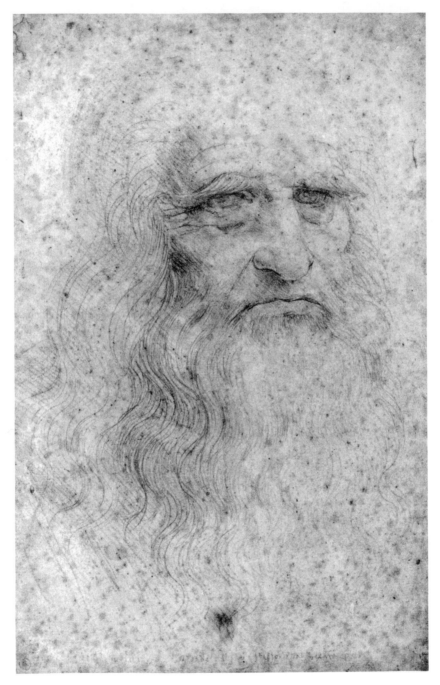

Fig. 2: Leonardo, So-called *Self-Portrait*. Royal Library, Turin

Introduction

THIS BOOK is about the cultural consequences of Leonardo da
Vinci. I write for a general reader who is basically conversant
with the languages of literature and the visual arts, curious about
Leonardo, but as yet perhaps not knowing very much about him or his
posthumous fortune.

Knowledge of the genesis of Leonardo, of the formative factors of his
cast of mind and work, speaks only partially to the question of why he
has been valued through the centuries, and why we value him today.
Why after his death did figures as diverse as Vasari, Goethe, Michelet,
Pater, Valéry, and Freud—to mention only a few—offer such passionate
but differing interpretations of Leonardo? What did they see in him?
Was it that each writer needed something from him? Why is it that
essays written on him today inevitably address different issues than essays written a century ago? Can we achieve anything like historical
certainty about Leonardo, or does the center of anything that could be
called the holding truth about him lie more in the manner in which
successive interpretations illuminate the nature of the era in which each
was written? These are some of the questions to be explored in what
might be called essays in cultural consequences.

Leonardo and his works are quicksilver in the hands of historians for
two reasons. First, he belongs to that select circle of men and women
who produced masterpieces. And second, Leonardo in his own day had
the honor, and perhaps the misfortune, to be called the New Apelles.

Masters and masterpieces tend to roil the waters of written history.
Mona Lisa, probably the world's best-known painting, is surely a masterpiece if ever there was one (fig. 1). The historian may tell us that the
portrait was painted in the first decade of the sixteenth century, and
may have a few things to report about its cultural context and the pos-

sible identity of the sitter. Yet that same historian usually does not go on to complain that *Mona Lisa* exasperatingly refuses to stay anchored in her time. Rather she floats on the stream of history down to our own day, claiming a perpetual relevance in a succession of ages. The rise and fall of reputations is not for her, nor will her obituary list positions held and surviving relatives. Indeed the living issues of which she partakes assure that there will be no need for an obituary, now or later.

This is to say no more than *Mona Lisa,* as we have come to understand her, is as much or more the creation of a succession of interpreters as she is of Leonardo himself. Masterpieces have not only something sufficiently provocative about them to sustain continuing interpretations, but also the resiliency and toughness to withstand the deluge of words. Masterpiece status, then, has to do with the fusion of an artifact and the words written about it. These words are intended to persuade us— persuade, not demonstrate—that the work in question embodies enduring values that transcend historical particularities.

What is true of *Mona Lisa* holds for Leonardo in general. An unambiguous history of the man and his work seems all but an impossibility, and in any event does not take us far in discovering just what it is that we so value in the cultural inheritance that bears the name Leonardo. The significance of the aura surrounding Leonardo is bound to the innumerable stories told about him, stories often shot through with affective issues couched in the rhetoric of persuasion. Of course, many of these stories can be shrugged off as bad history, yet their value, like that of imaginative literature, centers not in their historical veracity but rather in their capacity to suggest something of what it is to be human.

There is, I suppose, a tendency to make up more and better stories about people who seem to possess dimensions broader than those of ordinary lives. When relatively little is known about an individual, there are fewer constraints in telling the story. And that is where the problem of being the New Apelles comes in. It was normal practice in the Renaissance to link an illustrious contemporary with an ancient forerunner. For instance, Apelles was a famed painter of ancient Greece, and Leonardo's name was paired with his, it has been argued, in the belief that Leonardo had revived Apelles's dark manner of painting. However the coupling of these two names began, in retrospect it is problematic. Apelles is famous simply because ancient writers tell us so; not a paint-

ing survives to corroborate their assertions. Apelles, then, is all reputation and no surviving product. In this respect, Leonardo is a highly
plausible candidate to be the New Apelles, if not in the way the Renaissance intended the compliment. Until only a century ago, when publication of Leonardo's notebooks began, knowledge of him was sketchy.
His few paintings tended to be lost in the oblong blur of modest images
made by his Milanese followers; his most famous works were destroyed, never completed, or in ruin; the some seven thousand sheets of
his notes and drawings (surviving from a corpus perhaps three times as
large) lay in various libraries, mainly unseen, let alone carefully studied;
and of this man who spent much of his time as a technologist and
engineer, not a machine or battlement survives.

Leonardo had a great reputation, all right, provided for him in the
beginning by the writers of his own time. While not all that he did had
disappeared, as had happened to Apelles, what remained was fragmentary, inchoate, and the source of endless confusion. In this situation it
was easy enough to make up good stories about Leonardo. While "fact-
checkers" in the form of serious scholars began to emerge in some numbers around 1800, the history of Leonardo's fate until the late nineteenth
century is mainly a story of critical interpretations unhindered by the
protocols of what might be called systematic modern scholarship.

This book is largely about these critical interpretations and the con-
texts from which they arose. It is not a history of scholarship on Leonardo, nor is it about later artists' responses to him, both of which are
fascinating but quite different subjects.

The book is divided into three parts. The first is "A Working Life,"
using the word "working" to mean two things: a brief account of the
work he did, and a summary of the information that most scholars agree
on as the basis for any working interpretation. This may serve as an
introduction for the reader new to Leonardo, or as a quick review for
those already informed.

The second part is "The Anatomy of a Legend." In his copious notes
on anatomy, Leonardo records his frustration in attempting to distin-
guish among the various layers and systems when confronted with the
moist viscera of the body cavity. So it is with the layers of the legend
of Leonardo, extending from Vasari to Freud. There is a 1550 Leonardo,
an 1800 one, an 1850 one, and so on. Each is a different character based

on the needs of the given time that produced him, and each has ties to the Leonardo that went before.

The last part is "Leonardo Now." With no pretense to comprehensiveness or depth, these four final essays discuss issues by juxtaposing present concerns and Leonardo's themes in a way that I believe may be illuminating. I suggest neither that Leonardo is a precursor of our time, nor that the only codes worth considering in exploring him are those of the late twentieth century. Nevertheless, try as we may to transcend it, we cannot help but be partial prisoners of our own age.

Memories are essential to any wise perspective on the present. The significances of Leonardo, and surely they are multiple—as are those of any great figure—are only unearthed and made relevant to our own time through an archaeology of memory. Without those memories, the living present, which is the only holy ground we can know with certainty, is barren soil.

> Home is where one starts from. As we grow older
> The world becomes stranger, the pattern more complicated
> Of dead and living. Not the intense moment
> Isolated, with no before and after,
> But a lifetime burning in every moment
> And not the lifetime of one man only
> But of old stones that cannot be deciphered.
> —T.S. ELIOT, *Four Quartets*

PART I

A WORKING LIFE

*Being a brief account in three chapters of the life
and works of Leonardo da Vinci, stressing what
reasonably may be said to be known about him and—
just as important—what is not known about him.*

SELF-REVELATION was not Leonardo's strong suit. Although he kept copious notes for some thirty-five years, they yield little concerning his personal feelings, daily activities, or relationships to other people. This so-called universal man in fact possessed penetrating brilliance only in several delimited areas, most notably painting, engineering/technology, and the study of the human body. Other fields from the nineteenth century onward called history, politics, sociology, anthropology, and most of the humanities held slight if any interest for him. His written notes in his preferred areas of concentration have a strongly empirical and only at times hypothesizing flavor, concerned as they are with the close observation of phenomena and attempted explanations of how things work. They contain few expressions of Leonardo's subjective judgments or values.

The bits and pieces of testimony about Leonardo by his contemporaries are also disappointing. The picture emerges of a multitalented man, yet one diverted too often from his allegedly proper vocation as a painter, a vacillator unable to bring his projects to completion. But there is no commentary from his own time that can be called intimately revealing; and the literary portraits written after his death must be evaluated in terms of the conventions of biography of the day.

Our building blocks for a working life, then, will tell us far less than we would like to know about the man, but much about his work. Those blocks consist of documents—accidental and sporadic as documents from a distant time usually are—and the surviving words and images from Leonardo's own hand.

Words and images must be interpreted, and because images are mute, it is all too easy to tell stories about them of which they themselves are

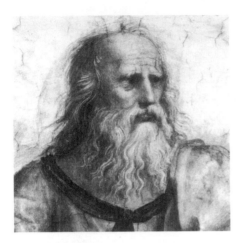

Fig. 3: Raphael, *School of Athens* (detail: Plato). Stanza della Segnatura, Vatican City

innocent. Before embarking on Leonardo's life, I offer an example as a cautionary note.

The striking red-chalk drawing of a bearded man, at Turin, is almost always identified as a self-portrait (fig. 2) and holds the place of honor as frontispiece in a number of books on Leonardo. An image almost too good to be true, it represents a man rich in years and filled with wisdom. This drawing has become a talisman of Leonardo, and indeed the embodiment of genius in general. But is it in fact a self-portrait? The drawing first came to light in the 1840s in Italy, although it (or a drawing like it) served as the model for an engraved frontispiece of a book on *The Last Supper* published in Milan in 1810. If it is indeed a faithful portrait of Leonardo, it would have to have been done late in his life (he died in 1519 at the age of sixty-seven, perhaps handicapped by a stroke in his last years).

Are there other images that might be self-portraits? Yes, for instance the drawing of a bearded old man by a pupil, which is similar to the famous woodcut that heads the chapter on Leonardo in Giorgio Vasari's *Lives of the Most Eminent Painters, Sculptors, and Architects* (edition of 1568), the first extended treatment of artists' lives and works written since antiquity. But these portraits are in profile, not full face. Barring some yet-to-be-made discovery, there was no tradition for three centuries of a frontal portrait of Leonardo; and the only exceptions have been forgeries, of which one of the most famous is in the portrait gallery of the Uffizi in Florence.

Could there be an alternative identification of the subject of the Turin drawing? In Raphael's *School of Athens* (1511), Plato and Aristotle hold court among the assembled philosophers of antiquity. Aristotle is younger and swarthy, Plato a balding and bearded sage (fig. 3) who bears a striking resemblance to the so-called *Self-Portrait* of Leonardo. What is to be concluded? Is the Turin drawing a straight self-portrait, an idealized philosopher type, or a self-portrait as a philosopher? There is no sure way to decide. All that is certain is that it was during the nineteenth century—not the sixteenth—that Leonardo's Turin drawing came to be regarded as a self-portrait.

To choose one identification over another is to choose one story as preferable to another. In our heart of hearts we know what we want the answer to be: somehow our idea of Leonardo is diminished if this old man is in fact not Leonardo. But in truth it may not be Leonardo, in which case the iconic center of our received image of Leonardo does not hold, and we are compelled to tell a different sort of story. *Caveat emptor!*

CHAPTER I

The Making of an Artist-Artisan

A BRIEF ACCOUNT of Leonardo and his work in the form that follows could have been written only during the past century, because it is based heavily on the notebooks. These were first systematically studied in the 1870s, with initial publication in facsimile and transcription in 1881. In 1883 J. P. Richter published his anthology of Leonardo's writings, *The Literary Works of Leonardo da Vinci,* and the way was opened to a wider public understanding of the man whose work had been so largely a mystery for several centuries.

Leonardo da Vinci was born on April 15, 1452 in or near Vinci on the slopes of Monte Albano west of Florence. He was the illegitimate son of a peasant woman named Caterina and a notary, Ser Piero di Antonio. Caterina soon married another man, and the young Leonardo was taken into his father's household, where he was joined by legitimate offspring of Ser Piero's third and fourth marriages.

Next to nothing is known of Leonardo's early education. Later in his life he described himself as an *"omo sanza lettere"*—a man without letters—and expressed contempt for those who favored book learning over direct experience. Nonetheless, at one point Leonardo recorded ownership of 116 books, and at about the age of forty made a valiant attempt, apparently not wholly successful, to learn Latin. Since Leonardo's father was a notary, and therefore literate, it is almost certain that Leonardo would have had a sound elementary education.

Leonardo was apprenticed to the artist Andrea del Verrocchio in about 1467 at age fifteen (if the year is correct), several years older than the norm for an apprentice.

While there were a number of artists' workshops in Florence in the 1460s, those of Verrocchio and the brothers Pollaiuolo were the most prestigious. Leonardo came to Florence when it was under the *de facto* rule of the Medici; and although it was a city in financial decline, Florence had, since shortly after Leonardo's birth, enjoyed both peace and a flourishing of the arts. Indeed, the city indisputably was the European capital of the arts, and while it lacked an important university, it was a stronghold of humanist learning.

In Florence during the course of the fifteenth century, the medieval view of the artist as a humble craftsman slowly gave way to that of the artist as a man worthy of intellectual and social respect. Leonardo later was to become the epitome of the artist raised to privileged status, his works sought by the great men of Europe. But around 1470 that was still a long way off for a youth in a traditional artist's workshop. Leonardo's day-to-day activities in Verrocchio's studio are not known, but like all apprentices he must have begun with the simple aspects of preparing materials, practiced drawing incessantly, and eventually assisted in the design and making of objects. Some of these objects were what today we call art, while others were strictly utilitarian. There was less of a distinction between the two categories then than there is now.

Very little is known about Leonardo until the late 1470s. Did he remain in Florence? Did he travel? He joined the Painters' Guild in 1472, and was a member of Verrocchio's household in 1476, a fact known through a court record of an anonymous charge of sodomy, of which Leonardo was cleared. (This incident aside, the cumulative evidence suggests that Leonardo was indeed a homosexual, something of which Freud was to make much in 1910.) In 1476 Leonardo may have been with Verrocchio for ten years, and it is likely that by then his apprenticeship status had evolved into some sort of business arrangement, probably a partnership. The works of these years attributed to Leonardo (but undocumented) suggest several things: that Leonardo was by an early age a brilliant draftsman but not particularly precocious as a painter, and that he confined himself to making art as opposed to the diverse activities that would engage him later (a judgment based on the limitations of what has survived from that period).

The earliest dated object from Leonardo's hand is a small sepia ink landscape drawing (fig. 4), inscribed in the upper-left corner in his usual right-to-left mirror writing "Day of Holy Mary of the Snows, 5 August 1473." (Rather than a way to disguise his thoughts, as many have claimed, Leonardo's mirror writing is probably more simply explained as the

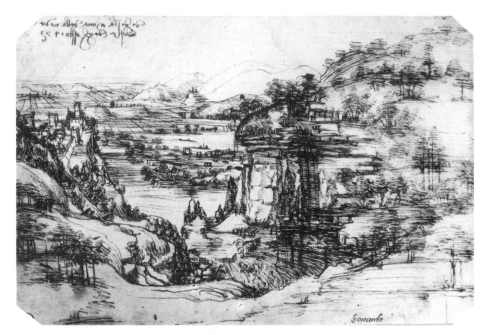

Fig. 4: Leonardo, Landscape 1473. Uffizi, Florence

natural way for a left-hander to write.) Is the little landscape drawn from nature? The inscription makes it tempting to think so—that, freed from his daily obligations on a feast day, Leonardo had gone to the hills above the Arno River and drawn one of the first pure landscapes since classical antiquity. But the hand of tradition may well have guided the pen.

With Leonardo's first dated work, questions arise that must inform any general inquiry about him. How much is original, how much borrowed? What is the relation between things observed, inherited visual conventions, and things imagined?

Any certainties about Leonardo's role as a painter in Verrocchio's workshop are lost in time. There is near-unanimity, concerning his authorship, about only one painting and part of another, and none of the works merely attributed to him are dated. Giorgio Vasari, in his *Lives of the Most Eminent Painters, Sculptors, and Architects,* more than once savors the literary device of having young artists make spectacular entries upon the artistic scene. According to his account, Leonardo painted one

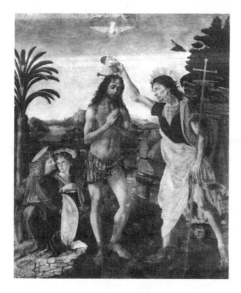

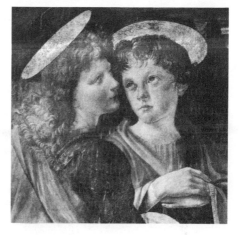

Fig. 5: Andrea del Verrocchio and Leonardo, *Baptism*. Uffizi, Florence
Fig. 6: *Baptism* (detail)

of the two angels in Verrocchio's *Baptism of Christ,* done originally for the monastery of San Salvi, and which today is in the Uffizi (figs. 5 and 6). Verrocchio, as Vasari tells it, was so overwhelmed at being surpassed by a mere youth that he gave up painting altogether. Whatever the improbability of the anecdote (Verrocchio was probably delighted to find himself freed for his main concern, sculpture), few have doubted the presence of Leonardo's hand in the softly modeled face and fluffy hair of the angel seen in profile, so in contrast to the tighter line and oily modeling of the hair of the pug-nosed angel on the right. The style of the latter is the same as in the figure of John the Baptist, and the landscape to the right exemplifies Verrocchio's version of the style generally prevalent in Florence around 1470, incisively linear with firm and taut surfaces. The center and the left side of the painting are handled less austerely, and analysis shows that Verrocchio's tempera painting (a mixture of egg yolk and water-based paint) was both extended and gone over in part in oils. The vaporous landscape to the left, the river, the foreground, and the reworking of the head and body of Christ are all by Leonardo.

When was the painting done, and what was the relationship between the two men and its execution? We simply do not know. The painting may have been begun in the early 1470s, for some reason left unfinished by Verrocchio, and later completed by Leonardo. Whether that may have been in 1472 or as much as six years later is anyone's guess.

If the *Baptism* leaves questions unanswered, another large painting of the period, the *Annunciation to the Virgin* (from Monteoliveto, and today in the Uffizi), compounds the difficulties of sorting out Leonardo's beginnings. It is undocumented, and until the mid-nineteenth century was not thought of in terms of Leonardo, but since then has been attributed to Leonardo in its entirety, or seen as a collaboration, as a design by Leonardo executed by others, and as a design by someone else in which Leonardo had a hand in the execution.

The ambiguities surrounding the *Baptism* and the *Annunciation* reveal the gaps in our understanding of the young Leonardo, a problem only intensified if several other paintings are also considered: a small *Madonna* (now in Washington), thought by some to be Leonardo's first work, a much-contested *Annunciation* (in Paris), and a *Madonna* (in Munich).

Verrocchio's workshop comprised a number of individuals who freely collaborated to complete a work of art in the style and to the standards of Verrocchio himself. There was a job to be done and an *ad hoc* team did it, something quite different from modern notions of art as creative activity in the hands of an autonomous individual. There is one painting from these years that is almost uncontested as a Leonardo, the *Portrait of Ginevra de' Benci,* now in Washington, D.C. (fig. 7). First attributed to Leonardo in the mid-nineteenth century, it was later identified as the painting, mentioned in early sources, of Ginevra, who married at age seventeen in 1474. *Ginevra* is the Italian word for "juniper," the species of evergreen that appears in the spray behind the woman's head. A truncated wreath on the back of the painting, and a variation on the painting showing crossed hands (done by another Verrocchio pupil later on), make it clear that at some time the panel was cut down and that about eight inches were removed from the bottom.

The portrait is hardly remarkable as a psychological study, for this light-complexioned, heavy-lidded beauty seems to reveal little of her inner self, apart from a certain seriousness. But as an object rendered in light and shade, it is a marvel. Firm bone structure is subordinated to a finely nuanced modeling of pearly flesh, working from the highlighted forehead to the light-infused shadows of the neck. The flesh is set in a

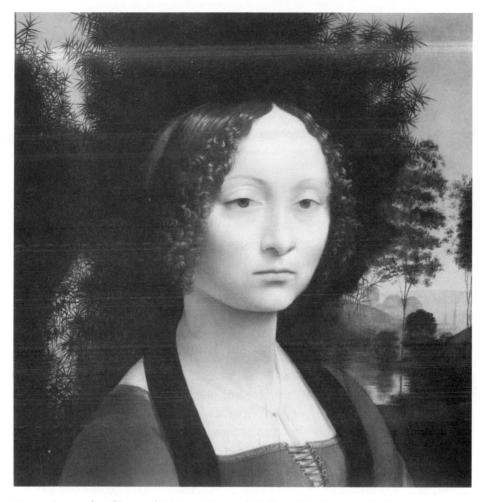

Fig. 7: Leonardo, *Ginevra de' Benci*. National Gallery, Washington, D.C.

frame created by the blacks and browns of the bodice, with blue-grays above in the heavy atmosphere of a humid day in the landscape to the right. Even allowing for darkening of the foliage through time, the picture is far more an exercise in monochrome than it is in color. Like the *Annunciation,* it lacks strong color spotting of the sort most usual in Florentine painting of the time. While Leonardo evidently considered Flemish painting in achieving his textures, he was thinking in tonalities rather than chromatics. Basically he is a draftsman.

For Leonardo, as for all young Florentine artists, drawing was the

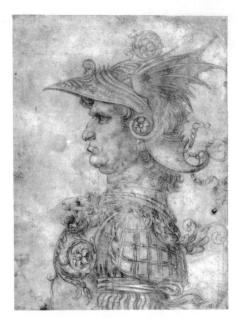

Fig. 8: Leonardo, *Warrior in Profile*.
British Museum, London

heart of the formation of artistic competence. Early on he made studies of drapery, sculpturally realized in light and shade. Other drawings seem ends in themselves, such as a masterful one in silverpoint (a silver stylus used on coated paper) of an ancient warrior in fantastic cuirass and helmet (fig. 8). Varying from taut, coiled lines to languid curves, the linear flow circumscribes surfaces with little tonal gradation between light and shadow. The rough topography of the man's face contrasts with the porcelain smoothness of Ginevra's, yet they share a subtly graded modeling.

Whatever the purpose of this sheet, in subject it is closely related to relief sculptures emanating from Verrocchio's studio during that period, raising the question as to what extent the young Leonardo may have had direct experience as a sculptor.

In 1478 the Pazzi family and their allies led a dramatic but failed attempt to overthrow the Medici, at a mass in Florence's cathedral. The conspirators attacked Lorenzo de' Medici and his younger brother Giuliano, killing the latter. Leonardo made a life sketch a year later of one of the extradited conspirators hanging from the ramparts of the Bargello (fig. 9). Beside the image is a curiously clinical written description of

Fig. 9: Leonardo, *Hanged Conspirator*. Musée Bonnat, Bayonne

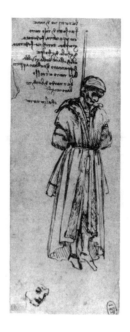

the traitor's clothing, one of the first symptoms of Leonardo's equipoise, if not indeed indifference, in the face of great public passions.

The year 1478 is the first in which Leonardo begins to emerge from the historical shadows. He received a public commission to do an altarpiece for the Chapel of Saint Bernard in the governmental Palazzo della Signoria, a sure sign that he already had a substantial reputation. Leonardo received a payment in March, but apparently never delivered the painting. It seems that the rising young artist inexplicably walked away from his first major opportunity as an independent practitioner. It was not to be the last time that Leonardo left major tasks unfinished.

A 1478 profile of a hook-nosed man, figuratively speaking a relative of the silverpoint warrior, is one of several images drawn by Leonardo in pen and ink on a single sheet now in the Uffizi. The sheet offers a couple of interesting pieces of information. The first is that Leonardo was now concerned with machinery, as he probably had been for a decade (although visual evidence for this assertion is slim). Leonardo's other pre–1481 material, done before he left for Milan, suggests that his focus was now broadening to engage a number of new fields from optics to war machinery. The second piece of information is an incomplete

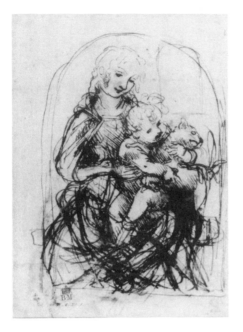

Fig. 10: Leonardo, *Madonna and Child with a Cat.* British Museum, London

inscription that states that the master began two Madonnas late in the year. A number of surviving sketches may relate to these, small and rapidly executed preliminary drawings that consider alternative ideas of mother and child, including one with fruit and another with a squirming cat (fig. 10). These drawings variously explore the positioning of masses in a compact figure group, and the overall effect of light and shade. The *Benois Madonna,* now in Saint Petersburg, whose closest prototype is a sketch in Paris, is one outcome of these explorations (fig. 11); it was first attributed to Leonardo early in the twentieth century, a judgment that is widely accepted today.

One of the most interesting of this group of drawings is at Windsor Castle (fig. 12). This complicated drawing raises questions pertinent to many of Leonardo's drawings: In what order were the parts done? At one sitting or at separate times? To what extent observed versus done from memory? The central and largest motif is a kneeling Madonna nursing her child, approached by the nude child John the Baptist, a compositional idea elaborated in several paintings by Raphael about twenty-five years later. The infant Saint John is reiterated in the upper-right corner, mirrored by a mature male, a pair similar in pose but

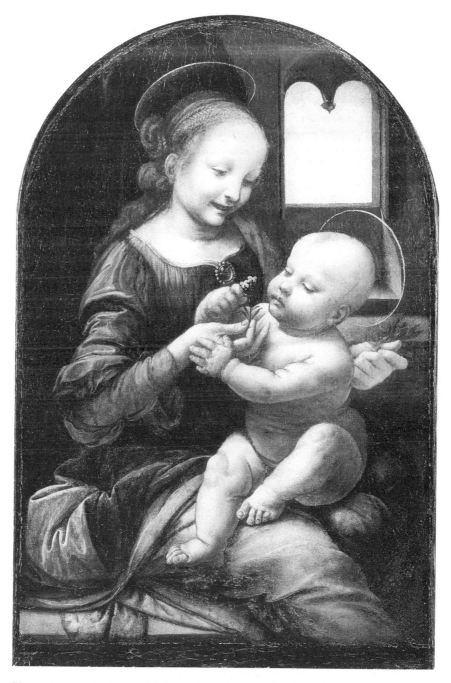

Fig. 11: Leonardo, *Benois Madonna*. Hermitage, Saint Petersburg

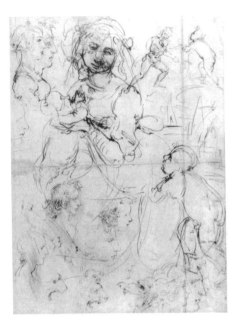

Fig. 12: Leonardo, *Madonna and Child and Other Studies*. Royal Library, Windsor

contrasting in physique. Several heads on the same page are in various states of finish and reveal Leonardo's strong interest in exploring types—youthful and old, male and female, ideal and particularized. Growling animals and a dragon at the bottom of the sheet imply an interest in comparative physiognomy, confirmed in Leonardo's later work. Throughout his career, extremes of ideal beauty and anomalous ugliness fascinated the master, the latter explored in his so-called grotesques, of which the *Five Grotesque Heads* (see fig. 13) is the most famous example.

In either 1480 or 1481, Leonardo was asked to do an altarpiece, subject unspecified, for the monks of San Donato a Scopeto outside Florence. The records of this commission run from March until September 1481, when payments break off. Almost all scholars agree that the unfinished painting is the *Adoration of the Magi,* today in the Uffizi (fig. 14). The painting is on a wood panel made of several pieces, about seven feet square. It is an underpainting—that is, a large monochrome in ochers and browns in which the outline mass of figures are defined prior to the application of color as the last stage. It is a perfect example of the Tuscan approach to art called *disegno. Disegno* literally means "drawing," and, as in English, can refer to either the process or the product, but as a process

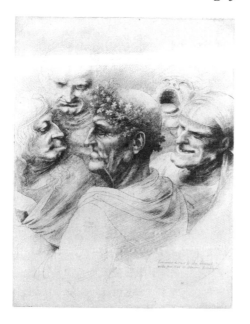

Fig. 13: Leonardo, *Five Grotesque Heads.*
Royal Library, Windsor

had a wider dimension which today we would associate with the word "design." Leonardo later proposed that the task of the painter is to create the illusion of relief where there is none, by giving a convincing effect of three-dimensional objects in a systematically rationalized space; *disegno* was the means to do this, and Leonardo addressed it in his notes in exhaustive detail.

The subject chosen, the adoration of the Magi, was a Florentine favorite. Earlier painters, such as Gentile da Fabriano in 1423, treated the subject as a discursive aristocratic pageant, replete with rich brocades and featuring caparisoned horses and exotic animals in a procession toward the Madonna and Child on one side of the painting. In the 1470s Botticelli moved the Madonna and Child to the center of the composition, an arrangement that Leonardo adopted to create an intellectualized picture whose diverse parts are integrated into a compelling unity.

In Leonardo's version, Mary and the Child, the kings, and the supporting retinue are placed in the foreground before a rise in the land. Ruins lie behind, and horsemen and footmen engage in skirmishes. The image of fighting juxtaposed to ruins possibly symbolizes the discord

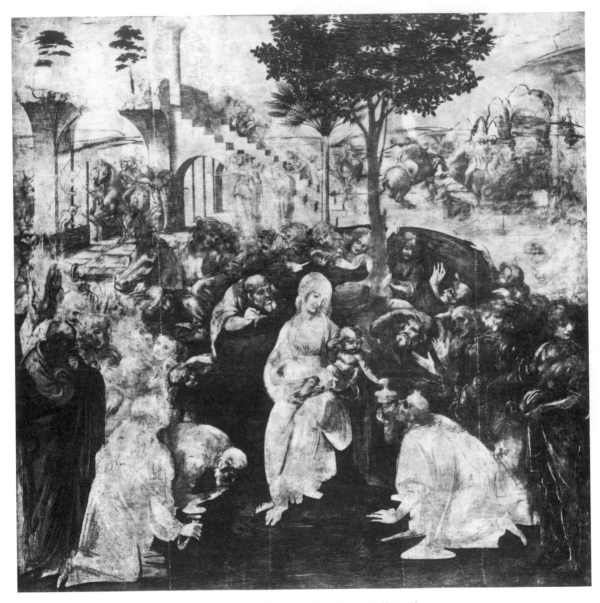

Fig. 14: Leonardo, *Adoration of the Magi*. Uffizi, Florence

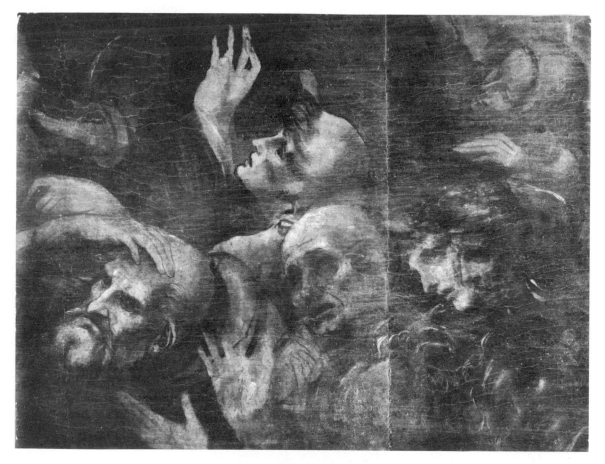

Fig. 15: *Adoration of the Magi* (detail)

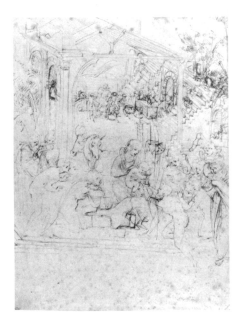

Fig. 16: Leonardo, Composition study for *Adoration of the Magi*. Louvre, Paris

and ruin of the era before Grace, in contrast to the serenity under Grace in the foreground. The painting's unity is achieved through the subordination of many parts to a lucidly simple geometric scheme. Mary's head is at the apex of a triangle formed by her and the attendant Magi. The retinue immediately behind them rings these figures in a half circle.

A diversity of calculated contrasts within a controlling unity is the painting's hallmark. A detail to the right of the Madonna shows Leonardo's mastery in microcosm (fig. 15). A bearded elder shades his eyes as he gazes upon the Madonna and Child, while above a beautiful youth turns his head to one side and gestures to the sky. To the right of the youth another figure gesticulates excitedly, while just below him is a skull-like head. The latter is a literal manifestation of a dictum that Leonardo wrote later, that in order properly to understand a figure one must paint from the bones outward. Contrast of age, variety of gesture, appropriateness of posture and action to the sorts of figures portrayed— all these characteristics also foreshadow Leonardo's later advice to painters. They constitute some of the subsets of his second major dictum, that the task of the painter is to reveal the mind of a person through his/her movement, posture, gesture, and facial expression.

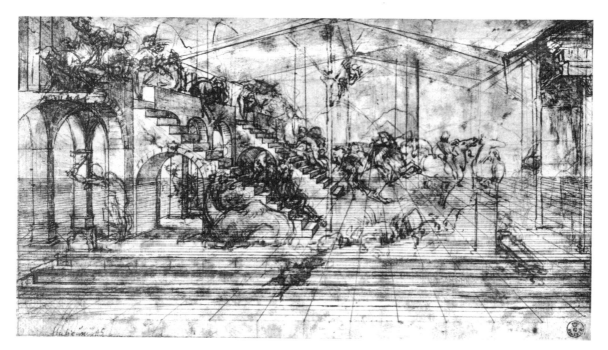

Fig. 17: Leonardo, Perspective study for *Adoration of the Magi*. Uffizi, Florence

Several preparatory drawings survive. A sketch in Paris is a loose version of the whole composition (fig. 16). The basics of the foreground group have been worked out, and, in order to understand the positions of the bodies, Leonardo has rendered most of them nude. Perspective is haphazard, for that is not his interest at the moment. The ruin is on the right instead of the left, and the traditional shed of the Nativity figures prominently, while in the underpainting it has been suppressed. Another drawing, now in the Uffizi (fig. 17), has a different purpose. If not wholly systematic by Leonardo's standards, it is nonetheless a rigorous perspective drawing for the background, in which the shed remains but the ruin has been moved to the left side. The dry science of the perspective grid melds with sketchy, almost spectral images of men, horses, and a camel. It is as if Leonardo's science and his art cannot be separated.

The *Adoration* was almost surely left unfinished because of Leonardo's departure for Milan. Possibly the same is true of his *Saint Jerome,*

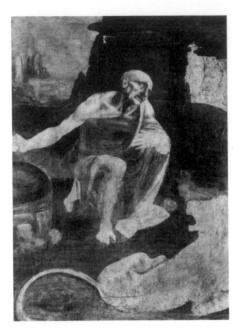

Fig. 18: Leonardo, *Saint Jerome*.
Pinacoteca, Vatican City

(fig. 18) close in style to the *Adoration*. The saint sits before the lion,
which looks two-dimensional in its unfinished state. Jerome's eyes
are sunken, and his neck tendons are painfully stretched as he clutches
the stone of flagellation in his right hand. Craggy rocks rise behind him,
a jagged mountain range is visible to the left, and a church can be seen
through an opening on the right. From the background of the *Baptism*
to the misty far landscape of the *Annunciation* and now in the *Saint
Jerome,* Leonardo reveals a sustained interest in depicting a tortuous
topography.

Leonardo in his twenty-ninth year is fourteen years beyond his probable beginnings with Verrocchio. And what do we now know of him?
Merely a couple of rites of passage, a few significant dates, and the
evidence of things from his hand. How much has been lost—and it must
be considerable—is simply not known.

It seems clear that the *Adoration* marks Leonardo's full coming of age
as an artist, the visual statement of principles he wrote down years later.
A few paintings over a period of fourteen years: that leaves a lot of time
to think about things, to attend to other matters. Probably technological

concerns were already important to him, but drawings and notes relating to these are but a trickle compared to the torrent that began to issue from his pen from the mid-1480s onward. We are left, then, with a picture of Leonardo that comes mainly from his art, and even here the outlines are blurred. Probably within months of receiving his last payment from the monks of San Donato, Leonardo was en route to Milan, where he was to live for nearly twenty years. Why? Had he an irresistible offer of which we have no record? Or had he come to find Florence uncongenial on intellectual, professional, or personal grounds? Or was it possibly a matter of undefined restlessness that seems to have marked Leonardo's life? There are no answers to this major conundrum, among the many that make Leonardo a largely unfathomable figure.

CHAPTER 2

Ducal Servant in Milan

ASARI WOULD HAVE IT that Leonardo brought to Ludovico
Sforza, the *de facto* ruler and later Duke of Milan, a gift—a silver
lyre that the artist himself had fashioned in the form of a horse's
head. There may be some truth to the story, but it hardly accounts for
Leonardo's permanent shift of residence. Possibly it had to do with
Ludovico's desire to erect a bronze equestrian monument to the glory
of his father, the *condottiere* Francesco Sforza. Both father and son were
usurpers of legitimate authority in Milan, and any art suggestive of their
dynastic continuity and stability would have been all to the point.
Equestrian monuments had the authority of antiquity (as with the imperial Marcus Aurelius in Rome and the destroyed *Regisole* at Pavia); and
in Francesco's own time, Donatello had made a monument for the outside of the Church of the Santo in Padua, to memorialize the Venetian
condottiere Erasmo da Narni, called Gattamelata.

It might have been more obvious to Ludovico through his Florentine
correspondents than it is to us that Leonardo was just the man for the
job. The artist had surely observed, and probably participated in, major
metalworking projects by Verrocchio—the Medici tomb in San Lorenzo, the planning for the *Doubting Thomas* group, the bronze *David*.
More to the point, Verrocchio had even competed for the equestrian
monument to the Venetian *condottiere* Bartolommeo Colleoni, and in 1481
a full-scale, leather-coated wooden model was taking shape in his studio. Equipped with the benefits of Verrocchio's example, and probably
well recommended on highest authority, Leonardo may have seized the
opportunity.

Milan in 1481 was considerably larger than Florence (it had a population of 200,000 compared with 65,000). It lay in a plain between the
Alps to the north and the river Po to the south, and was flanked by the

rivers Adda and Ticino to either side. Water was essential to the commercial transportation and sanitation of the city, and hydraulic engineering to provide the needed canals was a constant preoccupation from the later Middle Ages onward. The waterworks supported a considerable base of manufacturing, including armaments production. In short, the city was highly attractive to anyone interested in problems of technology.

While Milan had indigenous artists and a scattering of humanists, their number and illustriousness could not compare to those in Florence. So it must have been Milan's practical challenges rather than its high culture that led Leonardo there. That he saw things this way is revealed in a letter to Ludovico in which the artist offers his services. The letter is not in Leonardo's hand, has numerous corrections suggestive of a draft, is not dated, and has no addressee, though the salutation "Illustrious Lord" leaves little doubt about the identity of the intended recipient. Despite these uncertainties, most scholars believe—largely on the basis of records of later projects undertaken by Leonardo that seem related to the letter—that the letter substantively reflects his thought.

The letter opens with Leonardo's assurance that he has reviewed the available technology for instruments of war, and implies that he can do better. He goes on to list the accomplishments in his portfolio, from plans for siege bridges to mines and artillery. It is a shameless piece of bravura, for the closest Leonardo probably had come to such accomplishments was familiarity with them in books and manuscripts by others, notably the *De re militari* of 1472 by Roberto Valturio, secretary to Sigismondo Malatesta. About halfway into the letter, Leonardo unconsciously reveals his hand by slipping into the future and conditional tenses, and closes by saying he can demonstrate the feasibility of his suggestions in the ducal park. Only at the end of the letter does he claim his expertise in the three major arts, suggesting that "the bronze horse may be taken in hand, which is to the immortal glory and eternal honor of the prince, your happy father of memory."

Given Leonardo's announced agenda, and the participation of Milan in the defense of Ferrara against the Venetians, it is ironic that the first important record of Leonardo's activity in Milan is not as a technologist but as a painter. He shared a commission (dated April 25, 1483) for an altarpiece for the Chapel of the Confraternity of the Conception in San

Francesco Grande (since destroyed), with two local artists, the brothers Evangelista and Ambrogio de' Predis. Leonardo was responsible for the central panel, commonly known as the *Virgin of the Rocks,* which featured the Madonna and Child, young Saint John, and an angel.

There are two very similar surviving versions of the composition—one in the Louvre in Paris (fig. 19) and another in the National Gallery in London. The latter picture is traceable to the chapel itself, yet most scholars believe that it was made later than the picture in Paris. The common working hypotheses put forth to resolve this dilemma suggest the Paris picture (1483–86) was the original altarpiece for the chapel, but at some later point was replaced with the London picture (1490s, but perhaps finished as late as 1508) after the first version was given by Ludovico as a diplomatic gift, either to the French king or the German emperor, depending on the version of the hypotheses one accepts.

In the Paris picture, the four figures are disposed in a triangle just beyond a chasm in the foreground—a device used to separate the sacred world of the holy figures from the mundane space of the viewer. Mary extends her left hand over the blessing Child, while a kneeling angel draws the viewer's attention to the adoring infant Saint John. Despite the red of the angel's garment, this painting, like the *Ginevra de' Benci,* is more a study in tonality than in color. Compared to the *Ginevra,* shadows have deepened, to the degree that light seems a function of shadow rather than vice versa. It is Leonardo's use of sfumato, fully developed. The setting seems a visionary landscape of stalactite and stalagmite, with heavy air hanging over flowing waters. But if it is a vision, it is grounded in experience of the sort recorded in a drawing from these same years. Scholars have exhaustively searched the Bible and its exegetical literature to discover passages that might explain the juxtaposition of these particular figures with a rocky wilderness, and have come up with some plausible interpretations. But the real significance of Leonardo's visionary topography may lie far deeper.

Soon, painting ceased to be Leonardo's chief concern. There are about a half dozen additional pictures from his first stay in Milan, including several portraits attributed to him, the most elegant—and most surely by his hand—being the *Woman with an Ermine* (probably a portrait of

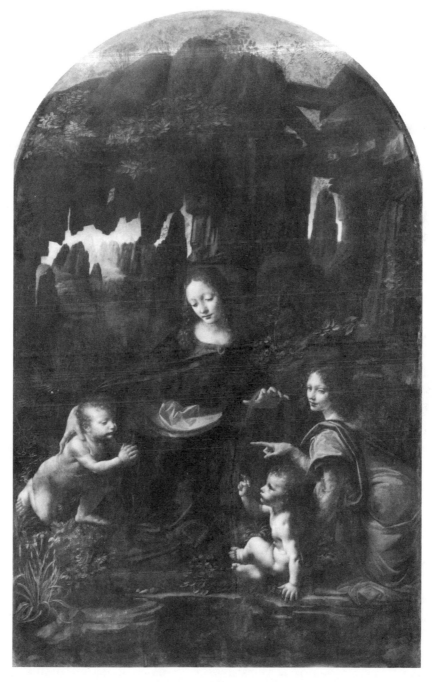

Fig. 19: Leonardo, *Virgin of the Rocks*. Louvre, Paris

Ludovico's mistress Cecilia Gallerani), the Paris version of the *Virgin of the Rocks,* and of course *The Last Supper.*

It is not known when Leonardo began to keep an extensive written and illustrated record of his works, nor what amount of material from the Florentine years has been lost. But barring evidence yet to be discovered, it is likely that Leonardo began keeping notebooks in earnest only in the mid-1480s. His early interest centered on architecture and military technology. A series of drawings from around 1487–90 involve a competition with Bramante and other local architects for the tambour of the Milanese cathedral. In June 1490 he was in Pavia to consult on work for the cathedral with Sienese architect Francesco di Giorgio, whose treatise on architecture Leonardo annotated.

In Pavia he came to know one of the better libraries in Italy. How much Leonardo read and how much he learned by word of mouth is an open question. A 1489 memorandum reads, "Get Messer Fazio to show you about proportionality." "Get the master of arithmetic to show you how to square a circle." "Try to get Vitelone, which is in the library of Pavia, and treats of mathematics." Leonardo was eagerly in search of knowledge, whatever the source.

In the field of architecture, Leonardo's book learning, his professional conversations, his technological skills, and his imagination all coalesced. In the years around 1490 he did a series of brilliant sketches of elevations and plans of centralized churches capped by a dome (see fig. 20). Leon Battista Alberti (1404–74) had earlier advocated a centralized church plan, claiming that the circle on which it is based is the most perfect of forms. Leonardo's church drawings are utterly lucid, based on carefully proportioned, repeated units, and the exterior elevations offer a clear idea of the interior space.

Leonardo also turned his hand to city planning, studying patterns of circulation, and—something that we tend to take for granted in the industrialized world—sanitation. One complex drawing proposes a double-tiered city, with the means for commercial transportation and sanitation afforded by a canal below, and amenable circulation for the citizenry above.

Despite all of this activity, not a building remains that can be attributed to Leonardo, nor is there reason to think that any of his major designs was ever executed. But his seminal ideas on centralized churches

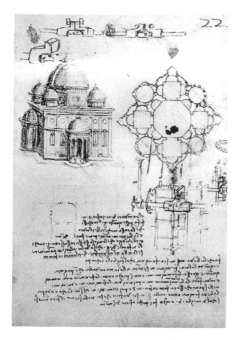

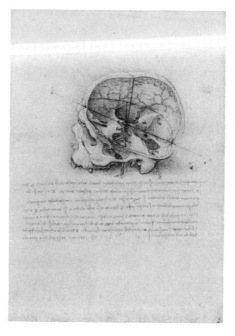

Fig. 20: Leonardo, *A Central Plan Church*. Institut de France, Paris

Fig. 21: Leonardo, *Human Skull*. Royal Library, Windsor

traveled to Rome with Bramante in the late 1490s and came to flower in the central plan for the new basilica of Saint Peter's, begun in 1506 at the behest of Pope Julius II.

In 1489 Leonardo did a series of drawings of the human skull (such as fig. 21), presumably to be associated with a book he intended to write, as reflected in a cryptic marginal note: "on 2 April 1489 book titled *Of the Human Figure.*" The scientific intent of the drawings is clear, yet at the same time these volumetric forms, like the volumes of his domed churches, are aesthetically pleasing, surely viewable in artistic terms. In few places is the art–technology nexus closer in Leonardo, revealing the fundamental importance of drawing to him. In an age before the microscope and telescope, when so much of the written word was freighted with conventional and often erroneous interpretations, the observations of the naked eye as recorded in drawings were a crucially important way to advance knowledge.

Through the 1480s and '90s Leonardo worked on his plans for "the

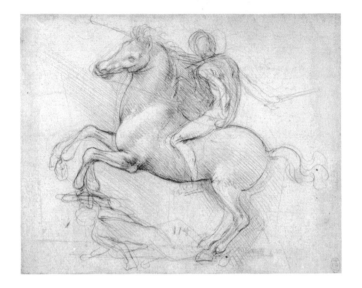

Fig. 22: Leonardo, *Study Related to the Sforza Monument*. Royal Library, Windsor

Horse,'' the great equestrian monument in memory of Francesco Sforza. It was to be some twenty feet high, and would have consumed about 200,000 pounds of bronze. As part of his preparation for the project, Leonardo studied horses, their movements, and their proportions. He considered the idea of Sforza on a horse that is rearing over a fallen warrior with a shield (fig. 22), an ancient motif known from sculpted reliefs, which would have been technically virtually impossible to realize in three dimensions on such a huge scale. Finally, Leonardo decided to portray Sforza on a striding horse, in the manner of Donatello's *Gattamelata* and Verrocchio's *Colleoni*. The work went slowly, and there is some indication that Leonardo withdrew from the project for a time, or was pulled from the job, only to begin again. A notebook in Madrid records ideas for the actual casting of the horse, yet it all came to naught, as was so often the case with Leonardo. This time it was not his fault. The bronze for the horse was diverted to the casting of a cannon, and in 1499 the French shattered the life-size clay model during target practice.

If war had its impact on Leonardo—he called it a *"bestialissima pazzia"* (a beastly madness)—he was nonetheless a master of weapons and fortifications. Yet there is a major question, to be returned to later, as to what extent his projects were practical. And were these schemes new, or merely his record of the work of others? This conundrum applies to Leonardo's technological work in general. Some drawings, such as those of textile machines, look like sketches of what he saw in the factories of Milan, while others, such as a gun barrel boring device, seem proposals for machinery to be fabricated. Whether machines were ever made from Leonardo's designs, none survive, and there is no clear record of them having existed.

The cumulative impression is of Leonardo as a designer with few practical achievements. In some areas his work may have been based on pre-existing technology, such as improvements in the waterworks of Milan, which spurred his interest in hydraulics in the 1490s. But there can be no doubt about the investigative nature, as opposed to applied research, of his approach. In a manuscript of the 1490s he writes, "beginning of the treatise on water," and refers to other books said to be done or promised, but none seems to have reached final fruition. Instead, his interests in these years widened to include optics, mechanics, writing about painting, and the flight of birds.

And then there was Leonardo the courtier. He prepared an elaborate "paradise festival" in 1490 for the marriage of Duke Gian Galeazzo (the *de jure* Duke of Milan, soon to be assassinated) to Isabella of Aragon; and he took part in arranging the festivities for the marriage of Ludovico's niece Bianca Maria Sforza to Emperor Maximilian I in 1493, with the model of "the Horse" as the centerpiece. Nights at court, probably, are reflected in the various riddles, prophecies, tales, and fables he recorded in his notes, as well as in drawings of costumed figures probably related to pageants.

The nineties also saw the beginnings of Leonardo's intense thoughts on the art of painting, which he developed after the turn of the century. These have come down to us in the compilation made by Leonardo's pupil Francesco Melzi after the master's death, and were first published in abridged form in 1651.

The most tangible, if severely damaged, work of the Milanese years is his mural *The Last Supper,* in the refectory of the church of Santa Maria delle Grazie, probably begun in 1495 and finished by 1498 (figs. 23 and 24). Painted in an experimental medium that proved to be disastrously flawed, the mural began to disintegrate during Leonardo's own lifetime, and was described by Vasari only several decades later as

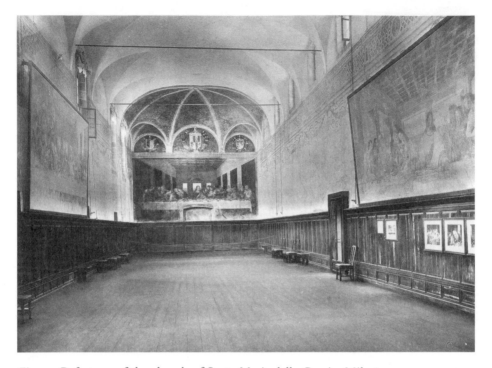

Fig. 23: Refectory of the church of Santa Maria delle Grazie, Milan

a mere spot on a wall. Cleaned and clumsily repainted more than once, the mural is being painstakingly conserved as of this writing, although at best it can be only a shadow of its original appearance.

Leonardo conceived the painting's setting as a trompe l'oeil extension of the end wall of the actual dining hall, with Jesus and the apostles understood as being at the head table, in the traditional Tuscan manner. (Compare it, for instance, to Domenico Ghirlandaio's *Last Supper,* fig. 25.) The painted space, however, belongs to an ideal world: the perspectival viewing point is well above a viewer's head, and the walls are skewed inward to create a trapezoidal rather than rectangular room, which has the visual effect of pushing the table with its thirteen men to the immediate foreground.

There has been much written about the narrative and theological nuances of the interpretation, but the basic point could not be more clear: Jesus has announced that one of the gathered company will betray him, and waves of emotion roll through his apostles.

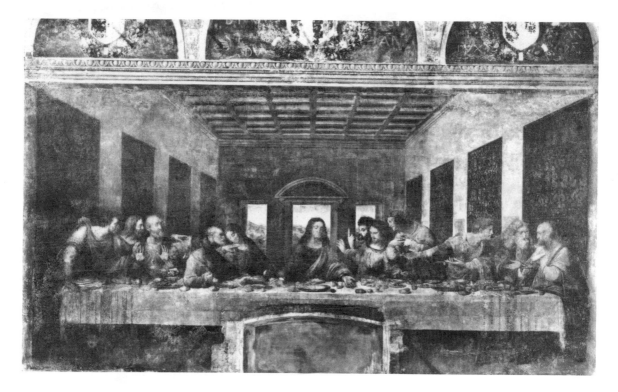

Fig. 24: Leonardo, *The Last Supper*. Santa Maria delle Grazie, Milan

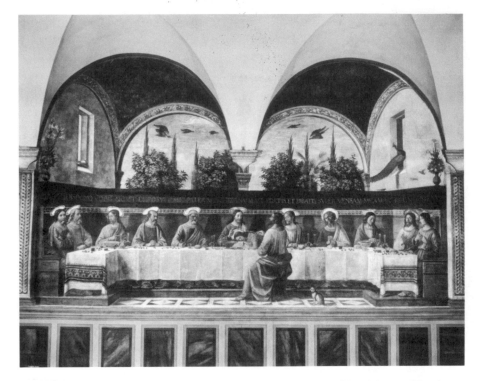

Fig. 25: Domenico Ghirlandaio, *The Last Supper.* Museum of San Marco, Florence

The calm figure of Jesus is the emotional center of this storm. He is disposed in a stable triangle, and clothed in the bright primary colors of red and blue. Largely removed from the groups of apostles to either side, he is framed by the central doorway, which creates a kind of natural halo. Space within the room is defined by the lines created by the wall tapestries, lines that recede into depth and at the same time function on the surface, leading the viewer's eye directly to the head of Jesus.

A painter who attempts this subject is challenged to differentiate the figures in the interest of lively diversity, which Ghirlandaio's somewhat wooden results fail to do. Leonardo, however, brilliantly conceives several contrasting types, from the beautiful young man to the grizzled elder, disposed in four groups of three persons each. These groups in turn establish a rhythm, from right to left: one group whose motion is toward Jesus, a second that pulls back, a third (of whom Judas is to the left) that again pulls away, and the last that inclines toward Jesus. These moves are countered here and there by a subordinate reverse flow, the mute dialogue of hands the thread that binds the figures into an ineluctable unity.

Sir Kenneth Clark called *The Last Supper* the most literary of paintings, and so it is. A story can be told about the whole, and about each of its protagonists. It is a story of anguish on the verge of explosion, but also anguish subsumed as a moment in the eternal stability of God's beneficence, reflected in the harmonic proportions of the mural's overall scheme. Here, as in so much of what he did, Leonardo turned to mathematics as the ordering principle in a world of endless, potentially chaotic phenomena.

Around the same time Leonardo painted a now lost decorative scheme in the Ducal Palace and a second, now much repainted, for the Sala delle Asse. Here, complex intertwining vegetal motifs spring from rocks painted on the side walls, a sharply observed continuation of Leonardo's geological interests. With this work, Leonardo and Ludovico's time together in Milan was at an end. The French invaded Milan in the summer of 1499, and at the fall of the Duke in September, Leonardo left the city. Ludovico returned briefly, only to be captured and spend his remaining years in prison. Around 1500, Leonardo wrote laconically, "The Duke lost his state and his property, and none of his works was completed for him." With "the Horse" probably his most bitter memory, Leonardo embarked on a final nineteen years of mixed fortunes.

CHAPTER 3

The Itinerant Engineer

FROM MILAN Leonardo traveled to Mantua, where he did a portrait of Isabella d'Este, usually acknowledged as being the chalk drawing of a woman in profile now in the Louvre. From Mantua he proceeded to Venice, where he is recorded, in March, planning defenses for the north of the city. By April he was back in Florence.

By 1501 Michelangelo also had returned to Florence, having been in Rome, where he had enjoyed the double triumph of his sculptures *Bacchus* and *Pietà*. The two masters entered what in retrospect might be called an informal competition that would culminate in their battle scenes for Florence's Palazzo della Signoria.

Leonardo may have brought back with him a cartoon (a 1:1 scale transfer drawing) identified as possibly his *Madonna and Child and Saint Anne,* now in London (fig. 26), although others believe, probably rightly, that this drawing was done several years later. It is an idealized vision of two women of the same age, their rolling, voluminous forms joined in a closely knit group. He is reported in 1501 by Fra Pietro da Novellara, Isabella d'Este's agent in Florence, to be at work on this subject, but Fra Pietro's description fits neither the London drawing, nor Vasari's description, nor the later painted version of the subject that is now in the Louvre (fig. 27). The puzzle as to the sequence of the various versions of this subject is too complicated to explore here, and in any event irresolvable. What is clear is that Leonardo was at work on a complex figure group, a likely spur to Michelangelo's similarly bold grouping in his *Doni Madonna* of several years later.

If a painting was Leonardo's task immediately at hand, it seems not to have been his only preoccupation. Late in the 1490s Leonardo had met the mathematician Luca Pacioli, who returned to Florence with the artist. Fra Pietro, in the same letter of 1501, wrote to Mantua that Leo-

Fig. 26: Leonardo, *Madonna and Child and Saint Anne*. National Gallery, London

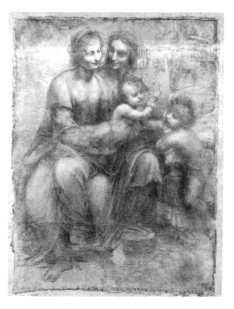

nardo's "mathematical experiments have distracted him so much from painting that he cannot suffer the brush."

But scholarly contemplation was quick to give way to the active life. In the summer of 1502 Leonardo was gone again, this time in the service of Cesare Borgia, nephew of Pope Alexander VI, and a paragon of efficacious cruelty, according to Niccolò Machiavelli. Leonardo was "Architect and General Engineer" to Borgia, a title similar to the one that he had held earlier in Milan, and to the ones he would hold again in Milan and later in France. Borgia was at work subduing the Romagna, and Leonardo's tasks were doubtless many and varied. He went from city to city and left traces of his work, such as the first flat plan of a city that is viewed directly from above (see fig. 48), as opposed to a traditional bird's-eye view, which is seen from an angle.

After the premature death of Borgia in 1503, Leonardo returned to Florence, where his engineering experience quickly was called upon. He worked on an unfeasible scheme to make the Arno navigable to the sea, which would have involved a tunnel at Serravalle between Florence and Empoli. He may also have had a part at the request of Machiavelli—the evidence is not clear—in a less pacific river project. Florence was locked in a war of attrition with Pisa, and it was proposed to isolate the Pisans

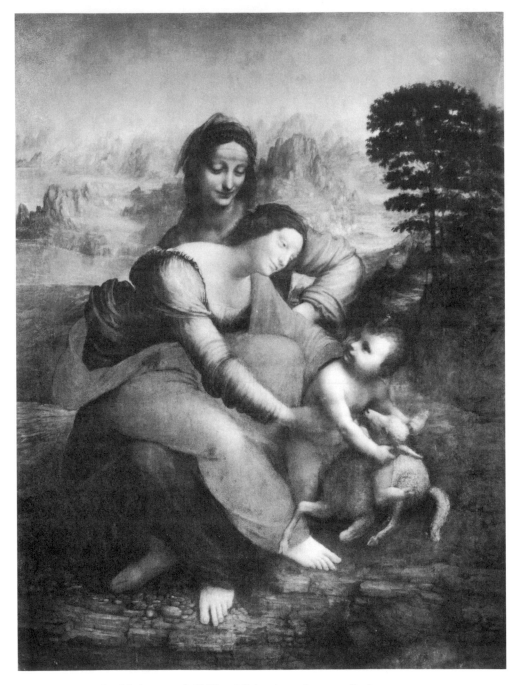

Fig. 27: Leonardo, *Madonna and Child and Saint Anne*. Louvre, Paris

from the sea by diverting the Arno. Two thousand men were set to work, but the project was soon abandoned. Some maps in manuscripts in Madrid and a few drawings of excavating machines may relate to this undertaking.

In 1503 Piombino, which had been captured by Borgia, was restored to its rightful owner, Jacopo Appiani. In November 1504 Leonardo was sent by the Florentines to plan the fortifications of the city. Little remains beyond a brilliant unexecuted proposal for an innovative fortress.

The Piombino assignment interrupted one of Leonardo's most important commissions as a painter. In the 1490s the new republican government of Florence built a large hall at the Palazzo della Signoria to accommodate its sizable Great Council. A decorative program was developed, including plans for two murals of historic Florentine victories, each to be about 20 by 50 feet. Leonardo was commissioned in 1503 to paint *The Battle of Anghiari* (a 1440 victory over the Milanese), and a little later Michelangelo was commissioned to execute *The Battle of Cascina* (1364 against the Pisans). Neither was brought to completion, for soon Michelangelo was called to Rome by Pope Julius II to work on the papal tomb, and Leonardo was persuaded to return to Milan. It is a pity, for the one clearly defined episode from each composition as known in copies suggests that the murals would have presented two brilliantly contrasting stylistic alternatives.

Moreover, Michelangelo never got beyond the drawing stage; and although Leonardo began to paint in the palace, his mural was either destroyed or else covered when Vasari frescoed battle scenes on the walls in the 1560s.

A part of Michelangelo's composition, preserved in a 1540 copy, shows a group of Florentine soldiers surprised by the enemy while bathing. The subject offered the artist an opportunity to display the heroic male nude in all manner of postures, a reprise of the early marble relief of *The Battle of the Centaurs,* and a harbinger of the nudes on the Sistine Ceiling. Michelangelo's surviving works suggest that the mural would have been a boldly sculptural rendition of men and horses in a bleak landscape setting.

The centerpiece of Leonardo's composition was to be a battle for a standard, a close encounter of horsemen in violent sword play, with fallen foot soldiers beneath them. The idea exists in several sketches by

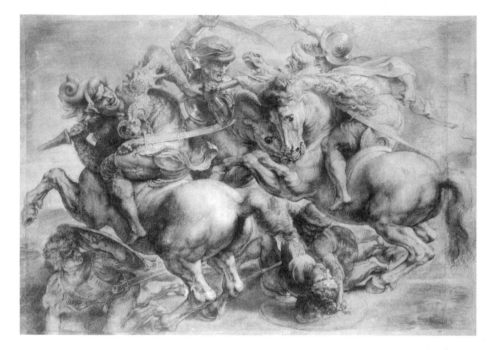

Fig. 28: Peter Paul Rubens, Copy of engraved copy of a portion of *The Battle of Anghiari*. Louvre, Paris

Leonardo, some contemporary copies, and most vividly in a drawing by Rubens (fig. 28). Other sketches suggest that the battle for a standard was but the centerpiece for a three-part panoramic scene (fig. 29). While there is little pictorial evidence, a description of such a battle in Leonardo's notebooks, combined with knowledge of the landscape backgrounds in most of his paintings, leads to speculation that the setting would have been an atmospheric plain below a mountain range. A drawing in Budapest for the head of one of the riders suggests an intensity of facial expression beyond anything that Leonardo had conceived before then (fig. 30).

Around 1504 Leonardo began developing a composition for *Leda and the Swan,* first planning a kneeling Leda, and several years later a standing version. The Leda myth tells of the union between a mortal woman and Jupiter in the guise of a swan, a perfect subject for a man profoundly interested in metamorphosis and comparative biology. The standing version, known only in copies, suggests that Leonardo's many plant

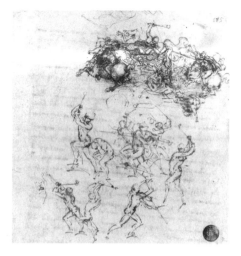

Fig. 29: Leonardo, Sketch for *The Battle of Anghiari*. Accademia, Venice

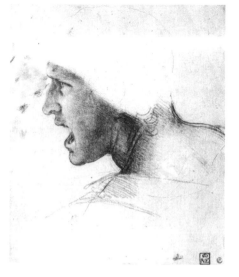

Fig. 30: Leonardo, *Rider's Head* (study for *The Battle of Anghiari*). Museum of Fine Arts, Budapest

studies of these years were done in connection with the thinking invested in the painting.

Also about 1504 Leonardo began the *Mona Lisa,* that ever so subtly modeled portrait of a faintly smiling woman on a balcony, before a barren, rocky terrain (see fig. 1). Vasari writes that Leonardo did a portrait of the wife of Francesco del Giocondo, also known as Mona Lisa, or La Gioconda. But who is the lady in the painting? Vasari describes the picture partially and inaccurately, which is not surprising, considering that it probably was in France by the time Vasari was seven years old. After Vasari, the written record concerning the portrait of Mona Lisa becomes muddled, to the extent that the connection between Vasari's words and the painting now in the Louvre is at best tenuous. The first reasonably accurate mention of the painting itself dates only from 1625.

Some scholars date the completion of the painting as late as the 1510s, but evidence in the form of paintings from the Raphael circle suggests that it or the design on which it is based was known by 1505. But is it in fact a portrait in the conventional sense, or an idealized figure like

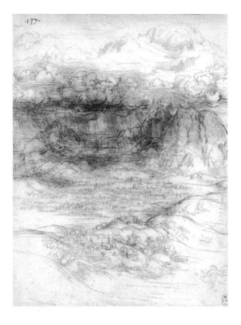

Fig. 31: Leonardo, *Thunderstorm in the Alps*. Royal Library, Windsor

the smiling women in Leonardo's altarpieces? One might speculate that it began as a portrait, and then over the years evolved into an idealized vision of womanhood. *Portrait of a Lady on a Balcony* is what we should now call it. She may have been a paragon of naturalism for Vasari and his contemporaries, but by the mid-nineteenth century she had become a femme fatale, the epitome of omniscience and forbidden knowledge. In any case, the painting is the most sophisticated study in light and shade that Leonardo had yet done, and is further testimony to his abiding fascination with rugged topography.

Art and science—how are they to be weighed in Leonardo's paintings or drawings? In a drawing of a *Thunderstorm in the Alps* (fig. 31), Leonardo looks from a high vantage point across a valley framed by mountains, whose flanks are lashed by wind and water. Is this view to be enjoyed as landscape pure and simple, or was the point to explore vortices of air and water? In Leonardo's terms is it even legitimate to make such a distinction?

While Leonardo was actively engaged as an artist during these years, his scientific interests were unabated and probably took up the majority of his time. About 1505 he wrote a short treatise on the flight of birds, anticipating observations by others that would find their way into print only centuries later. And, probably in the same year, he mentioned in his notes "A book entitled 'On the transformation of one body into another without diminution or increase of substance,' " a book that does not survive if indeed it ever existed, but was inspired by the same thinking that produced drawings of the transformation of geometrical solids. And finally, the master turned to anatomy, a subject that was to occupy him for most of his remaining years.

In 1506 Leonardo was called back to Milan, and late in the year the French governor of Milan formally petitioned the Florentines for his services. During the next couple of years he went back and forth between the two cities, his notebooks filling with observations on mechanics, anatomy, geometry, geology, and painting. In 1508 he began work on an unrealized project for a bypass of the River Adda at Tre Corni, but soon was back in Florence to assist the sculptor Rustici with a bronze group for the Baptistry. In Florence he makes a note that could stand as an epitaph for his chaotic written material: "Begun in Florence in the house of Piero di Braccio Martelli on the 22nd day of March 1508. And this is to be a collection without order taken from many papers that I have copied here, hoping afterward to arrange them in order in their proper places according to the subjects of which they treat."

By the end of 1508 Leonardo was back in Milan, now concentrating on the study of muscles and the dynamics of fluids. His most exact anatomical drawings come from the next several years, and in 1510 he indicated in his notes his intention to finish his book on anatomy. In 1511 he met the young anatomist Marcantonio della Torre, but a promise of collaboration vanished with the latter's death a short time later.

Art still engaged much of Leonardo's time. He worked on a second equestrian monument, this time to Gian Giacomo Trivulzio, which never got beyond the sketch stage. The Paris version of the *Madonna and Child and Saint Anne* (see fig. 27) probably dates from these years (it is undated). It is the most mature version of this subject. Mary, seated on the lap of her mother, is reaching down for the Child, who grasps the lamb. Rounded, volumetric forms are counterpointed by diagonals that yield a more active composition than the drawing in London. A patch of scrupulously observed pebble-strewn earth is at the foot of the figures, while ice blue mountains rise in the distance. Seemingly born of the imagination, they in fact resemble the master's geological studies done at about the same time.

In 1512 the Sforza family returned to power in Milan in the person of Ludovico's son Maximilian. His patrons expelled, Leonardo departed for Rome on September 24 with his pupil Francesco Melzi. He took up residence in the Vatican under Medici patronage, but, it being the Roman heyday of Raphael and Michelangelo, we hear little of a public Leonardo. If Vasari is to be believed, the sixty-year-old man was denied access to cadavers and was subverted by a feckless assistant. It was a time of frustration and fruitless experimentation, but his anatomical investigations continued nonetheless, with studies of the heart based upon animal parts.

About this time the fanatical student of anatomy painted his strangest and most unanatomical pictures, a pneumatic and androgynous *Saint John the Baptist* who emerges from the penumbral shade, signaling He who shall come afterward (fig. 32). Just as strange are the master's meditations on the end of the world, embodied in that fantastic series known as the deluge drawings (see figs. 67–68), in which his hydraulic expertise and rare imagination are united.

Of his practical work during the Roman years we hear of little beyond a plan to drain the Pontine Marshes (which was not executed until the 1930s). There is a hint in 1515 that Leonardo was ill, possibly a victim of a cardiovascular ailment.

Leonardo for some time had been admired by the French. Louis XII (1462–1515) had coveted *The Last Supper,* and even thought of having it transported to France. At the death of his Roman patron, Duke Giuliano de' Medici, Leonardo accepted the invitation of the new French king, Francis I (1494–1547), and in the summer of 1516 settled in the Loire Valley at the country house of Cloux, which was only a short walk from the royal château at Amboise. Here he assumed the title "First Painter and Architect and Engineer of the King."

At Cloux, Leonardo worked on the canalization of the Loire, and did designs for a never-executed royal palace complex at Romorantin, to the east of Amboise. He had brought his work with him from Italy— according to a letter recounting a 1517 visit by Cardinal Luigi d'Aragona, which mentions the *Madonna and Child and Saint Anne,* a painting of a young *John the Baptist,* and a portrait of "a certain Florentine lady done

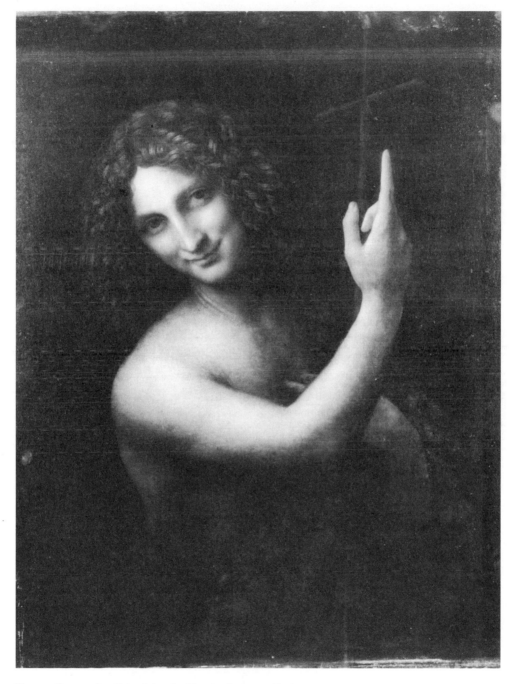

Fig. 32: Leonardo, *Saint John the Baptist*. Louvre, Paris

from life for the late Magnificent Giuliano de' Medici" (*Portrait of a Lady on a Balcony?*)—but he apparently painted no more after that. The same letter mentions paralysis of a hand.

Rather, Leonardo was now a sage at court, the embodiment of the sort of wisdom recorded in the so-called self-portrait (fig. 2). Decades later, the sculptor Benvenuto Cellini, himself a Florentine and servant of the King, wrote in his *Treatise on Architecture:*

> King Francis, being extremely taken with [Leonardo's] great *virtù,* took so much pleasure in hearing him reason, that he was apart from him but a few days a year. . . . I do not wish to neglect repeating the words I heard the King say of him, which he said to me—that he believed there had never been another man born in the world who knew as much as Leonardo, not so much about sculpture, painting and architecture, as that he was a very great philosopher.

In 1518 Leonardo wrote, "I shall go on." On May 2, 1519 he died, leaving his brothers 400 ducats, and his favorite pupil, Francesco Melzi, his artistic and scientific legacy. Melzi carried the material back to Lombardy, where it suffered centuries of obscurity as sheets were lost, dispersed, and lay buried in various collections.

Leonardo was said to have been buried in the Church of Saint Florentine at Amboise, but that, too, is destroyed, like so much of his own work.

PART II

THE ANATOMY OF
A LEGEND

*Being an exploration in five chapters of how
Leonardo became all but lost, then was invented and
reinvented by those who needed him.*

CHAPTER 4

Giorgio Vasari Invents Leonardo

AT THE CLOSE of his life of Leonardo, Vasari reports that the great man expired in the arms of King Francis I. However, Francesco Melzi's letter announcing Leonardo's death to the latter's brothers makes no mention of these extraordinary circumstances, and some two centuries ago it was shown that Francis and his court were far from Amboise on May 2, 1519, the day that Leonardo died.

Not true, then, but what a story! It says volumes about the fine discrimination of a world-class patron, and the exalted position that an artist might attain in the corridors of wealth and power. Why did Vasari recount this anecdote? Could it be that Vasari, jockeying for the position he would soon attain as chief artistic entrepreneur for the Medici court, was more interested in making a point about the status of artists than he was in the historical truth of a particular case? If nothing else, the fictional death scene suggests that Vasari's *Lives* should be read with a critical sense of its implicit ideological agendas.

The matter is important, for Vasari's life of Leonardo is the starting point in our extended knowledge of Leonardo, and a continuous locus of reference down to our own time. It preserves information that otherwise would be lost, and beyond that deals with a host of issues that have as much or more to do with the world of the mid-sixteenth century than they do with Leonardo and his time. Although Vasari gives us some facts about Leonardo, his central importance in matters of Leonardo is to have invented him. With his version of the death scene, the legend of Leonardo began to take shape.

The reasons for the need to invent Leonardo lay in the chaotic state of knowledge about him, even shortly after his death. Understanding this confusion is prerequisite to examining the Leonardo that Vasari invented.

Today, scholars agree that about a dozen paintings are by Leonardo, and a handful of others are known only through copies. Of the dozen, a quarter were not recognized as Leonardo's until the nineteenth or early twentieth century. Of the remaining nine, *The Last Supper* was acknowledged to be a wreck already in the sixteenth century, and four— the *Virgin of the Rocks* (Paris version), *Portrait of a Lady on a Balcony,* the *Madonna and Child and Saint Anne,* and *Saint John the Baptist*—appear to have left Italy with Leonardo, and for centuries were not publicly accessible.

The Tuscans remembered Leonardo as the harbinger of a new style, as described by Vasari in 1550, but there was little actual work to be seen with one's own eyes. In northern Italy, where Leonardo spent the bulk of his working life, his main traces were the often inferior copies and adaptations of his work produced by pupils and followers.

Unlike almost any other old master, Leonardo bequeathed posterity no artistic Mecca. Michelangelo created the Sistine Chapel, Raphael the Vatican Stanze, Titian the great altarpieces of the Frari in Venice, Correggio his domes at Parma. And Leonardo? Only a disintegrating mural on a humid and flaking wall at the Santa Maria delle Grazie in Milan.

Leonardo's artistic oeuvre was riddled with holes—works lost, destroyed, or never finished, such as the Sforza monument, which would have been the most spectacular bronze of post-classical times, and *The Battle of Anghiari,* which, with Michelangelo's *Cascina,* might have been the touchstones of mature Florentine style, had they been completed. Only when the Louvre became publicly accessible in Paris around 1800 did the master have his belated Mecca. In the absence of a core of available and accepted works, attributions to Leonardo were invented freely. Most inventories of major seventeenth- and eighteenth-century collections include at least one alleged "Leonardo," and even as late as the mid-nineteenth century some ninety works were associated with Leonardo's name. These objects were scattered across Europe, along with the heterogeneous output of his Milanese followers; indeed, most of the works attributed to Leonardo were by these men.

Painters such as Raphael had their works disseminated by prints, but not so Leonardo. With the exception of a few undistinguished prints after *The Last Supper,* reproductions of Leonardo's works were few and far between until the late eighteenth century. Several were not reproduced at all.

Today we recognize the core of Leonardo's genius in his notes and drawings, but the whereabouts of this material left them largely inaccessible for centuries. The material inherited by Melzi lay dormant, with one notable exception: toward 1550, or possibly earlier, Melzi organized some of the material into a treatise on painting, which today is in the Vatican Library. Most of the rest of Leonardo's legacy passed to Melzi's heir Orazio, thence through various hands to the sculptor Leoni at the end of the sixteenth century. Leoni divided the loose material into two groups by subject: one on technology, and the other on anatomy and artistic studies. The first is the Codex Atlanticus, in Milan; the second is in the Royal Library at Windsor Castle. The remainder of the manuscripts were dispersed, the bulk of which are now in France, England, and Spain.

Some of the material was studied avidly by *eruditi* on a Milan-Paris-Rome axis in the seventeenth century. But this aside, there were only sporadic advances in knowledge of the source material—for example, the publication of engravings of some of the drawings in the 1780s, or a summary and brief anthology of Leonardo's scientific thought offered by a Modenese applied scientist in 1797. The Windsor drawings were first published in 1881. Before the last quarter of the nineteenth century, then, Leonardo's accomplishment wasn't well known, let alone critically evaluated.

A final important reason for a Leonardo badly out of focus is that he was a man without a country. Born a Tuscan, he left for Milan at about the age of thirty just as his reputation was established, serving there until the downfall of Ludovico. He wandered for the last twenty years of his life—on the road with Cesare Borgia, back and forth between Milan and Florence, stayed three short years in Rome, and ended finally in France, where he died an expatriate in 1519. So Leonardo did not have the advantage of the history and traditions of one proud place to perpetuate the facts and myths of his life and work. Instead, his natal and various adopted homes had different stories to tell about "their" Leonardo. Ironically, considering that he was one of the most famous of a galaxy of notable Tuscans, it was Milan where a solid historical understanding of Leonardo was first put forth around 1800, and Paris and Oxford that interpreted him for the modern world.

If all these circumstances taken together suggest why for centuries Leonardo was an ill-defined figure, it seems that Leonardo himself set in motion the obfuscation that attaches to his name. His eccentric behavior begins with the 1478 Palazzo della Signoria commission for the altarpiece of the Chapel of Saint Bernard. Why did he not deliver it, and what reading of his character did his contemporaries place upon this failure? Does this event have anything to do with his absence from the group of distinguished Tuscan and Umbrian painters invited to fresco the side walls of the Sistine Chapel in 1481, or was it simply that he was not invited because of his lack of experience in the medium of fresco painting? And why in 1482 did he choose a fresh start in a foreign city? Was he leaving an uncongenial situation, or was he drawn to Milan by a compelling challenge? Whatever the answers to these questions, early on Leonardo seems unconcerned with conventional opportunism and the sort of flatteries that make a man sought after.

Leonardo is often called a universal man, and doubtless the scope of his investigations is wide. Yet, as has already been suggested, the notion of universality is applicable only if the fields of interest that we today call the humanities and social sciences are not considered. Usually this lack of interest on his part is explained as characteristic of an intellect oriented toward direct experience of nature in preference to the conventions of the written word. But might there not be a complementary explanation—that Leonardo disliked the subjectivity, value judgments, and exploration of interpersonal relations inherent in the humanities and social sciences? Be that as it may, in the thousands of pages of notes that Leonardo penned he tells us virtually nothing about himself or his relations to other people. An apparently private person, he even avoided self-revelation in writing intended for his eyes only.

One startling fact attests to Leonardo's public reticence. Although he was born at about the same time as the invention of movable type, and came of age during the rapid spread of the printed book, Leonardo never published anything. It is truly extraordinary that a great investigator should have turned his back on one of the most important inventions of his age.

Leonardo also abjured another contemporary innovation—the dissemination of visual images by means of engraving. Here was the ideal mode to spread the astounding knowledge embodied in his drawings, but the few prints associated with his name are by others, and are tangential to the major themes of his thinking (the one exception being simple designs of the Platonic solids for a book by his friend Pacioli).

One can only speculate that either indifference to or fear of public disclosure of his work constituted an essential feature of Leonardo's psyche. His reputation evolved almost in spite of himself, and it is little wonder that his privatism combined with the scarcity and inaccessibility of what he produced resulted in a dissonance between a large but vague reputation and any agreed-upon core of publicly available work. More than any other notable figure of his time, Leonardo was vulnerable to being misinterpreted—indeed, to being willfully invented anew. How, or whether at all, he would be understood after his death and the death of his immediate contemporaries would depend on the character of the critical interpretations that might appear to fill the information void. Some thirty years after his death a biography appeared that not only assured that he would have a reputation, but that also fundamentally colored comment for centuries to come.

Vasari's *Lives of the Most Eminent Painters, Sculptors, and Architects* was first published in 1550, and again in a revised and expanded form in 1568 to include lives of living artists. The work is fundamentally important for three reasons. It is the first extensive account of Italian art between about 1250 and 1550, based on considerable factual inquiry. Were it not for Vasari, our nuts-and-bolts knowledge of the art and artists of these years would be much diminished. Second, Vasari, beyond a sequence of biographies, offers a developmental view of the history of the period that holds the achievement of the ancients as the norm against which the art of the moderns should be measured. Last, Vasari writes about objects in a specific, vivid way unmatched in his age. This combination of qualities merits his status as one of the best art historians of any time.

Earlier scholars often dwelled on Vasari's lack of factual completeness and accuracy. Today we are more inclined to look at his strategies as an author, bearing in mind that various ancient literary models helped to shape his enterprise, and that pointing out artistic and/or moral lessons was one of his primary intentions.

The idea for the *Lives* originated in Rome in the 1540s, among a circle

of men at the papal court. One of this group was the physician and man
of letters Paolo Giovio, a seasoned biographer who had written a few
brief lives of artists in the late 1520s, including that of Leonardo. Giovio
was the obvious choice for the project, but he begged off. Instead the
lot fell to Vasari, an artist in his mid-thirties who had enjoyed a privileged literary education at the Medici court in Florence.

A long prologue to the *Lives* (which, misleadingly, is often abridged
or omitted entirely in translations) is aimed squarely at his fellow artists,
and describes the bedrock of his artistic theory, the concept of *disegno:*

> Seeing that Design, the parent of our three arts, Architecture,
> Sculpture, and Painting, having its origin in the intellect, draws out
> from many single things a general judgment, it is like a form or
> idea of all the objects in nature, most marvelous in what it com-
> passes, for not only in the bodies of men and of animals but also
> in plants, in buildings, in sculpture, and in painting, design is cog-
> nizant of the proportion of the whole to the parts and of the parts
> to each other and to the whole. Seeing too that from this knowl-
> edge there arises a certain conception and judgment, so that there
> is formed in the mind that something which afterward, when ex-
> pressed by the hands, is called design, we may conclude that design
> is not other than a visible expression and declaration of our inner
> conception and of that which others have imagined and given form
> to in their idea.

So *disegno* has to do with universal harmony and order and their perception in the artist's mind, the successful committing of this perception
to the forms of an art object, and the apprehension of those qualities by
a viewer. Accomplished *disegno* was seen as a specifically Tuscan triumph
and, for Vasari, Leonardo was one of its greatest practitioners.

If Leonardo was a perfect technical exemplar for Vasari, he also occupied a crucial position in the author's concept of art-historical development. Vasari, inheriting a commonplace view, believed that art had
reached a pinnacle of perfection under the Greeks and Romans. This
achievement was the norm against which the entire history should be
evaluated. With the fall of Rome, a precipitous artistic decline began at
the hands of Christians who effaced pagan works and the memory of
their creators. Around 1150, after centuries of darkness (the image of the

Dark Ages was invented by Petrarch in the fourteenth century), an artistic revival began, and over a period of three and a half centuries art simply got better and better until a peak of perfection was reached in Michelangelo, whose divine gift overshadowed even that of the ancients. So Vasari's overarching scheme is inscribed within the cycle of florescence, decay, and reflorescence, and includes a dynamic of incremental progress within that cyclical scheme.

If antiquity marked the first case of incremental progress, Vasari's story of art from the mid-thirteenth century to his own time is the reprise, "the age of the rebirth of the arts up to our own time." He divides the latter era into three periods, corresponding roughly to the late thirteenth and fourteenth centuries, the fifteenth century, and the sixteenth. The first two periods are marked by a steady advance in naturalism, but even as the second neared its close, vestiges of stiffness and dryness remained in the artists' manner. The formulas of naturalism had been mastered, and lacked only a greater fluidity to bring works of art to life.

The period opening around 1500—"which," according to Vasari, "we like to call the modern age"—is characterized in the Prologue to the third part of the *Lives*. The pioneer was Leonardo, "who beyond his subtle and exact reproduction of every detail in nature, showed in his works an understanding of rule, a better knowledge of order, correct proportion, perfect design, and an inspired grace. An artist of great vision and skill and abundant resources, Leonardo may be said to have painted figures that moved and breathed."

For Vasari, then, faithful rendition of observed nature was not enough, but had to be enhanced by the qualities he finds in Leonardo. Leonardo was the artist after whom art simply would not be the same.

The life of Leonardo is pivotal in Vasari's scheme and opens the third part of a tripartite structure. Positioned as it is, this particular life bears a burden of literary strategy that goes well beyond the task of recounting one man's life and work.

While Leonardo and Raphael died only a year apart, Vasari's accounts of their lives are quite different. Raphael's is much longer and more richly documented, and to a large degree factually accurate. This is not surprising; Vasari was in Rome for an extended period just a decade after Raphael's death in that city, and he had access to many people who knew Raphael both in Florence and Rome. Leonardo, however, was born a generation earlier, left little of his work behind, and moved from place to place. The most knowledgeable informants would have been in Milan and France, and thus known to Vasari mainly at second hand. Vasari may have been hampered by what he did not know, but it left him plenty of room for invention.

Probably Vasari's main source was Paolo Giovio himself. Giovio fled to the island of Ischia after the sack of Rome in 1527, and there wrote a posthumously published life of Leonardo. Giovio's Leonardo was not only an artist in several media, but also a student of optics, anatomy, and music. As appropriate to a learned man, Leonardo required solid founding for the fledgling artist in both the sciences and the liberal arts. He made severe demands upon himself, and would cast aside work that did not come up to his personal standards. His character was exemplary; according to Giovio:

> His charm of disposition, his brilliance, and generosity were not less than the beauty of his appearance. His genius was astounding, and he was the arbiter of all questions relating to beauty and elegance, especially in pageantry.

Some, but by no means all, of Vasari's Leonardesque themes are here *in nuce*.

Vasari opens his account with maximum firepower: Leonardo is nothing less than a *deus ex machina*. "Endowed by heaven" with beauty, grace, and talent, everything Leonardo does "comes clearly from God" and is "divinely inspired." Exemplary character is projected through physical and mental beauty, and it is intimated that these qualities are prerequisites to the production of excellent works. Leonardo "was an artist of outstanding physical beauty who displayed infinite grace in everything he did and who cultivated his genius so brilliantly that all problems he studied he solved with ease." He possessed great strength and dexterity; he was a man of regal spirit, tremendous breadth, and a lovable disposition, and was esteemed by all. Leonardo's compassion was such that he bought caged birds for the sole purpose of setting them free.

But even such a paragon of God-given excellence was touched by human frailty. Vasari describes Leonardo as "volatile and unstable, for he was always setting himself to learn many things, only to abandon them almost immediately." This shortcoming is explained: "Clearly it was because of his profound knowledge of painting that Leonardo started so many things without finishing them; for he was convinced that his hands, for all their skill, could never perfectly express the subtle and wonderful ideas of his imagination." As T. S. Eliot later wrote,

> Between the idea
> And the reality
> Between the motion
> And the act
> Falls the shadow
> —"The Hollow Men"

If vision outran the manual capacity to realize it, there is also innuendo of the master's overreaching ambition. Vasari quotes Petrarch apropos the unfinished horse: "Desire outran performance."

Vasari praises Leonardo's breadth of interests and accomplishments—master of the visual arts, architect, geometrician, engineer capable of altering the course of the Arno—but, understandably, it is the painter who interested him most. Leonardo's greatness as a student of nature lay in his ability to infuse his products with a pervasive grace, implicit in the notion the idea that the grace of God infuses the gracefulness of the artist, which grace in turn permeates the work of art.

Vasari occasionally employs a set piece in which he describes a particular work of art to capture in microcosm the general qualities that he prizes. In his account of Leonardo's life, that moment comes near the end in an inspired description of the *Mona Lisa* (see fig. 1):

For Francesco del Giocondo, Leonardo undertook to execute the portrait of his wife, Mona Lisa. He worked on this painting for four years, and then left it still unfinished; and today it is in the possession of King Francis of France, at Fontainebleau. If one wanted to see how faithfully art can imitate nature, one could readily perceive it from this head; for here Leonardo subtly reproduced every living detail. The eyes had their natural luster and moistness, and around them were the lashes and all those rosy and pearly tints that demand the greatest delicacy of execution. The eyebrows were completely natural, growing thickly in one place and lightly in another and following the pores of the skin. The nose was finely painted, with rosy and delicate nostrils as in life. The mouth, joined to the flesh tints of the face by the red of the lips, appeared to be living flesh rather than paint. On looking closely at the pit of her throat, one could swear that the pulses were beating. Altogether this picture was painted in a manner to make the most confident artist—no matter who—despair and lose heart. Leonardo also made use of this device: while he was painting Mona Lisa, who was a very beautiful woman, he employed singers and musicians or jesters to keep her full of merriment and so chase away the melancholy that paints usually give to portraits. As a result, in this painting of Leonardo's there was a smile so pleasing that it seemed divine rather than human; and those who saw it were amazed to find that it was as alive as the original.

According to this account, the artificer-conjuror Leonardo has produced a counterfeit interchangeable with life itself. However, as mentioned earlier, the description diverges from the painting today in Paris. Contrary to Vasari, the picture is finished, and the eyebrows he describes are not to be seen; and he fails even to point out such prominent features of the painting as the crossed hands and rocky landscape. But no matter; Vasari's intent was not to describe accurately a work that he probably never saw, but to advocate mimesis—the faithful imitation of nature—as the first principle of *disegno*. The power of his words to drive this point home smothered any possible qualms as to whether or not those words were faithful to the appearance of a particular painting in a distant land.

The *Mona Lisa* passage is then an encomium to mimesis, a credo that runs as a theme throughout Vasari's life of Leonardo. Yet this devotion to nature would seem to have a dark underside, for excessive devotion to nature can have serious costs—an idea brought home by two passages that figuratively serve as bookends to the main discussion of Leonardo's oeuvre.

The first is a description of a work that, if indeed it ever existed (there is some evidence that it did), seems to have left no trace. Had Leonardo not painted it, then Vasari would have had to invent it, which possibly he did. This description is the longest in the life and concerns a buck-ler, or shield, painted by Leonardo when he was young:

The story goes that once when Piero da Vinci was at his house in the country one of the peasants on his farm, who had made himself a buckler out of a fig tree that he had cut down, asked him as a favor to have it painted for him in Florence. Piero was very happy to do this, since the man was very adept at snaring birds and fishing and Piero himself very often made use of him in these pursuits. He took the buckler to Florence, and without saying a word about whom it belonged to he asked Leonardo to paint something on it. Some days later Leonardo examined the buckler, and finding that it was warped, badly made, and clumsy, he straightened it in the fire and then gave it to a turner who, from the rough and clumsy thing that it was, made it smooth and even. Then having given it a coat of gesso and prepared it in his own way Leonardo started to think what he could paint on it so as to terrify anyone who saw it and produce the same effect as the head of Medusa. To do what he wanted Leonardo carried it into a room of his own, which no one ever entered except himself, a number of green and other kinds of lizards, crickets, serpents, butterflies, locusts, bats, and various strange creatures of this nature; from all these he took and assem-bled different parts to create a fearsome and horrible monster which emitted a poisonous breath and turned the air to fire. He depicted the creature emerging from the dark cleft of a rock, belching forth venom from its open throat, fire from its eyes and smoke from its nostrils in so macabre a fashion that the effect was altogether monstrous and horrible. Leonardo took so long over the work that the stench of the dead animals in his room became unbearable, although he himself failed to notice because of his great love of painting. By the time he had finished the painting, both the peasant and his father had stopped inquiring after it; but all the same he told his father that he could send for the buckler when convenient, since his work on it was completed. So one morning Piero went along to the room in order to get the buckler, knocked at the door and was told by Leonardo to wait for a moment. Leonardo went back into the room, put the buckler on an easel in the light, and shaded the window; then he asked Piero to come in and see it. When his eyes fell on it Piero was completely taken by surprise and gave a sudden start, not realizing that he was looking at the buckler and that the form he saw was, in fact, painted on it. As he backed away, Leonardo checked him and said: "This work certainly serves its purpose. It has produced the right reaction, so now you can take it away."

There seems something unclean about this project: a secret room, obsessiveness, work carried out in disregard of the physically revolting. And to any educated reader of Vasari's time, the description must have seemed a delightfully bizarre inversion of the expected order of things. One of the most famous anecdotes on art to come down from antiquity was the story of Zeuxis, a *typos* of the virtues of idealization. In order to paint a picture of Venus, the artist assembled the five most beautiful maidens of Croton, and chose from each the best parts in order to create an idealized representation. What is the story of the buckler but the opposite of this, a selection of the most bizarre features to constitute a terrifying whole? Like the *Lady on a Balcony,* the buckler was consummate naturalism, but a composite naturalism unmediated by grace.

Obsessiveness is a trait of Leonardo that Vasari brought up more than once—for instance, in recounting that the artist would follow someone whose face fascinated him for an entire day. And it is that obsession with the study of nature and of technique that passes beyond art that Vasari uses as a second bookend at the close of the life. Leonardo was at the Vatican, apparently in lonely isolation, pursuing purposeless and fruitless investigations; and Pope Leo X was a student of natural philosophy and alchemy, but according to Vasari even his Holiness gave up on Leonardo:

Leonardo went to Rome with Duke Giuliano de' Medici on the election of Pope Leo, who was a great student of alchemy and natural philosophy, and particularly alchemy. And in Rome he [Leonardo] experimented with a paste made out of a certain kind of wax and made some light billowy figures in the form of animals which he inflated with his mouth as he walked along and which flew above the ground until all the air escaped. To the back of a very odd-looking lizard that was found by the gardener of the Belvedere he attached with a mixture of quicksilver some wings, made from the scales stripped from other lizards, which quivered as it walked along. Then, after he had given it eyes, horns, and a beard he tamed the creature, and, keeping it in a box, he used to show it to friends and frighten the life out of them. Again, Leonardo used to get the intestines of a bullock scraped completely free of fat, cleaned and made so fine that they could be compressed into the palm of one hand; then he would fix one end of them to a pair of bellows lying in another room, and when they were inflated they filled the room in which they were and forced anyone standing there into a corner. Thus he could expand the translucent and airy stuff to fill a large space after occupying only a little, and he compared it to genius (or virtue). He perpetrated hundreds of follies of this kind, and he also experimented with mirrors and made the most outlandish experiments to discover oils for painting and varnish for preserving the finished works.

Vasari continues to record Pope Leo's despair at Leonardo's working habits:

Once, when he was commissioned a work by the Pope, Leonardo is said to have started at once to distill oils and various plants in order to prepare the varnish; and the Pope is supposed to have exclaimed, "O dear, this man will never do anything. Here he is thinking about finishing the work before he even starts it!"

These two bookends to the discussion of Leonardo's work—the set piece on the fantastic shield and the caprices of the old Leonardo in Rome—invite speculation. In a prologue to the section on the third period of art—i.e., the sixteenth century—Vasari praises Leonardo for advancing those qualities (rule, order, measure, *disegno*) necessary to accomplished art, and, in the life proper, for having imbued the study of nature with grace. Vasari's lives of Raphael, Michelangelo, and other sixteenth-century artists reveal how important stylization, grace, facility, and effortlessness were to him. In his view, mastery of nature is the basis of excellent art, but the greatest art moves beyond nature to marvelous artifice.

Vasari's Leonardo is a genius, but a flawed genius. His passionate devotion to the investigation of nature moves from the youthful bizarre shield to the Roman caprices of his old age. In joining natural parts in unnatural combinations, Leonardo evinces qualities of the necromancer or alchemist, although Vasari stops short of such a description.

For better or worse, by 1568 Vasari had drawn the literary portrait of Leonardo da Vinci that would become the point of departure for future generations. A divine genius, possessing the highest qualities of physical beauty, intelligence, and benign disposition, Leonardo had explored the physical phenomena of the world as no one before. But his mind conceived of ideas that ran beyond his powers of execution; hence, his frequent inability to finish what he started. Unconstrained by convention and blessed by a transforming grace, this genius recognized no God—at least in Vasari's 1550 version, in which there are allegations of unbelief; in the 1568 edition, sanitized by the Catholic Counter-Reformation climate, Leonardo dies a good Christian.

That death and its occurrence in the arms of the French king mark the true beginning of the myth of Leonardo, a myth subsequently elaborated by others, but always indebted to Giorgio Vasari.

CHAPTER 5

Playing by the Rules

IN DISCOURSES delivered to the students of the Royal Academy between 1769 and 1790, Sir Joshua Reynolds offered a clear-minded version of what over a couple of centuries had become the mainstream of academic art theory. The goal of art was the embodiment of Virtue, whose manifestation was universal rectitude and harmony in a painting. This was attainable by proper attention to intellectual beauty, achieved by the disciplined study of generalized, as opposed to a particularized, nature. Study of the best examples of ancient art and of the old masters would help the eye and hand to move toward a goal whose perfect realization could exist only in the mind. Progression toward that perfection had to be founded on rules, which, in Reynolds's view, were particularly important for the formation of a young artist.

These *Discourses* range over a number of artists, of whom Raphael and Michelangelo were for Reynolds the greatest exemplars, displaying most of the supreme qualities of high art. And where does Leonardo fit into Reynolds's scheme of things? Quite simply he is a bit player, mentioned only a few times as an illustration of this or that point, as formulator of useful rules for specific applications, as a source for Raphael, a student of Masaccio's work, and so forth. But Reynolds does not pause to offer a general assessment.

In fact, few writers in the century and a half before Reynolds had much to say about Leonardo. To be sure, Leonardo was recognized as a pioneer of the mature phase of Western painting, the man who brought the quest for verisimilitude in art to perfection, a master of modeling in light and dark, and the author of useful precepts for painters.

But not many of these writers got down to cases, for there was little of Leonardo's art to see. Take the only major surviving work in a relatively public place, *The Last Supper* (see fig. 23). In 1642 Francesco

Scanelli ended his description of the mural: "The good relics of the work rendered almost wholly useless, there is nothing to look at now but the fame of the past." The Richardsons in England were less poetic and more specific in 1722: "In the refectory over a very high Door, is the famous picture of the Last Supper, Figures as big as Life; it is exceedingly ruined and all the Apostles on the Right-hand of Christ are entirely defaced and those on his Left-hand appear pretty plain, but the Colours are quite faded and in several places only the bare wall is left."

To be sure, other works were known. In 1649 Abraham Bosse wrote a brief appreciation of Leonardo's handling of color and chiaroscuro, but cited only two examples—"La Gioconde a Fontainbelle-eau," and a painting entitled *Flora* (owned by Queen Marie de' Medici) that is actually a Leonardesque imitation. In 1667 André Félibien published his *Entretiens,* a set of lives à la Vasari culminating in the life of the French Raphael, Félibien's contemporary Nicolas Poussin. He devotes more than forty pages to Raphael but can eke out only eleven on Leonardo, in which *The Last Supper* and the paintings now in the Louvre figure most prominently. While Félibien praises Leonardo's meticulous sense of surfaces, he questions the intense darkness of his shadows. Expressiveness is the quality that intrigues him most, and it turns out that this is the harbinger of a new view of Leonardo.

Despite such instances, knowledge of Leonardo was sporadic and diffuse. Charles Alphonse du Fresnoy's *Art of Painting* was published in 1667; Dryden's English translation appends a qualitative evaluation of Italian artists, from which Leonardo is inexplicably omitted. Only at the end does the compiler explain himself: "I say nothing of Leonardo, because I have seen little of his; though he restored the arts at Milan and had many disciples there." Even such an astute student as the Frenchman Roger de Piles in 1699 found Leonardo to be an elusive shadow: "But that which the historians of his oeuvre have written of his works, which are today almost ruined, ought to persuade us that he had an abundant vein, that his movements were lively, his mind solid and adorned with much knowledge, and thus that his inventions ought to have been of great beauty." Arguably the most perspicacious writer on art around 1700 is reduced to writing about Leonardo as if he were some vanished artist of antiquity.

Leonardo's case was not helped by the general character of writing on art after Vasari, in the late sixteenth century in Italy or in France past the middle of the following century. A student in Paris or Rome around 1650 would have found that all the available didactic treatises on art were a half century old. Vasari held pride of place as a biographer for a century, while writings by others from about 1550 to 1600 dealt mainly with practical, technical, theological, and, above all, theoretical issues.

Several characteristics of these books, taken collectively, are germane to the image of Leonardo. First, while they supplement Vasari by adding new information, what they add has to be harvested assiduously, for the comments are fragments scattered in larger works dedicated to other matters. Second, these writers make unequivocally explicit what had been implied by writers from the early fifteenth century on—that production of good art depends on following rules. By 1600 these rules were stern, motivated by a feeling that excessive license had led to a precipitous decline in the quality of art after the death of Michelangelo in 1564. Last, because principles, rules, and precepts were the order of the day, it tended to follow that Vasari's example of descriptive set pieces on individual works of art was now rarely followed. Instead categories were treated one by one—*disegno,* use of color, movement, expression, and so forth. For instance, the notion of movement might be considered in several different paintings, each only discussed in terms of the chosen category. Holistic analytical description of a painting gives way to a mining of a single aspect of that painting, according to the needs of the argument at hand.

The most popular of these writers was the Milanese Gian Paolo Lomazzo, who published his *Treatise on the Arts of Painting, Sculpture, and Architecture* in 1584, and his shorter *Idea of the Temple of Painting* in 1590. Like Leonardo he was a painter and writer, loved music, promoted a scientific approach to art, and had a voracious curiosity. But Lomazzo's curiosity focused on combing through the flotsam and jetsam of pedantic learning so characteristic of later sixteenth-century scholarship. Lacking an adequate education, he compensated by socializing with learned men, joining scholarly academies, and getting secondhand knowledge from the encyclopedic compilations of the day. Lomazzo's table of contents suggests a lucidly organized system; the appearance is illusory. His hundreds of pages are in fact badly organized, rambling, and often crammed with factual trivia to suggest a veneer of learning.

Lomazzo's manner of thinking led to emphasis on certain "parts" (that is to say, "elements") of painting identified with specific masters. Although he praised Raphael, Lomazzo wrote that Raphael would have to yield to Michelangelo in the anatomy of bodies, to Leonardo in divine and celestial *moti* (expressive, characteristic movements) and light, and to Titian in color. The *reductio ad absurdum* of such thinking was the mental creation of all-time "superstar" paintings: "I'll say in my opinion, if one wanted to do two paintings of highest perfection, as one would need an Adam and an Eve, Adam given to Michelangelo to draw, to Titian to color . . . and Eve drawn by Raphael and colored by Antonio da Correggio; these would be the best pictures ever done."

While Lomazzo provides new information (e.g., that Leonardo painted a *Leda*) and apparent misinformation (e.g., that he painted portraits of Mona Lisa *and* La Gioconda), clearly his abstract mode of thought shed little light on an elusive and largely lost Leonardo. One could not *see* anything more in Leonardo by reading Lomazzo, and the fact that the latter went blind at the age of thirty-three may explain in part why he wrote as he did. As an overall characterization of Leonardo, Vasari's life was still unchallenged.

The second way of writing about art emerged in the circle of the French Royal Academy of Fine Arts, founded in 1648 in Paris. It was modeled on the Académie Française, which was established in 1635 under the patronage of Richelieu to create a standard dictionary and grammar of the French language. The Academy of Fine Arts was established for much the same reason: to sponsor an art whose premises and standards would be clearly understood by producers and consumers alike— in short, to establish a public art. Academic doctrine drew heavily on the paintings of Poussin, although it is not wholly clear whether Poussin was the John the Baptist of the situation or co-opted by the Parisian pedants. The Academy's position over its first twenty-five years can be stated as follows (though allowing for shades of difference between the various writers): History painting—i.e., subjects from the Bible or from history, preferably ancient—is the highest genre of painting; *disegno* is the foundation of painting, and color is subordinate; nature is not to be rendered directly but "corrected" to achieve idealization, following the model of the best examples of ancient art; the pose and the facial expression of figures are to be cultivated; and decorum is to be observed (that is, the suitability of figures to the roles they play in the narrative).

Art writing within the Academy concentrated on the subject matter of a painting as centrally important. And of all possible subject matters, history was most worthy. Invention was considered to be analogous in literature and in painting, and while painting lacked a rich tradition of criticism, there was abundant commentary on literature from as far back as Aristotle. It was natural, then, to adapt the critical strategies appropriate to literature and apply them to the visual arts. Paintings were now "read" in terms of the traditional Aristotelian literary unities of time, place, and action. Under this system, forms are to be treated as allusions before being considered as visual phenomena in their own right. Paintings, frequently those by Poussin, were thus analyzed in depth by writers such as Félibien and Charles Le Brun, chief artistic entrepreneur to the monarchy.

In order to be a candidate for such readings, a painter had to have produced history paintings. Poussin was the perfect exemplar, as was Raphael, with his Vatican Stanze and tapestry cartoons. But what of Leonardo? His major narratives were but three: the unfinished and little cited *Adoration of the Magi,* the never completed *Battle of Anghiari,* and the ruined *Last Supper.* Lacking an oeuvre in history painting, Leonardo could hardly be a subject of discussion. Leonardo languished between Lomazzo's abstract categories and the Academy's focus on the subject matter of history painting, a lost figure from the distant past according to de Piles, and acknowledged only in passing by an English compiler of old masters.

What Lomazzo and the French academicians had in common was the conviction that art is a game to be played by the rules, and here Leonardo gained new stature. The thinking that lies behind academic doctrine gathered momentum in Paris and Rome during the 1630s in a highly intellectualized way of talking about painting, culminating in the proposition that art should be based upon correct *a priori* principles and executed according to clear rules. The legacy of Lomazzo and other late sixteenth-century writers took hold, and a renewed outpouring of writing during the second half of the seventeenth century engaged in clarifying, emending, and contesting those rules.

Leonardo became a cornerstone of this activity. Well before most of the writings by the French appeared, a treatise on painting attributed to Leonardo was published in Italian in 1651, *Treatise on Painting of Leonardo da Vinci, Newly Brought to Light, with the Life of the Author Written by Raffaelle du Fresne, to Which is Added the Three Books on Painting and the Treatise on Sculpture by Leon Battista Alberti.* The engraved illustrations are by Errard after original drawings by Poussin. In the same year a French edition was published by Roland Fréart Sieur de Chambray with a dedicatory letter to Poussin. What was the origin of this posthumous publication, which became perhaps the all-time best-seller on art, with sixty-two editions, eleven in five languages alone before the end of the eighteenth century? While Lomazzo reports that Leonardo's friend Pacioli had read such a treatise by 1498, surviving material in Leonardo's notes suggests that much on painting was written toward the end of his life. After Leonardo's death in France in 1519, his pupil Francesco Melzi brought his papers back to Italy. Here Melzi loosely organized the notes on painting into a treatise consisting of 994 mini-chapters, copied the work, and illustrated it with drawings. (This manuscript is now in the Vatican Library.) While only a part of it is traceable to Leonardo's own notes, the fidelity of that part suggests that the treatise represents Leonardo's thought accurately. By Melzi's death in 1570, the treatise had been around for at least two decades, but it is unclear who saw it. It was first published in 1817.

It was a long road from Leonardo's tentative and presumably unfinished treatise to the Paris editions of 1651. At some point someone made an abridged version of the Melzi compilation, and unpublished close variants of that version proliferated. The 1651 editions were based on two of the manuscript abridgments, and were the culmination of combined efforts of scholars in the 1630s and 1640s in Paris, Milan, and Rome. The impetus seems to have come from Cassiano del Pozzo, secretary to Cardinal Francesco Barberini. Cassiano studied Leonardo material in Rome, corresponded with the Milanese scholar Galeazzo Arconati, had materials sent from Milan, and copied an abridged version of the treatise for himself. He commissioned the illustrations from Poussin, who also made a manuscript copy of the edition (and later in 1651 painted the *Landscape with Pyramus and Thisbe,* apparently inspired by Leonardo's description of a storm).

The main tenets of Leonardo's views on painting are clear enough, and consonant with the seventeenth-century French academic consensus. The eye is the primary instrument by which to achieve knowledge of the world, and painting is the handmaiden of sight. A philosopher with creative powers analogous to God, the artist can conjure whatever scenes please him. The goal of painting is faithful imitation of nature, reached by a close observation of specifics conjoined to the ordering power of mathematics, particularly geometry as applied to correct proportions and the perspectival definition of space. Mastery of these tools presupposes practice undergirded by theory, and armed with theory Leonardo regards the practice of painting as a methodical one taken in steps, the results verifiable by the judgment of both eye and mind. As stated, *disegno* is the general term for this procedure, the basic discipline of the painter as he seeks to create the illusion of three-dimensional relief where there is none.

The subject matter of the painter can be anything under creation, but his abiding concern is humankind. As Alberti had already suggested some eighty years earlier, *istoria*—history painting—is the noblest genre of painting. To undertake it successfully, a painter requires some learning in letters as well as training in art. His success depends upon his ability to render posture, gesture, and facial expression in such a way that they reveal the workings of the mind of the figure represented. Indeed, the representation of the emotional and mental life of figures in forms that give them the effect of three-dimensional substantiality are the dual requirements of successful painting. In order to be convincing, figures must be represented in specific ways appropriate to the role each plays in a narrative, in terms of age, occupation, social status, etc.—for instance, the posture, movements, and dress of an old man to be distinguished from those of a youth. Last, the underlying assumption of Leonardo, often repeated, is that art is an intellectual undertaking, rational in its procedures, whose products may be evaluated on the basis of tangible experience.

Such a capsule summary greatly oversimplifies the not always well organized treatise, and it would be a mistake to assume that it in any sense became regarded as canonical doctrine by the French academicians. On the contrary, from the beginning it was recognized as tentative and incomplete, and not often cited in the writings of the time. Yet

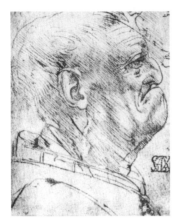

Fig. 33: Leonardo, *Grotesque Head*. Ambrosiana, Milan

the correspondence between Leonardo's writings and those of the French is striking. In general, the latter both expanded and rigidified Leonardo's ideas, and in one very significant respect differed from his. In place of close fidelity to nature observed, they counseled creation of an idealized nature through the corrective lessons offered by ancient art, which in practice mostly meant sculpture.

Whatever the correlations between Leonardo's writings and those of his French successors, and whatever authority they may or may not have accorded him, the fact remains that essentially private writings probably addressed to a circle of students ended up becoming one of the cornerstones of a public, national art policy. Although Leonardo the artist had all but faded from view, Leonardo the teacher-theorist was born. It hardly could be otherwise, since his one universally accepted and accessible artifact, existing in multiples, was a book.

This is not to say that Leonardo's visual imagery was ignored entirely. Soon after his death, people became fascinated with a series of grotesque drawings, compelling and at times bizarre depictions of human heads that push far beyond the boundaries of physical normality (fig. 33). There are dozens and dozens of these, and even today there is little agreement on criteria for distinguishing Leonardo's from those by his followers.

Leonardo, we remember, held that a major function of the painter is to reveal the mind of a depicted figure through proper attention to that person's posture, gesture, and facial expression, a tenet that finds its most powerful exemplification in *The Last Supper*. Character and mood can be read in the countenance, as well as elaborated through physical distinctions. Arguably the grotesques are a subset of this idea, the outer limit of Leonardo's constant preoccupation with comparison and varied contrast.

From the mid-seventeenth century on, interest in Leonardo's notion of revelation through facial expression and in the grotesque heads intensified, and it is worth exploring what these two enthusiasms had to do with one another.

In 1662 Fréart de Chambray wrote of *The Last Supper* that "expression, the movements of the mind, is excellent above all others [i.e., the parts of painting], and wholly admirable: for it gives not only life to figures by representation of their gestures and passions, but it seems that they speak and reason." And Félibien a few years later: "And of all the parts of painting, it is expression that [Leonardo] the most possesses, for as he who has lively imagination, and meditates profoundly on all things, enters into the passions and most hidden sentiments of men, and represents them so forcefully to the eyes, so he never fails to draw them well when he sets out to paint them."

Notions of expression and the passions seem interchangeable in much of the writing of the time, and in 1708 Roger de Piles clarified the distinction:

> The word Expression is ordinarily confused with Passions when discussing painting. They differ nonetheless in that expression is a general term which signifies representation of an object according to the character of its nature, and according to the disposition the painter who in drawing gives it in the composition of his work. Passion in painting is a movement of the body accompanied by certain expressions on the face that signify an agitation of the soul. Thus all passion is an expression, but not all expression a passion.

The strongest statement on the passions in de Piles's sense is contained in a lecture delivered in 1667 by Charles Le Brun, first painter to the King and director of the Academy of Fine Arts. It was published posthumously in 1698, with an editor's note that it was part of a longer intended work on physiognomy that Le Brun never completed. Le Brun's views had an immediate and continuing fascination,

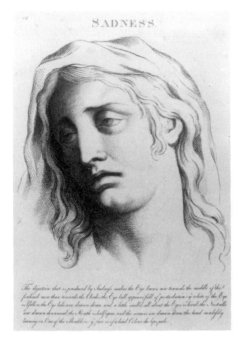

SADNESS.

The dejection that is produced by Sadness makes the Eye brows rise towards the middle of the forehead more than towards the Cheeks, the Eye ball appears full of perturbation: ye white of the Eye is Yellow the Eye lids are drawn down and a little swell'd all about the Eye is livid, the Nostrils are drawn downward, the Mouth is half open and the corners are drawn down, the head carelessly leaning on One of the Shoulders, ye face is of a lead Colour the lips pale.

Fig. 34: Engraving of *Sadness*. From Le Brun, London, 1813

with reprints and variants appearing well into the nineteenth century. Figures as varied as Hogarth and Diderot were attracted to the rigid taxonomy of what in life are the most elusive and fleeting human qualities.

For Le Brun, the passions could be enumerated and described precisely in both writing and visual illustration. Attraction, weeping, compassion, terror, desire, scorn, laughter—these and many more emotional states were specified. This is how sadness is described and illustrated in the London edition of 1813 (fig. 34):

The dejection that is produced by Sadness makes the Eye brows rise towards the middle of the forehead more than towards the Cheeks; the Eye ball appears full of perturbation: ye white of the Eye is yellow, the Eye lids are drawn down and a little swelled; all about the eye is livid; the Nostrils are drawn downward; the Mouth is half open and the corners are drawn downward; the head is carelessly leaning on one of the Shoulders; ye face is a lead Colour the lips pale.

Le Brun's "pop" version of what was an ancient idea derived most immediately from an essay by Descartes, the man who for better or for worse set the human mind apart from everything else in the world. Whatever the origins of Le Brun's idea of physiognomy as the key to a comprehensive taxonomy of the emotions, it was a success, attuned to such diverse enterprises in systematizing as Diderot's encyclopedia and Buffon's natural history. In my view, popular fascination with the paired ideas of expression of the passions and classification brought Leonardo the draftsman of grotesque heads to center stage together with Leonardo the theoretician. It is necessary to drop back to the sixteenth century to see how this happened.

The so-called grotesque heads by Leonardo represent striking instances of physiognomic curiosities and malformations. They appear to be rendered dispassionately, with no will to caricature in the sense of humor or mockery, and certainly never to sentimentalize what is observed. Some of the heads are isolated vignettes, while others are intruders on sheets dedicated to entirely different concerns, as if in daydreaming Leonardo had shifted mental gears before proceeding with the work at hand. The heads only rarely are juxtaposed in a way that might suggest a symbolic or narrative meaning.

Leonardo nowhere tells us just what he intended by these studies. He does record his subjects (for example, "Giovannina—fantastic face—in the Hospital of Saint Catherine") and remarks on the contrasting juxtapositions ("Beautiful and ugly features are mutually enhancing"). He further comments in the *Treatise on Painting* that faces reveal the character behind them through the traces left on flesh and muscle by habitual expression. The objective tone of these grotesque heads suggests that they are accurate transcriptions of specific models or imaginative extensions of concrete observation. Vasari's account of Leonardo stalking subjects that interested him and the later elaboration of this idea by other writers suggest that they believed these drawings to be the direct recording of bizarre aberrations of humanity, a reading that complements Vasari's general interpretation of Leonardo's passion for the singularities of nature. Anyone who has traveled in impoverished Third World countries, or even the New York subway, should have little problem with this explanation.

The late nineteenth century saw a seriousness of purpose in the gro-

tesques, and surmised that they were preparatory to a treatise on physiognomy. This was a reasonable view, given the large number of these
drawings and the fact that they often appear in ordered groupings. But
these groupings are for the most part by followers, and their relationship to drawings by Leonardo often tangential. There is a strong possibility, then, that Leonardo's grotesques took on a significance quite
other than what he intended. Indeed, the original context of the grotesques suggests no systematic pattern. The heads are often marginalia,
and discoveries published some thirty years ago by Carlo Pedretti shed
light on how the original intent was obfuscated.

To abridge a complex story, at the end of the sixteenth century Leonardo's sheets were organized into two collections, one devoted to technology, and the other to anatomy and art. Unfortunately this clean
distinction did not always correspond to the way that Leonardo laid
things out, for a number of his drawings with written commentary mix
these concerns. To "correct" this deficiency, the compiler would take a
sheet dedicated to technological studies and cut out art vignettes that
had nothing to do with the material on the rest of the page. He would
then fill in the gaps that he had created with fresh paper, being sure to
copy in writing removed by the excisions.

A falsification of the original context has resulted. A grotesque head
might appear as an autonomous drawing in the Windsor Castle collection while in fact it really belongs to a page in Milan that Leonardo
inscribed with notes and illustration having to do with cannon boring.
It seems that the grotesques would surface from time to time in Leonardo's thinking. Since several types are repeated, some may be memory
images, raising psychological issues far more subtle than any implied by
the assumption of a workaday project to systematically record physiognomic types.

The urge to order these heads seems already to have emerged in Leonardo's circle. A sheet by a follower in Milan and one possibly by Melzi
show series of grotesque heads ordered in profile, like so many butterflies pinned to a mounting board (fig. 35).

The public manifestation of this systematic interest comes in several
series of engraved grotesques issued during the seventeenth and eighteenth centuries. Various albums of drawings copied from originals by

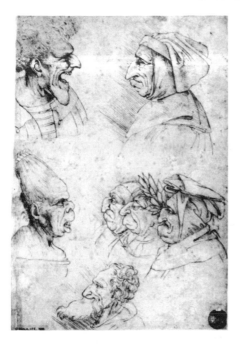

Fig. 35: Followers of Leonardo, *Grotesque Heads*. Ambrosiana, Milan

Leonardo and sheets erroneously presumed to be originals served as models, some done as late as the seventeenth century. One such album in the New York Public Library consists of 104 pencil drawings by a seventeenth-century hand, many copied from Leonardo drawings now dispersed in various European collections.

The first engraved series was done by Wenceslaus Hollar between 1637 and 1642, and was sufficiently popular to be reissued in 1648 and 1666. In 1652 Jacob Sandrart, a German, issued a similar series entitled *Variae figurae monstruose*. These series are in sympathy with a characteristically northern taste for the bizarre, a taste also shared in Italy. The album in New York is bound with a text by Rabelais, and the word "monstrous" in Sandrart's title suggests that the association of these images with the French normative, unribald academic notion of the passions could be off the mark. Yet a publication from 1730 suggests that interest in the grotesque and the issue of the passions have come together. In that year the distinguished collector and connoisseur Mariette had another series engraved by the Comte de Caylus, and in a twenty-two-page preface addressed to Crozat he summarized the state of knowledge about Leonardo. He speculates that the collection upon which these engravings are based may be one of the notebooks that Lomazzo reported Leonardo keeping to record unusual-looking heads, and that perhaps it was the very group used by Hollar. Mariette considered the drawings a striking instance of Leonardo's originality and beauty.

Mariette believed that Leonardo was the first to have founded a style based on the close study of nature, and to have understood that art is guided by rules, a dual achievement that rescued art from the barbarisms of earlier centuries. While fidelity to nature informed Leonardo's art, to Mariette this was subordinate to variety and avoidance of uniformity. That variety was achieved in good measure through expression of the passions. Leonardo was a calculating man who would throw a dinner party for peasants in order to observe their changing expressions. "Singular physiognomies being that which contribute most to characterizing the passions, Leonardo was no less attentive in doing exact research." Not a poser of light jokes like the Carracci and others in their caricatures, "Leonardo, whose views were much more noble, had the passions as the object of study. An angry, contemptuous, stupid man almost always has his character painted on his face. Leonardo by virtue of this study became a great physiognomist, and, it is said, left a fairly large treatise on this subject."

It seems that for Mariette two ideas came together: the grotesques as testimony to the variety of nature, and a Le Brunian concern with classification of the passions. Hardly the same thing, they nonetheless fed off one another, and lay at the heart of academic enthusiasm for Leonardo.

This chapter began with Joshua Reynolds, that wise and tolerant summarizer and ameliorator of much doctrinaire academic writing that had gone before. Yet, as we have seen, Leonardo was merely a background figure on a stage starring Michelangelo, Raphael, Titian, and others. How could it be otherwise with so few Leonardos to be seen? But, as this chapter suggests, Leonardo was far from forgotten. Chance and some manipulation had substituted the father of theory for the artist, the investigator of grotesque heads for the draftsman and painter of idealized Virgins, angels, and epicene youths. Leonardo the scientific-technological investigator was acknowledged in passing, but materials to substantiate that version of Leonardo lay forgotten in a library in Milan. Until the will arose to constitute a broader-based, more public Leonardo, there matters rested.

CHAPTER 6

Leonardo Goes Public

AROUND 1800, through the efforts of various artists and scholars, Leonardo went public. No longer merely the theoretician and draftsman of grotesque heads, Leonardo was now revealed as a man of wider-ranging interests, an anticipatory scientific thinker, his renovated *Last Supper* the painting of the academic tradition. At last there was a shared sense of his work and its significance.

In retrospect it almost seems as if there was a conscious program of rehabilitation, a view that surely oversimplifies the story. But it is clear that Milan triumphantly celebrated its greatest adopted son, in no small measure through the workings of Napoleonic cultural propaganda.

Several events of the 1780s are harbingers of this expanded view of Leonardo. The French painter François Ménageot composed a Leonardo deathbed scene for the Salon of 1784, thus joining Vasari's bit of myth-making to the tradition of noble and stoic deaths of great men, of which the Neoclassical painters were so enamored. In the same year a young scholar at the Ambrosian Library in Milan, Carlo Amoretti, based on years of work by the library's prefect Baldassare Oltrocchi, wrote a preface to a series of engravings done by Carlo Giuseppe Gerli after drawings by Leonardo (and drawings presumed to be by Leonardo), a project meant to offer "so much instruction to the art of *disegno,* shed so much light on the story of the human spirit, and bring so much glory to Leonardo and the city where [the drawings] are conserved." Gerli was encouraged by the collector Don Venanzo da Pagave, who owned many of the drawings. In accord with the taste of the time, Gerli first planned to confine his engravings to heads and parts of the body. But his learned friends persuaded him to omit some heads in favor of a more varied selection, including even drawings whose chief intent was not artistic.

Gerli's choice of images brought to the fore the vexed question of the relation of the true Leonardo to the Leonardesque. On the plus side, it offered the first wide dissemination of the range of Leonardo's interests, including the famous *Vitruvian Man* (see fig. 59)—now in Venice, as is the Pagave Collection—as well as mechanical-technical drawings, grotesques, and drawings preparatory to artistic projects. However, as would become evident later, the majority of the engraved drawings were not by Leonardo at all, but derived from work by him, on the borderlines between originals and direct copies—student derivations, pastiches of indeterminate origin, and free variations hard to establish. From Gerli on, sorting Leonardo from the Leonardesque would be a tortuous and unfinished business. If in a sense Gerli's project obfuscated knowledge of the true Leonardo, this was more than made up for by its demonstration of the sheer range of the Leonardesque vision.

During this period, a painting was attributed to Leonardo, but later it became notorious as a misattribution. In 1782 Luigi Lanzi, later famous for his biographies of Italian artists, reattributed a circa 1600 Flemish painting of a Medusa head in the Uffizi to Leonardo, presumably because he associated it with a painting of that subject mentioned by Vasari (see fig. 39). This attribution triggered the invention of a new Leonardo by the mid-nineteenth century.

If these 1780s events are harbingers, the manufacture of a new Leonardo accelerated in the years around 1800. The core of Leonardo's works—the *Lady on a Balcony,* the *Saint John the Baptist,* the *Madonna and Child and Saint Anne,* the *Virgin of the Rocks*—went on display in the newly opened museum at the Louvre, and in 1803 Gault de Saint-Germain published the first catalogue of Leonardo's work. Visual knowledge was furthered in 1797 by Chamberlaine's engravings of Leonardo drawings in England. Around the same time, serious work on Leonardo's manuscripts and on the archives was undertaken, primarily at the hands of Giovanni Battista Venturi and Carlo Amoretti.

Venturi was one of the finest students of Leonardo, but ironically, like the work of his famous subject, most of Venturi's scholarship was never published. He did manage to issue a prolegomenon in 1797, an essay derived from a lecture he gave to the French Institute of Sciences and Arts, *Essay on the Physical-Mathematical Works of Leonardo da Vinci, with Extracts from the Manuscripts Brought from Italy.*

It is hard to imagine anyone better suited to probe the manuscripts than Venturi. Trained in mathematics and physics, he was what today we would call an applied scientist, consulting on projects as diverse as dirigibles, bridge construction, and hydraulics. His encounter with the Leonardo material was intense and to an extent fortuitous. Sent on a diplomatic mission to Paris from the Cisalpine Republic in 1796, Venturi found himself out of a job when the delegation's credentials were refused. As it happened, Leonardo's manuscripts arrived in Paris that November along with other cultural booty taken by Napoleon. In an exhausting eleven months of work, Venturi studied and transcribed large portions of them before returning to Italy.

Venturi's lecture-essay, which he wrote halfway through his Parisian stay, was more a tantalizing outline of possibilities than a developed argument. But the publication is fundamentally important as offering the first printed, broad-based selection of Leonardo's scientific thought.

Venturi begins by characterizing the Leonardo that his studies have revealed: "The rational intellect (*l'esprit géometrique*) guided him in everything, whether in the art of analyzing an object, in the structure of his discourse, or in the care always to generalize his ideas." In natural science, Leonardo was never satisfied with a proposition unless he verified it by experience. Venturi lists a number of Leonardo's alleged discoveries, such as the theory of forces applied obliquely to a lever, the influence of gravity on bodies at rest and in motion, movements of the iris, studies in hydraulics, and the invention of the camera obscura. Saying that in the space allowed him he can give only the "hors d'oeuvres" of Leonardo's thought, he offers excerpts translated into French, each followed by a brief commentary.

The collective message of these commentaries is that Leonardo anticipated important aspects of modern science: "One must put Leonardo first among the moderns who concerned themselves with the physical-mathematical sciences and the true method of research. It is a shame that he did not publish his views in his own time . . . and [so] the age of true interpretation of nature was delayed by a century." This became the near-unanimous assessment of scholars throughout the nineteenth century: Leonardo the *deus ex machina* who anticipated the great late sixteenth- and seventeenth-century pioneers of modern science.

On his return to Milan in 1797, Venturi was received by Napoleon, and four years later entered the diplomatic corps, where the press of administration consumed his time until his death. What Venturi's contribution might have been is suggested by three thick notebooks of transcriptions from Leonardo in the library at Reggio Emilia, knowledge buried and forgotten for some eighty years.

Carlo Amoretti was the other substantial Leonardo scholar around 1800. Having succeeded Oltrocchi as librarian of the Ambrosiana, he published the fruit of two decades of research on Leonardo in his 1804 *Historical Memoirs,* a lengthy preface to a new edition of Leonardo's *Treatise on Painting.* Building on the work of Oltrocchi and Venturi, whom he warmly acknowledges, Amoretti's book marks the third substantial advance, after Vasari and Lomazzo, in factual knowledge about Leonardo. Rather than a source of critical insights, it dwells on historical specifics. He confirms Venturi's assertion that Leonardo was born in 1452 rather than 1445, weighs all the evidence to reach the conclusion—universally accepted today—that Leonardo went to Milan in about 1482 rather than a decade later, offers an exhaustive account of Leonardo's activities in Milan on an almost year-to-year basis, counters Vasari's 1550 intimations of Leonardo's atheism by finding nothing to support such a view in the notebooks, and supports Venturi's debunking of Vasari's assertion that Leonardo died in the presence of King Francis.

While Leonardo's universality had been affirmed from Vasari onward, Amoretti is the first to elaborate specifics, building on Venturi and using Gerli's engravings. He is not always factual, for instance in his perpetuation of the Vasarian portrait of a bizarre, magus-like Leonardo: "His youth and his vivacity gave rise to thoughts that appeal and were extravagant, like creating horrible smells that today we would call gas, with mixtures of odorless things, and introducing them invisibly into rooms to drive out whoever was there."

On the whole, Amoretti's Leonardo is a man of high intellectual seriousness. Amoretti picks up on Mariette's interpretation of the significance of the grotesques: "He studied them not only to paint in the face and attitudes of the beautiful and deformed, but also to express the ideas, the affects, the soul itself." He surmises that the *Treatise on Painting* is but a fragment of an intended longer work, of which he suspects the first book would have been devoted to perspective.

Amoretti seems not to have been overly interested in art, so his ner-

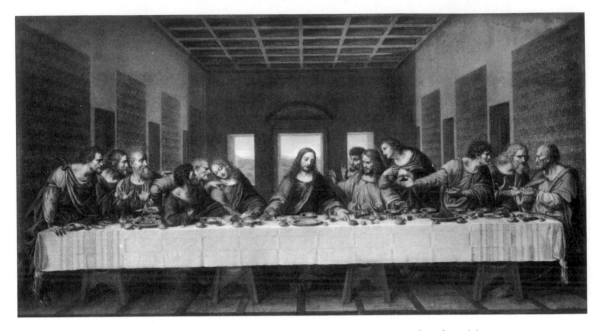

Fig. 36: André Dutertre, gouache copy of *The Last Supper*. Ashmolean Museum, Oxford

vousness about attributions comes as a surprise. He believes that a good catalogue of Leonardo's work would be lengthy if it took into account all the paintings by, or claimed to be by, Leonardo: "One will feel equally, as I do, that when a painting through popular or domestic tradition is said to be by Leonardo, it is as perilous to affirm it as to deny it," a predicament complicated by the sheer number of Leonardo's students. Notwithstanding, Amoretti finds eighteen Leonardos in Milan alone (although he is uncertain about several of them) and nearly fifty elsewhere.

Despite these doubts, Amoretti found one work, though damaged, holding a central position in Leonardo's oeuvre—*The Last Supper* (see fig. 23): "This year (1496) and perhaps earlier, Leonardo began the greatest of his works, which, according to Lanzi, is the compendium of all his studies and writings, and by which he acquired great celebrity, that is to say, *The Last Supper* in the refectory of the convent of the Grazie." Amoretti painstakingly discusses the history and condition of the mural, and reviews the evidence offered by various copies. For him the mural

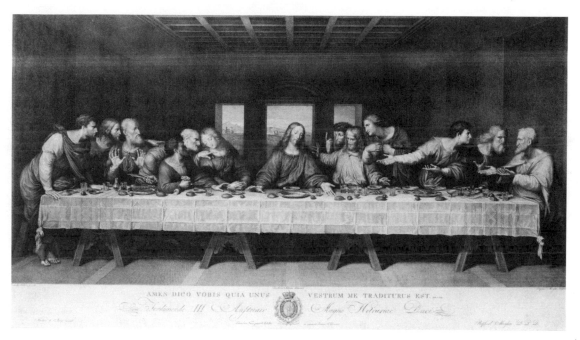

Fig. 37: Raphael Morghen, engraved copy of *The Last Supper*. Private collection

hovers between a physical fact and an idea: "I went to see *The Last Supper* a few days ago. Having just entered the refectory I turned to look at it close up, and saw almost nothing: I stepped further back, and it appeared to me less deteriorated."

If the image of a public Leonardo was to be more than a matter of books, then something had to be done about *The Last Supper*. It soon was, and though initiated in Milan, the impetus was clearly French.

The French had always had a special affinity for *The Last Supper*. Paolo Giovio reported that Louis XII hoped to transport the original to France, an oft-repeated story with Francis I the alleged coveter. Napoleon himself gave orders that the mural be protected from damage, unfortunately to little avail. This French interest is hardly surprising. After all, as far as the French were concerned, Leonardo had come to his true homeland to die, and *The Last Supper* was a great French academic "machine" (a large academic history painting) *avant la lettre*.

To seventeenth- and eighteenth-century eyes, *The Last Supper* was either badly damaged or indeed destroyed. But because it was the memory of a masterpiece, no one seems to have violated its surface for two hundred years. In the eighteenth century, however, it was "restored" or, more accurately, manhandled in botched cleanings and repaintings. In 1796 the Milanese Domenico Pino recounted the sad fortunes of the mural. While he is careful to point out that he is not a painter, and that his main concern is to establish theological correctness, Pino tells of the restorations, concluding, "It is better in my opinion to have a retouched painting than not to have one at all."

In some quarters this sort of resignation would not do, although it was realized that cleaning the surface would not reveal the lost Leonardo. Rather, one would have to make the best copy possible, availing oneself of supplementary evidence, most notably the surviving early copies. This new copy would be, in a sense, the result of "archaeological" investigation, and would serve as a surrogate original to stand in for Leonardo's largely perished work.

In 1789 Louis XVI commissioned such a project from André Dutertre, and the five years he spent on it suggest the extreme care taken. This reconstitution took the form of a small gouache, now in Oxford, which in 1794 received the Prix de Dessin of the Louvre (fig. 36). The work is especially valuable in documenting Leonardo's mural before the damage inflicted on it between 1796 and 1801, for, despite Napoleon's decree, the refectory was used as a powder magazine and stable, and for feed storage. The wider value of Dutertre's copy is as the most complete and faithful of all copies, including the earliest ones. The disposition of masses in space, the arrangement of the feet beneath the table, the placement of the objects on the table—all these are clarified.

Unfortunately, because of political vicissitudes, Dutertre's copy was never engraved and disseminated as planned. The engraver was to have been Raphael Morghen, who did in fact publish in 1800 an engraving derived from other sources in an edition of five hundred (fig. 37). It was to prove to be the most famous of numerous nineteenth-century prints of *The Last Supper,* although in comparison to Dutertre's work it is somewhat murky and wooden. Once again through an accident of history, Leonardo's reputation was not as well served as it might have been.

While Morghen's engraving gave *The Last Supper* a new life across Europe, it still did not give Milan what was so badly needed—a full-scale presence of a revivified *Last Supper,* a Mecca of the sort that existed for other painters in the other major cities of Italy. That was to happen at the hands of Giuseppe Bossi, who was one of the two leading Neo-classical painters in Lombardy, and at the behest of Napoleon's viceroy in Italy, Eugène de Beauharnais. Leonardo was about to be reborn as a creature of Napoleonic cultural politics.

In 1797 the French, having expelled the occupying Austrians, set up the Cisalpine Republic. A creation of the French, the Republic embodied the goal of fulfilling the ideals of the Revolution, and the possibility of a united Italy. These hopes played against the reality of widespread looting of the Italian cultural patrimony, including the removal in 1796 of Leonardo's Milan manuscripts to Paris.

The Cisalpine interlude was brief and disillusioning, succeeded by the new Kingdom of Italy, whose ceremonial centerpiece was Napoleon's self-anointment as emperor in June 1805. Outwardly the Kingdom was a boon for its capital city, Milan, with much money and energy dedicated to urban projects. Yet it was a highly controlled government, censorious of any remaining revolutionary or democratic leanings. The writer Ugo Foscolo, perhaps the leading critic of French repression, shrewdly observed that Napoleon had simply co-opted the intellectuals, giving each a well-defined bureaucratic position in which the expectations were clear and the incumbent beholden to a generous patron. There is no doubt that Napoleon loved Milan, nor that he indirectly ruled it with an iron hand through his stepson Beauharnais. He was a despot, but as Antonio Gramsci observed much later, an "example of progressive Caesarism."

The unhappy story of Milan in the history of freedom, so poignantly recorded in the writings of Foscolo and the historian Carlo Botta, are not part of our story. Rather, the surface of things is our story, and that surface clearly glittered. Milan flared incandescently to become a major center of literature and the arts, behind only Paris in all of Europe. Some, such as Mme de Staël in 1805, saw the city with a clear eye as a mixture of beauty and ugliness, wealth and deprivation. Yet others, of whom the most eloquent was the young Stendhal, found Paris wanting in comparison to Milan, a city of strikingly beautiful streets and courtyards. In 1819 the Duc de Richelieu exclaimed, "What a magnificent city! such riches!" In his opinion, Milan would doubtless have been the most superb city in the world had fate not led Napoleon to his fall in 1815, bringing the return of the Austrians to rule the city.

In cultural matters, Napoleon realized the potency of well-honed propaganda. In a letter of 1796 he wrote: "The sciences that honor the human spirit, the arts that embellish life and transmit great acts to posterity, ought to be especially noted in free governments. All men of genius, all who have attained a distinguished rank in the republic of letters are French, whatever the country that gave them birth. . . . The French people place more value in the acquisition of a learned mathematician, a painter of high reputation, of a distinguished man whatever the matter he professes, than on that of the richest and most populous city."

Under Beauharnais, Milan was endowed with a new cultural pride, and a new physical face, of which the most potent symbol was the rapid completion of the façade of the cathedral at a cost of 8.5 million lire, a project that had languished for four centuries. Not the least part of this cultural refurbishment had to do with Leonardo's *Last Supper*. In 1839 Stendhal published a novel of adventure and intrigue, *The Charterhouse of Parma,* in which its young hero, Fabrizio, finds himself a fugitive in Parma. Prepared for any contingency, he is armed with three passports, one for a fictitious student of philosophy named Giuseppe Bossi. The name would have immediately rung a bell for any cultivated reader of the time, and must have evoked puzzlement, for the real Giuseppe Bossi (who died in 1815) had been a leading figure in the cultural circles of Napoleonic Milan. Bossi, educated in letters and in painting, was a friend of such writers as Stendhal, Foscolo, and Manzoni, and the artist Canova. Trained as a painter in Rome, he returned to Lombardy to become one of its leading Neoclassical artists and the chief exponent of a strictly theoretical position. In 1802 he became secretary of the Academy of Art. Under his auspices its plant and curriculum were revised, and the museum later to be called the Brera was inaugurated. A man of wide culture, Bossi collected art, wrote poetry and critical essays on art, and was a dedicated administrator and teacher. But today he is remembered, more than for any of those capacities, as one of the earliest and best of Leonardo scholars.

In 1806, on commission from the Viceroy of Italy, Bossi began intensive studies of Leonardo, which resulted in two related projects: a meticulous full-size "copy" of *The Last Supper,* and a large scholarly book in which the painting and evidence concerning it are reviewed. But was Bossi's painting merely a copy? Quite evidently not, for early in 1808 he wrote to the greatest sculptor of the age, Antonio Canova, that "it is not a copy but rather a renovation (*rinnovazione*) based on good authorities, without which work moreover the memory of the original would be lost with great shame to our city." Evidently Bossi understood his task to be the creation of a surrogate original in the context of fostering civic pride. In 1805, in his *Discourse on the Public Utility of the Arts of Design,* he argued that from the beginning the arts had no other purpose than to contribute to the felicity of nations and to public morals, and that therefore they deserve the protection of enlightened governments. The subjects chosen by the artist should honor humanity and respect virtue and homeland. In an 1807 letter to Venturi he underscores the civic nature of the Leonardo commission, "all done for the glory of our country."

Bossi's *"rinnovazione"* was the culmination of a process that, after close study of the surviving copies, produced a full-scale cartoon and a completed oil painting. Ironically, like the original, Bossi's painting was ruined, destroyed in a World War II air raid along with the only known photographic negative. It is, however, preserved in the work for which the whole process was finally intended, a mosaic by the Roman Raffaelli. This was completed in 1816, but in the political vagaries of the times ended up in the Minorite Church in Vienna, where it may still be seen.

On April 14, 1807, Bossi wrote to the interior minister, the Conte di Mejan, to convey his understanding of the Viceroy's commission: "Note then his desire that an inscription indicate the noble idea of the Prince to restore to the world and put before the eyes of posterity the work of painting judged by three centuries to be the best that this art has produced, and through the medium more than any other the conqueror of time, mosaic. But this inscription, instead of being sculpted in the usual stonework and so easily removed or altered, ought to be itself in mosaic so that it can perish only with the work itself."

Bossi's determination, then, was that the end product would be a surrogate original done in an imperishable medium, in the manner of the mosaics after famous seventeenth-century painted altarpieces on the piers of Saint Peter's. A series of letters to Canova and others record his painful progress, requests for information, complaints of an obsession that drove him to illness and spitting blood.

By 1810, Bossi was finishing his book, entitled *The Last Supper of Leonardo da Vinci: Four Books* (published in 1811, but dated 1810). Even by modern standards the book has scholarly authority, the work of a man who had a comprehensive grasp on just about everything written on Leonardo up to his own time. His Leonardo is a man of austere seriousness: "I wish to defend him from the character trait given by some, that he was distracted and bizarre." As for *The Last Supper* itself, Bossi has surprisingly little to say about the composition as a whole, concentrating instead on detailed descriptions of Jesus and each of the apostles. These descriptions read like Le Brun, and indeed Bossi is faithful to Le Brun's categories of the passions.

Bossi is the observer of a *tableau vivant,* closely noting individual actors as a drama coach might do. He is not overly concerned with seeing things in terms of Leonardo's intentions, rather assuming that what one sees and the artist's intention are synonymous—that is, that academic values are the common ground of painter and spectator. Made by the rules and received by the rules, the mural suggested no conundrum about Leonardo nor asked for anything more than a communal response on the part of spectators. *The Last Supper* was more than ever a comprehensible, public monument in the grand tradition of classical painting, and an icon of civic pride.

After all of Bossi's comprehensive and labored accomplishment, it was one of the great minds of the time who in a brief review gave resonance to Bossi's work. This was Goethe, the Sage of Weimar, who published his essay in the periodical *On Art and Antiquity* number III, in 1817. Goethe first saw *The Last Supper* when he visited Milan in 1788, but his interest in Leonardo began earlier. In a letter from Rome in July 1787 he wrote: "In the evening I took a walk with a fellow countryman, arguing about the primacy of Michelangelo versus Raphael: I maintained the former, he the latter; we ended up raising a hymn to Leonardo." The following year he wrote to his patron Karl August in Weimar: *"The Last Supper* is the true key to the vault of artistic concepts. In its genre it is a unique work to which nothing can be compared."

Despite this interest, the great polymath did not write on Leonardo until some decades afterward. The opportunity came in the form of a trip to Milan by the Grand Duke Karl August. His guide was Gaetano Cattaneo, a close friend of Bossi's. Duke Karl was given first choice of Bossi's collection, and took some eighty sheets of tracings and drawings done in connection with the *Last Supper* project. He returned to Weimar with this material and a copy of Bossi's book. From November 1815 to January 1816, Goethe studied the materials and wrote his review.

Goethe wrote it in German, but it was soon translated into French and English. A summary can hardly do justice to the beautifully structured essay, but may at least suggest how he brought Bossi's long and somewhat dry account to vibrant life. He opens with an account of Leonardo's life, exploring his learning: ". . . but what, above all, he had at heart was the variety of human countenance, in which not only the permanent character of the mind, but also temporary emotion is presented to the eye. And this will be the point which, contemplating *The Last Supper,* we shall have chiefly to dwell."

Goethe invites the reader to have Morghen's print before him or her as the description unfolds. In one sense the choice could not have been better, for the print anticipates Goethe's secularizing invocation by suppressing the eucharistic glass of wine at Christ's right hand, and omitting the halos found in some early copies. Goethe begins by evoking the setting, a refectory in which the actual table of the prior faces the illusionistic table of Jesus and the apostles:

It must, at the hour of the meal, have been an interesting sight, to view the tables of the prior and Christ, thus facing each other, as two counterparts, and the monks at their head, enclosed between them. For this reason, it was consonant with the judgement of the painter to take the tables of the monks as models; and there is no doubt that the table-cloth, with its pleated folds, its stripes and figures, and even the knots, at the corners, was borrowed from the laundry of the convent. Dishes, plates, cups, and other utensils were probably likewise copied from those, which the monks made use of.

There was, consequently, no idea of imitating some ancient and uncertain costume. It would have been unsuitable, in the extreme, in this place, to lay the holy company on couches; on the contrary, it was to be assimilated to those present. Christ was to celebrate his last supper among the Dominicans, at Milan.

Goethe notes the setting of the fresco within the room, the perspective view, the height from the floor, and the genius of concentrating on the upper half of the bodies, the most potent locus of expression. But he does not allow his recitation to distance the viewer from the drama itself:

> Transfer yourself into this place, and picture to your mind the decorous and undisturbed calm, which reigns in such a monkish refectory; then you will admire the artist who knew how to inspire into his work a powerful emotion and active life, and, while approximating to nature, as much as possible, at the same time, effected a contrast with the scenes of real existence, that immediately surrounded it.

Rarely if ever had a writer evoked so well the impression and function of a work of art *in situ* for the audience for which it was intended, and been able to bring his contemporaries to empathize with the historical condition of the work's genesis.

Goethe describes the trigger of emotion in the room:

> The means of excitement, which he employed to agitate the holy and tranquil company, at table, are the words of the Master, "There is one among you who betrays me." The words are uttered, and the whole company is thrown into consternation, but he inclines his head, with bent-down look, while the whole attitude, the motion of the arms, the hands, and everything, seems to repeat the inauspicious expressions, which silence itself confirms. "Verily, verily, there is one among you who betrays me."

Leonardo's treatment of hands is the great expressive device that Goethe finds to be particularly Italian: "The countenance and action are in perfect union, and there seems to be a cooperation of the parts, and at the same time a contrast, most admirably harmonized."

Goethe observes that the apostles are arranged in four groups of three, and his description leaves each figure embedded in the wider context of the mural as a whole. We do not sense a writer trapped in the jargon of

Le Brunian concepts, but rather a reporter with acute vision who gives an eyewitness account of what befalls before his very eyes. The effect is enhanced by his having these mute figures speak, as does Philip: " 'Lord, I am not he—Thou knowest it—thou seest my pure heart—I am not he.' "

Yes, we are there, but without the names to give it away, we might think that it is a secular event. The subject is betrayal among friends, and betrayed and suspects alike suffer. Surely this is no God of power or majesty, but simply the carpenter's son, a man among thirteen men. In place of the cosmic Christ is a historical Jesus, teacher rather than miracle worker, purveyor of common sense rather than dogma. In the space of a few pages Goethe has brought these ideas to bear on Leonardo's masterpiece, transferring a divine sacrament into the most human of occasions. With variations, this interpretation stood throughout the nineteenth century. As Goethe saw it, what he and Bossi had written were requiems: "It is to be desired since the work is as good as lost, the vestiges of it may be preserved, as a melancholy, but pious memorial, for future ages."

The other major popularizer of the fruits of the Bossi years was Stendhal. In 1811 he began a translation of Luigi Lanzi's *History of Painting,* which had first appeared a couple of decades earlier. Ill-prepared in terms of knowledge of art or the earlier critical and historical literature, Stendhal nonetheless plunged in, taking notes in preparation for a project that would carry the history of painting down to his own day. The undertaking soon evolved from a translation to an original work, the scope narrowing to Central Italian painting of the Renaissance. It appeared in 1817 as the *History of Painting in Italy,* a set of striking personal anecdotes and judgments combined with borrowings from, and outright plagiarism of, earlier writers.

Michelangelo and Leonardo are the paired heroes of Stendhal's history, and the contrast drawn between them is based upon their emotional qualities: "The only emotion which divinity can inspire in feeble mortals is terror and this is the emotion Michelangelo seemed born to imprint into souls by means of marble and color." In contrast to the impetuosity of Michelangelo, "the gentleness and calmer character of Leonardo permitted him on the contrary to please in each instance, and to attach grace alike to all his actions and works."

Calm, gentleness, grace—these qualities infuse the content and the prose style of Stendhal's description of *The Last Supper:*

The painter had to represent that poignant moment when Jesus, seen simply as a young philosopher surrounded by his followers on the eve of his death, says to them with deep emotion: "Verily I say unto you, that one of you shall betray me." Such a loving heart must have been profoundly moved at the thought that among his twelve chosen friends—with whom he had taken refuge to escape an unjust persecution, and whom he wished to see assembled that day at a fraternal meal as a symbol of the union of hearts and universal love he wanted to bring about on earth—there was a traitor about to hand him over to his enemies in return for a sum of money. To be expressed in painting, such sublime and moving grief demanded the simplest disposition of the figures, in order to fix the whole of our attention on the words uttered by Jesus at this moment. The expressions of the disciples had to be of great beauty and their gestures exceptionally noble to make it clear that Jesus' suffering was not due to a base fear of death. An ordinary man would not have wasted time on dangerous pity; he would have stabbed Judas, or at least taken flight with the faithful disciples.

Leonardo da Vinci sensed the heavenly purity and profound sensibility which mark the action of Jesus. Racked by the detestable indignity of an act of such treachery, appalled at the sight of such human wickedness, he turns away from life in disgust, preferring to abandon himself to the divine sadness which overwhelms his soul. Rather than attempt to save an unhappy life constantly surrounded by such thankless men, Jesus watches the collapse of his system of universal love. "I was wrong," he said, "I judged men after my own heart." His emotion is so strong that, as he pronounces to the disciples these sad words, "One of you shall betray me," he dares not look one of them in the face. . . .

But we sense that all the men surrounding Jesus are only disciples, and the eye, after surveying the various characters, soon returns to their sublime master.

Such dignity in suffering is truly heart-rending. Our hearts are brought back to the sight of one of the great misfortunes of humanity, the betrayal of friendship. In order to relieve the feeling of claustrophobia, an impression of open air was needed. So the artist painted the open door and two windows at the far end of the room. The eye finds repose as it perceives a peaceful landscape in the distance. A longing of the heart is satisfied by this calm silence, which reigned on Mount Sion, where Jesus used to assemble his disciples. The evening light with its dying beams falling over the landscape imparts to it a tinge of sadness in harmony with the state of the action. He knows that this will be the last evening the Friend of Man will pass on earth. The next day at sunset he will no longer be alive.

With the prints of Morghen and others, with Bossi's life-size renovation and accompanying book, and with the words of Goethe and Stendhal, *The Last Supper* had returned to the consciousness of the West. A classical tradition of centuries' standing was triumphantly affirmed. *The Last Supper* shone as a paragon of art, and a jewel in the crown of the city that it adorned.

But above all, as Stendhal's passage makes so clear, *The Last Supper* was literature embodied in an image, a story heroic yet poignant. It was, to be sure, a religious story, yet creed and dogma are incidental to it. Betrayal by a friend: such was a drama that everyone could understand, a motif unequivocally in the domain of secular significances. If he was anything, Leonardo was now a public man, unattended by private ambiguities.

However, Stendhal's words evoke thoughts that are not always based on what is actually to be seen in the mural. For him, the picture itself is to a degree only the starting point for a new work of art, a passage in prose. In this respect, he is a forerunner of writers at mid-century at whose hands Leonardo would once again be invented anew.

CHAPTER 7

Leonardo the Harbinger of Modernity

D URING THE SECOND PART of the nineteenth century, Leonardo probably gave rise to more historical and critical literature than any other historical figure. If one item had to be selected as the most seminal, it probably would be an essay by Walter Pater, an influential Oxford don, that was first published in 1869 and included in Pater's famous *Studies in the History of the Renaissance* of 1873. The essay's extraordinary prose paints an unsettling portrait of Leonardo as an apostle of the modern condition. Yet there is no new fact or science in the presentation, only a rare persuasiveness that continues to hold sway well into our century. To understand Pater's position, his debt, and his originality, it is necessary to cross the Channel and to drop back several decades in time.

A JUXTAPOSITION of two passages on *The Last Supper,* the first written in 1810 and the second in 1850, suggests vividly that Leonardo had passed from one literary world into quite another in the intervening years.

Giuseppe Bossi wrote in 1810:

The space accorded him took up the width of the refectory, and such part of the height of the wall that the work was about half as high as it is wide. He adapted his composition perfectly to this field, placing across it a large table at which Christ sits in the middle with six apostles to either side, the outermost seated in profile. The figures are about half life-size, suitable to a place that admits spectators up to 120 feet away. It will be appropriate to name them one by one, in order to be aware with what finesse of artifice Leonardo in juxtaposing the characters, alternating the physiognomies and ages, varying the effects, the attitudes and customs, knew how to compose a whole so varied and at once so balanced and harmonious, that the more one contemplates this work, the more the mind is occupied and the soul filled with wonder and delight.

And then Théophile Gautier, in a travel piece posted from Milan and published in Paris in *La Presse* on October 2, 1850:

Certainly the state of degradation into which this masterpiece of human genius has fallen is regrettable; but it is less injured than one could believe possible. Leonardo is, par excellence, the painter of the mysterious, the ineffable, the crepuscular. His painting has the air of music in a minor key. His shadows are veils that he half removes, or that he thickens in order to make us divine a secret thought; his tones are deadened like the colors of objects in the moonlight, and time, which is hateful to other painters, aids him by strengthening the harmonious shadows in which he loves to plunge himself.

The first impression made by that marvelous fresco is in the nature of a dream. All trace of art has disappeared; it seems to float on the surface of the wall, which absorbs it as a light vapor. It is the ghost of a painting, the specter of a masterpiece returned to earth. The effect is more solemn and more religious even than if the picture were alive. The body has disappeared but the soul survives in its entirety.

In one description, the mural is seen in an objective way, while in the other it is the subjectively recorded impression of a viewer in a dreamlike state. Writing on art by the rules had given way to a projection of the writer's personal sensibility.

The story of the sea change in writing on art, of which these two excerpts provide a particular example, lies beyond the scope of this book. Here, only the most basic factors can be cited. After the French Revolution—which was both cause and symptom of a collapse of traditional political systems and arrangements, of creeds and dogmas—old truths were suspect, with competing ideas trying to stake claims to truth. More particularly in the affairs of art, several developments were relevant to the fate of Leonardo. The first was the slow but progressive demise of Neoclassicism—along with the attendant dogmas of history painting, presented through the rule of *disegno*—as the dominant European style. This was not simply the demise of a style, but that of the official art of an old order. Second, accompanying this development, other genres of painting proliferated and tended increasingly to be seen on an equal footing, rather than hierarchically ranked in value, as had been the French academic position. For instance, Géricault could set tradition on its head by using academic formulas of history painting to present the rude imagery of a blacksmith's shop, and could look unflinchingly at the forms of severed hands and limbs. Last, for the first time the writing of history and criticism began to go their separate ways, the former addressed to the art of the dead, the latter to that of the living. When at times these two separate genres of writing crossed over, as happened in the case of Leonardo, strategies and judgments occurred that had little precedent.

In few places is this more clear than in the work of Edgar Quinet and Jules Michelet, professors at the Collège de France in the 1840s. Protagonists in the most dramatic educational battle in France in the nineteenth century—the defense of secular control of education against the claims of the Jesuit order—they found in Leonardo, among others, a harbinger of the modern secular spirit, and thus a weapon to use against the dead hand of oppressive religious tradition.

Michelet and Quinet had been appointed to the Collège de France in 1838. The Jesuits, whose *de jure* and *de facto* claims to legitimacy in France had had varying fortunes, launched an offensive in 1841 to gain control of secondary education. In 1842 they accused eighteen professors at the Collège, including Quinet and Michelet, of "subversive" teaching, and singled out Michelet as an "impure blasphemer" the following year.

In 1843, in separate sets of lectures, the two professors undertook a counterattack, published as *The Jesuits*. Other tracts by Michelet followed—*The Priest, Woman and the Family* in 1845, and *The People* in 1846. In the former, Michelet's scorn turns to priests and Catholicism in general. The old religion is seen to seek control of the minds of women and children. Distrusting human nature, it would replace the will to freedom and liberty with obedient passivity. *The People* identifies living religion as France herself, conceived as a feminine principle, whose fulfillment demands a fusion of the warmth of the people with the intellectual sophistication of the middle class. The Revolution transformed France into a religious entity based upon Enlightenment principles, a purveyor of justice on behalf of the urban and rural poor. In an outburst of energy, Michelet turned out six volumes on the Revolution between 1846 and 1853.

Thinking of this sort became an inextricable thread in the fabric of events leading to the Revolution of 1848. A conservative government found Quinet's and Michelet's views to be sufficiently extreme to be a danger to social stability. Overflow audiences in excess of a thousand people led to government monitoring of the lectures, then suspension of the lectures and student protest—events that resulted in 1851 in the permanent expulsion of Quinet and Michelet from the Collège de France. All this occurred on the heels of a failed revolution and the ascendancy of Napoleon's nephew Louis-Bonaparte, soon to become emperor through a coup d'état.

Over a period of several decades, Michelet had undergone a remarkable intellectual odyssey and became France's most famous nineteenth-century historian. In his *Introduction to Universal History* of 1831, Michelet equated the progress of humanity with France herself—*La Patrie*—which he identified as the fecund nurse of spiritual and moral authority. Michelet was the son of free thinkers, and had embraced the Church in his teens. In the opening volumes (1833) of the *History of France*—a series that was to occupy Michelet over the next thirty-four years—he presents a sympathetic portrait of Christian society in the Middle Ages.

But by 1840 his view had changed. In an August diary entry Michelet writes: "Two ways to bear the world: accept it, approve it, like the Christians, [or] remake it like the artists. The epoch of the Renaissance is when Christian resignation was missing; no longer accepting the world, they turned to the task of remaking it." In December he records the thought that only one thing is fixed in human affairs, and that is change.

The diary entries of 1841 and 1842 dwell on death and rebirth, and describe a constant current that runs through the generations toward a beneficent future. In 1843 Michelet writes: "Christianity has two chances, to perish or transform itself. Will it transform itself, and in what proportion will it remain?" And later, "Good-bye past, good-bye Adele [his daughter], good-bye Pauline [his first wife, who had died in 1839]! All that is finished. Also my dreams of the Middle Ages. To me, then, O future! . . . All that I loved and knew, I have taken leave of for an unknown infinity, for a somber depth. I sense, without knowing it yet, the new God of the future."

While Michelet had lectured on the Renaissance at the Collège beginning in 1839, the seventh volume of his history of the Renaissance was written only in 1854 and published the following year. It followed an experience of personal renewal after years of turmoil, a renaissance in the mud baths of the Italian town of Acqui. Entered in his diary on April 10: "I'm involved in the mountain cure—and more than mine— the cure of Italy. . . . This sick people will assume moral vigor, and will purify itself in the fire of liberty." With his hopes for France dashed, he now looked to Italy to carry the torch of freedom. The emotional foundation had been laid for him finally to address the cradle of Italian civilization, the Renaissance.

Before looking at Michelet's 1855 idea of the Renaissance and Leonardo's place in it, it is useful to assess his earlier encounters with Leonardo. Already in 1833–34 Michelet had sensed a Leonardo foreign to the world of 1800:

> He seems to have, in this calm . . . something of the fantastic that makes us doubt the sincerity of inspiration. In spite of yourself, you listen to see if some bizarre sounds pierce these tranquil rocks, and if an insulting laugh will not escape these delicate figures: it is as if the profound solitudes of the New World, whose majesty may from moment to moment be troubled by the boffo intonations of the magpie. (*Cours de 1833–34,* Leçon 20)

Michelet perceives an atmosphere of disquietude, indeed of possible perversity, a particular instance of the seductive Circe that is the Renaissance.

Michelet returned to the subject of the Renaissance in the conclusion of his course at the Collège in 1838–39: "Renaissance, that is to say resurrection of Nature, of Christianity, and pagan antiquity, of Europe and of Asia." In his course of 1839–40 he stressed the importance of the invention of printing, and included a lecture on painting from Giotto to the High Renaissance. Leonardo is characterized as displaying a grace attuned to nature and paganized, so that "Saint John becomes Bacchus who becomes La Gioconda. . . . The spirit of transformation informed an age promising a *vita nuova*—a new life."

Concerning Leonardo, the exact priority of opinion by Quinet, Michelet, and the latter's son-in-law Alfred Dumesnil lies buried in conversations of the 1840s. In any event, Quinet was the first to publish on Leonardo, but it is likely that Michelet was in good measure the source of many of the ideas.

Edgar Quinet wrote about Leonardo in the *Revolutions of Italy*, published 1848–52. In his preface he makes clear his intent not to record the historical details of the communes, but the history of the soul of a people. Italy had been enslaved, at times by the emperor and at others by the Church, and the people waited to become their own master. The conscience and instincts of that people shine in Dante's *Divine Comedy*. Quinet invokes the courage of heroic individuals—Joachim da Fiore, Saint Francis, Columbus, Michelangelo, Savonarola, Campanella—who said a resounding "No!" to the perpetuation of a moribund world.

For Quinet, the sky in Michelangelo's *Last Judgment* is charged with storms that burst upon modern society, a modernism in which Dante and Michelangelo represent, respectively, adolescence and old age. The trajectory between the two is one of growing spiritual complexity, doubt, and ambiguity, and it is these very qualities that make Leonardo a quintessentially modern man:

> He had about him the distinctive trait of the Italian without a country, the same immense effort to not allow himself to be enclosed by any horizon, to be limited by any special form. Citizen of the world, he would wish to place himself in the foyer of the universe, to identify with the intimate genius of creation.

Quinet describes the variety of Leonardo's investigations, finding it most effective to use paintings as a refracting lens to reveal the colors of the master's accomplishments. He writes of the Louvre *Bacchus* (fig. 38), now long recognized as having been done by a follower:

> Look at his young Bacchus, in the midst of the first days. What silence! What curiosity! He is a seeker in the solitude of the first origin of things, the rustle of nature in the process of being born:

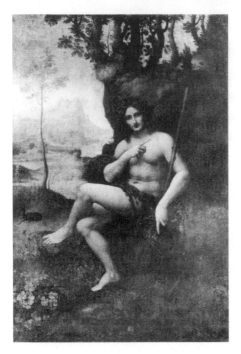

Fig. 38: Follower of Leonardo, *Bacchus.*
Louvre, Paris

he listens through the Cyclops to the surrounding murmur of the gods.

And of the Louvre *Saint John the Baptist* (see fig. 32):

I believe I find the same curiosity about good and evil in his Saint John the Precursor: a blinding look, who carries in himself the light and laughs from the obscurity of time and things; the infinite avidity of the new spirit which seeks science and cries, I have found it; the movement of the revolution of time in an expanding intelligence; the ravishment of discourse mixed with an undefinable skepticism. I do not recognize there the submissive prophet diluted by Christ and the Passion. Is this not rather the curious genius, inventive, precursor of the Renaissance, who pierces the shadows? And this mysterious finger raised in the night, what does it point to afar? What future? What unknown? Is it the rejuvenated Christ of Savonarola in the waters of another Jordan? Is it the vault of the heavens expanded by Galileo? Is it the sail of Christopher Colbus's ship? The religion of science, the Word of modern times, crying out in the new precursor?

The *Lady on a Balcony* (see fig. 1) is further witness to Leonardo's modernity:

> The smile of the Mona Lisa, is it not again the same half ironic smile of the human soul that parades in peace as it looks upon a world liberated from human terror? I cannot see this young woman without thinking that she hears about her the happy melody of the poems of Pulci and Ariosto.

Leonardo is the new secular man, and *The Last Supper* (see fig. 23) a meeting of modern minds:

> In removing the halo from the saints, Leonardo removes the crown from the Middle Age. In the *Last Supper* the guests no longer possess anything of consecrated character. The modern personages announced a new Christianity among them. . . . It is the hour when the spirits evoked in the Middle Age pale and disappear. In the *Last Supper* the banquet of Plato begins anew.

Leonardo is the prelude to Raphael, to whom Florence gave liberty and Rome grandeur. His catholicism was greater than that of the Church, for it embraced paganism, and his orthodoxy a matter of all that was beautiful. In his vision were joined two religions, two worlds. Raphael was the ideal painter announced by Leonardo:

> One sees a Church founded lower than the ideals that these painters realized through their eyes; and art, in this infinite expansion, shattered the limits of doctrine, rebelled against tradition, showed itself more universal than the Church, more beautiful than the cult, more catholic than Catholicism. It was the religious revolution of Italy.

The book concludes on a passionate note, with a charge to the Italians not to resuscitate a nation, but to create one anew: "The opportunity is unique; the voluntary servitude of France gives over to Italy the opportunity to seize with audacity the crown of civilization." One realizes now what in the course of the narrative had been implicit: that the situation in Italy is being read through French eyes, that Leonardo and his fellow pioneers of modernity were betrayed by the failure of the French Revolution. The time was ripe for the Italians to take the moral high ground. No wonder that on hearing of Quinet's death in 1875 Garibaldi called him one of the greatest of patriots.

Quinet believed in the possibility of a rejuvenated Christianity, and on this point he and Michelet drifted apart. But the latter followed Quinet's lead concerning the Renaissance, for, like Quinet, he saw a select race of individual heroes struggling against oppressive collectives, and used individual works of art to mirror wider issues.

Michelet saw the Renaissance as a rebirth, after centuries of spiritual death. It was a holistic renewal of life, a "discovery of the world and man"—a notion posited five years before the similar position taken by Jacob Burckhardt in his famous *Civilization of the Renaissance in Italy*. For Michelet, the place of renewal was Italy, in isolated instances in the fifteenth century, in full flower in the sixteenth, and then spreading across Europe. The heroes are not statesmen and soldiers, but artist-prophets, explorers, discoverers, contesters of the old order—Brunelleschi, Leonardo, Copernicus, Luther, Rabelais, and others.

Michelet's two prophets of the new order were Michelangelo and Leonardo, the former (as with Quinet) the conscience of the age, the latter the first to see the universal source of knowledge in nature. In the mid-fifteenth century, there "appeared a great Italian, the complete man, balanced, all-powerful in all things, who summarized all the past, anticipated the future—one understands that I speak of Leonardo da Vinci."

Michelet was a most visual man in both his published writings and diaries and, like Quinet, relished registering his argument through evocation of specific works of art:

> You enter the Louvre Museum in the Grand Gallery: on the left you have the old world, on the right the new. On one side the listless figures of Fra Angelico of Fiesole of the Virgin of the Middle Age. . . . Opposite the old mysticism shine the paintings of Vinci, the genius of the Renaissance, in its ruder disquietude, in its more piercing lance, [and] between these contemporaries there is more than a thousand years. . . .
>
> Bacchus, Saint John, La Gioconda direct their looks at you: you are fascinated and troubled, an infinity acts upon you through a

strange magnetism. Art, nature, genius of mystery and discovery, master of the profundities of the world, of the unknown abyss of the ages, speak, what do you wish of me? This canvas attracts me, calls me, invades me, absorbs me; I go to it in spite of myself, like the bird to the serpent. . . .

Only one thing needs to be said: these are gods, but sick. They are not a victory. The Bacchus and Saint John, these rude prophets of the new spirit, in suffering are consumed. You gaze upon their looks. A desert separates them, with a hundred uncertain images. A strange isle of Alcina is in the eyes of La Gioconda, gracious and smiling phantom. You believe her attentive to light readings by Boccaccio. Beware! Vinci himself, the great master of illusion, was taken in by the snare; long years he remained there without power to ever emerge from this mobile labyrinth, fluid and changing, that he painted in the background of this dangerous picture.

No one was more admired than Leonardo da Vinci. No one was less followed. This surprising magician, this Italian brother of Faust.

This interpretation agrees with Quinet, to whom Michelet expresses his debt, but it is more morbid, somehow unclean, the flowering of Vasari's treatment of the buckler. Alfred Dumesnil, in his *Italian Art* of 1854, transforms the *Mona Lisa* into a death-chamber portrait:

It goes so well with La Gioconda, only rendering better this insidious sweetness, in making rise from beneath the warmth of this slight swollen flesh an almost funereal pallor. A tragic and somber sign wells up in this mirage of fantasy, the enchantment of the smile, the brilliant beauty. The smile is full of attraction, but it is the treacherous attraction of a sick soul that renders sickness. This so soft a look, but avid like the sea, devours.

The almost macabre mood of such writing surely owes much to Gautier, whose description of *The Last Supper* was quoted earlier in this chapter. His *La Presse* articles of 1850 were gathered in 1852 in *Italy,* a book exuding an aesthetic of indeterminacy and mystery. What Gautier likes he frequently describes as mysterious: the Milan cathedral seems "veiled in mystery," the prints of Piranesi endowed with a "mysterious reality," and Venice is entered by night, when "the evening shadows restore the mystery which the day lays bare—and give the most simple moments of life the charm of intrigue or of crime."

Gautier presented his views on Leonardo in an 1858 article, then in *The Gods and Demi-Gods of Painting* (an 1864 series of unsigned essays by Gautier, Arsène Houssaye, and Paul Saint-Victor), and finally posthumously, to a wide audience, in *Guide to the Louvre for the Amateur.* He stresses the combination of exactitude and vision, reality and dream, and the singular, enigmatic, and mysterious quality of the paintings. He registers two new themes, androgyny and unbelief, writing of the *Saint John:* "... but his mask, effeminate, enough to make one doubt his sex, is so sardonic, so deceiving, so full of reticence and mysteries, that he upsets and inspires in you vague suspicions about his orthodoxy....[He] believes not at all in the Christ that he announces; nonetheless for the benefit of the vulgar he makes the conventional gesture, and puts the religious in the confidence of his diabolical smile."

Gautier devotes a long set piece to the *Lady on a Balcony,* a woman who, "under the *expressed* form, one senses a vague thought, infinite, *inexpressible,* like a musical idea; one is moved, troubled." Leonardo was a repository of strangeness and otherness. One senses in Gautier a drift away from the polemical patriotism of Quinet and Michelet to a taste savored entirely for its own sake, the world of darkness, shadows, and mystery, a night world of sfumato. It is the monochromatic verbal parallel to the veiled shadows of Leonardo's paintings, Charles Baudelaire's "deep and shadowed unity as limitless as darkness" (from the poem "Correspondences"), evoked in his poem "The Beacons":

> Leonardo da Vinci, profound and somber mirror,
> Where charming angels with sweet mysterious smile
> Appear in the shadow
> Of glaciers and pines which girdle their land.

It was to Gautier that Baudelaire dedicated his book of poems *The Flowers of Evil,* in which he compares Leonardo to "a mournful mirror, or darkened glass" (in the poem "Spleen and Ideal").

How this French mid-nineteenth-century portrait of Leonardo would fare in the popular mind would depend on its dissemination in books on art written for a wide audience. (Quinet's and Michelet's Leonardo were in long texts mainly about other matters.)

Charles Clément's *Michelangelo, Leonardo da Vinci, and Raphael* appeared in 1861 (followed by three more editions in the next two decades). Clément's Michelangelo is the supreme hero of the Renaissance, the anguished modern titan as Rodin was soon to understand him. Leonardo, in contrast, is the cool observer, devoid of transcendental aspirations. "He would attach himself, but without passion, to all things of the intellect" in works that lack the "moral flavor" of Raphael and Michelangelo. "The author of *The Last Supper* is neither liturgical, nor Christian, nor religious in any degree." Clément found no contradiction of such attitudes in Leonardo's notebooks, which reveal "never a word issued from the heart, never a sentiment that goes beyond reality."

In Clément's descriptions of the Louvre pictures, the heady prose elaborated by Quinet-Michelet-Dumesnil-Gautier is adopted so closely that it would be a redundancy to quote him. His concluding assessment is that Leonardo "had neither vices nor great virtues . . . he never penetrated so far as the moral world. . . . Leonardo never knew the storms of sentiment and the heart where lightning is divine light, and thunder sacred words."

In 1865 the prolific Hippolyte Taine published his *Voyage in Italy,* an enormously popular work that had reached its sixth printing by 1889. Issues of Leonardo's sensuality, sexual ambiguity, and questionable religiosity are polished artfully. On the *Saint John*: "Is it even a man? It is a woman, the body of a woman, or the body of a beautiful ambiguous adolescent similar to the hermaphrodites of the imperial epoch, and which, like them, seems to announce an art more advanced, less healthy, and almost sickly." Leonardo's paintings seem figuratively to have double and triple layers, "like a delicate unknown vegetation beneath the depths of transparent water."

During this period, the new Leonardo started out as a hero of modernity exhumed by the historians, was promptly co-opted by the literati as a morbid proto-decadent creature and wrapped in the most purple of prose, and reached an extreme at century's end in the encomiums of the bizarre Rosicrucian Josephin Péladan, for whom the *Saint John* was the greatest painting in the world. Leonardo's role in the Decadent period touched figures as diverse as Mallarmé and Moreau.

None of this could have been overly palatable to those deep in the faith. Leonardo's religion had been an issue ever since Vasari seemed to convert his 1550 unbeliever into a proper 1568 observant. The leading French writer on early religious art was Alexis F. Rio, a champion of the Italian primitives, and supporter in general of Catholic art. In 1836 Rio published *Of Christian Poetry, in Its Principles, Material, and Form*. He expresses a warm appreciation of fourteenth-century Italian art, suggesting that the germ of decadence is already present in the fifteenth century (for instance, in its fatal attraction to ancient art). To Rio, Fra Angelico is the quintessential Christian painter, but he also heaps praise upon Ghirlandaio, Perugino, and Giovanni Bellini. Leonardo is mentioned only tangentially, for Rio considered him *de facto* Milanese, someone from a region beyond the purview of his book.

Given his preferences, it is somewhat surprising that Rio published a monograph on Leonardo in 1855 (*Leonardo da Vinci and His School*) in which Leonardo is called "if not the most interesting and most pure figure in the history of art, certainly the most grandiose, not excepting Michelangelo himself." Rio tackles the question of Leonardo's religiosity head-on, although it is not the main purpose of Rio's book (perhaps it would have been had it been written a few years later). *The Last Supper* is described as "a great mystical composition" that has not always been interpreted correctly: "Goethe, who is often mistaken when it comes to Christian art, has made too much of naturalism in the interpretation of this masterpiece." Further on: "It is the work of Leonardo, independent of its intrinsic merit, that protests in favor of a dogma that one has justly called the generative dogma of Christian piety, and this protestation holds that one inspired by a prophetic instinct came just in time to revive in artists the consciousness of their Christian mission." Praise, however, is not unqualified; to Rio the *Saint John* lacks the requisite asceticism, and, in general, Leonardo's obsessive naturalism prevented him from reaching the pinnacle of Christian art.

In 1869 Arsène Houssaye published his *History of Leonardo da Vinci*. Four years earlier the author had directed an archaeological dig at the destroyed Church of Saint Florentin, near Amboise, the reputed place of Leonardo's burial. With the assistance of the clairvoyant memories of a local centenarian, Houssaye managed to unearth the supposed skull of Leonardo and fragments of his tomb. Faced with such "evidence," Houssaye had no emotional choice but to embrace Vasari's story of the death of the painter in the arms of the King.

Houssaye's Leonardo is a man without flaws, a paragon of Christian art. Like Rio earlier, he takes issue with Goethe: "It is in vain that Goethe sees in this grand page only a work of naturalism, in affirming that the portrait is but a portrait. Leonardo was too much the philosopher, if not too much the Christian, in such a representation, not to rise above the types he met during his strolls." Indeed the man Houssaye evokes is a Christian-Artist-Hero. "Leonardo is a doctor of the faith and Father of the Church. Great patriarch of Christian painting, he dared put science before the Faith, but his will proves that the former did not kill the latter. For Leonardo da Vinci, science illuminates the image of God with an ever brilliant light. The earth denied not God, but explained him."

Whatever Houssaye, like Rio before him, might write to buttress Leonardo's Christian integrity, the secular Leonardo launched by Quinet, Michelet, and others was to dominate. Only in the matter of the future could Houssaye agree with them: "He is too living to turn toward the past. His country is the Future. He will come to France to die because Athens is not at Athens, because Rome is no longer Rome, because France already suspends the new spirit from her fecund breasts."

By 1869, Houssaye notwithstanding, most commentaries on Leonardo's Louvre pictures involved a verbal web spun of strangeness, mystery, and ambiguity. Across the Channel, in the year that Houssaye published his book, Walter Pater undertook to review it. That review soon metamorphosed into the most memorable piece on Leonardo ever written. Even though there is hardly an idea in it not owed to the French, this nuanced, private meditation on modernity couched in extraordinary prose assured Pater his unique place in the writing on Leonardo.

There is doubtless a certain shallowness about the new French Leonardo. In just what did his modernity consist? He is a rebel, a discoverer, a man who says "No!" to the Christian tradition, a man who finds himself in a select company of individual cultural heroes who displayed such characteristics, ranging from Brunelleschi to Copernicus. But one looks in vain for any subtle elaboration of this argument. Rather, various passages on Leonardo, woven around the images he made, suggest an unsanctified knowledge calculated to shock the traditional-minded. Walter Pater took over this French Leonardo, accepting many of the ideas about him, but modeling a creature of more nuanced ambiguity.

To be sure, the English had earlier attempted to form a usable Leonardo. In 1828 William Brown wrote what is arguably the first monograph (it depends on one's definition) on Leonardo, *The Life of Leonardo da Vinci with a Critical Account of His Works*. The book's chief significance is as a transmitter of circa 1800 Milanese scholarship to the English-speaking world. Leonardo certainly interested the artists, as evidenced by Ralph Wornum's 1848 *Lectures on Painting by the Royal Academicians Barry, Opie, and Fuseli,* a compendium of lectures given (and published separately earlier) by the three artists. Passing on familiar views, these men are also both passionate and original about Leonardo's pioneering role in the use of chiaroscuro, which opened the way to Antonio da Correggio, that charming artist who for a few brief decades was esteemed one of the greatest painters of the West.

In 1820 in *Memorials of a Tour on the Continent,* William Wordsworth devoted a lackluster sonnet to the faded *Last Supper*. Much more suggestive was Shelley's poem "On the Medusa of Leonardo da Vinci in the Florentine Gallery," written a year earlier, and published in his *Posthumous Poems* of 1824.

I

It lieth, gazing on the midnight sky,
    Upon the cloudy mountain-peak supine;
Below, far lands are seen tremblingly;
    Its horror and its beauty are divine.
Upon its lips and eyelids seems to lie
    Loveliness like a shadow, from which shine,
Fiery and lurid, struggling underneath,
The agonies of anguish and of death.

II

Yet it is less the horror than the grace
    Which turns the gazer's spirit into stone,
Whereon the lineaments of that dead face
    Are graven, till the characters be grown
Into itself, and thought no more can trace;
    'Tis the melodious hue of beauty thrown

Athwart the darkness and the glare of pain,
Which humanize and harmonize the strain.

III

And from its head as from one body grow,
  As grass out of a watery rock.
Hairs which are vipers, and they curl and flow
  And their long tangles in each other lock,
And with unending involutions show
  Their mailèd radiance, as it were to mock
The torture and the death within, and saw
The solid air with many a ragged jaw.

IV

And, from a stone beside, a poisonous eft
  Peeps idly into those Gorgonian eyes;
Whilst in the air a ghastly bat, bereft
  Of sense, has flitted with a mad surprise

Out of the cave this hideous light had cleft,
  And he comes hastening like a moth that hies
After a taper, and the midnight sky
Flares, a light more dread than obscurity.

V

'Tis the tempestuous loveliness of terror;
  For from the serpents gleams a brazen glare
Kindled by that inextricable error,
  Which makes a thrilling vapour of the air
Become a—and ever-shifting mirror
  Of all the beauty and the terror there—
A woman's countenance, with serpent-locks,
Gazing in death on Heaven from those wet rocks.

Shelley's poem is based on the small oil painting in the Uffizi (fig. 39)
that had originally been inventoried as a Flemish painting of around

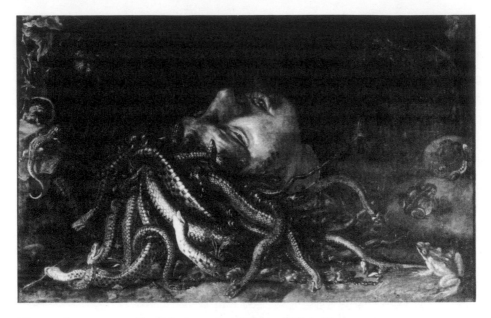

Fig. 39: Anonymous, Flemish circa 1600, *Medusa*. Uffizi, Florence

1600, until in 1782 Luigi Lanzi apparently connected it with a passage in Vasari's life of Leonardo that mentions a painting of the Medusa. Lanzi identified it as a long-lost Leonardo said in the 1540s to have hung in the Palazzo della Signoria. Wrote Lanzi in his gallery guide:

> Finally on the following wall one sees the head of Medusa with serpents so realistic that it makes credible what we read of Vinci; where in a painting produced like this in which one saw fear and fled; something that does no less honor to modern painting than did the grapes of Zeuxis or the horses of Apelles. . . . Nevertheless the work lacks the final finish, as do the works of Vinci for the most part.

However fallacious the attribution, it was an instant success. The next year Zacchiroli published a guide to the Uffizi in French, writing explicitly that the painting was believed to be the one mentioned by Vasari. Henceforth the attribution recurs in guides to the Uffizi, and the

painting is reproduced as a full-page engraving in the multivolume illustrated catalogue of the Uffizi that appeared in the 1820s. In the late
1820s the excellent German scholar Rumohr tried to stem the tide, but
it was too late. The *Medusa* had become a favored exemplar in the canon
of Leonardo's work. Already in 1851 across the Channel, Gustav Planche
had written enthusiastically of this recaptured Leonardo, claiming for it,
as Shelley had, a combination of horror and beauty, requisite qualities
of what later would be called the "horrific sublime." Planche associated
the picture with *Portrait of a Lady on a Balcony:* "I do not hesitate to say
that in the Medusa of the Uffizi there is the germ of what we admire in
the Gioconda of the Louvre." But the picture was dropped by subsequent French writers, fixed as they were on the core of Leonardos in
the Louvre. It was quite otherwise in England, where Pater would accord the picture an important place in his 1869 essay, and where a prose
appropriate to the serpentine content of the painting evolved before
Pater.

At mid-century, apparently independently of the Parisians, Dante
Gabriel Rossetti, in meditating on the *Virgin of the Rocks* (see fig. 19), saw
Leonardo as a master of the occult:

For
'OUR LADY OF THE ROCKS'
By Leonardo Da Vinci

> Mother, is this the darkness of the end,
>   The Shadow of Death? and is that outer sea
>   Infinite imminent Eternity?
> And does the death-pang by man's seed sustain'd
> In Time's each instant cause thy face to bend
>   Its silent prayer upon the Son, while he
>   Blesses the dead with his hand silently
> To his long day which hours no more offend?
>
> Mother of grace, the pass is difficult,
>   Keen as these rocks, and bewildered souls
>   Throng it like echoes, blindly shuddering through.
>   Thy name, O Lord, each spirit's voice extols,

Whose peace abides in the dark avenue
Amid the bitterness of things occult.

The writing is rich, though not as rich as that of Algernon Charles Swinburne, who published his "Notes on the Designs of the Old Masters in Florence" in the *Fortnightly Review,* just a year before Pater's essay on Leonardo appeared in the same journal:

Of Leonardo the examples are choice and few; full of that indefinable grace and grave mystery which belong to his slightest and wildest world. Fair strange faces of women full of dim doubt and faint scorn; touched by the shadows of an obscure fate; eager and weary as it seems at once, pale and fervent with patience and passion; allure and perplex the eyes and thoughts of men. There is a study here of Youth and Age meeting; it may be of a young man coming suddenly upon the ghostly figure of himself as he one day will be; the brilliant life in his face is struck into sudden pallor and silence, the clear eyes startled, the happy lips confused. A fair straight-featured face, with full circles fallen or blown against the eyelids; and confronting it, a keen, wan, mournful mask of flesh: the wise ironical face of one made subtle and feeble by great age. The vivid and various imagination of Leonardo never fell into a form more poetical than this design. Grotesques of course are not wanting; and there is a noble sketch of a griffen and a lion locked or dashed together in the hardest throes of a final fright, which is full of violent beauty, and again, a study of the painter's chosen type of woman: thin-lipped with a forehead too high and weighty for perfection or sweetness of form; cheeks exquisitely carved, clear pure chin and neck, and grave eyes full of cold charm; folded hands, and massive hair gathered into a net; shapely and splendid, as a study for Pallas or Artemis.

Another long passage by Swinburne, on a drawing of a woman's head by Michelangelo, portrays a classic example of the femme fatale—the fatal woman to whom Swinburne often turned in his poetry, his Faustine, his Dolores, inhabitants of a sin-tinged, sunless world that was to be that of Pater's *Mona Lisa.*

Swinburne was the main conduit of French literature to England in these years, and was deeply influenced by writers such as Gautier and Baudelaire. He and the French had moved from describing aesthetic qualities understood as inherent in the work of art to the writer's projection of his own sensibility onto the work of art, in turn to be interpreted freely by the sensibility of an individual viewer. This sea change in writing on art is already present in Burke and Blake, and is at the heart of the move from Neoclassicism.

So things stood on the eve of Pater's essay on Leonardo, with the ever popular Anna Brownwell Jameson in 1868 declaring Leonardo to be "*the* miracle of that age of miracles." There was but one dissenting voice, that of the new Slade Professor, John Ruskin, who was the shadow over Pater's career. In the 1869 *Queen of the Air,* a brilliant and at once inchoate exploration of the dark side of Greek mythology, Ruskin praised the bland Luini at the expense of Leonardo: "a man ten times greater than Leonardo". . . "Leonardo depraved his finer instincts by caricature, and remained to the end of his days a slave to an archaic smile" . . . "Leonardo's design is only an agony of science, admired chiefly because it is painful, and capable of analysis in this best accomplishment."

Pater's 1869 essay was included in his most famous book, *Studies in the History of the Renaissance* of 1873, thereby achieving a renown it would not have had if it had been simply a piece buried in a journal. The structure of the essays in the book and the place of the Leonardo essay among them lie beyond my purpose here. Rather, before turning to Pater's Leonardo, it may help to explore three essays that preceded it, in which Pater's view of the modern condition is established.

Pater wrote about Coleridge in 1866, allowing that the great poet-critic clung to the idea of the absolute spirit to the detriment of his well-being. Coleridge failed to grasp that a new spirit was abroad, the spirit of the relative, whose characteristics were flux, ambiguity, and contingency. The only remaining certainty was the certainty of change.

Pater's essay on Winckelmann followed the next year, in 1867. The great German classicist, the first art historian in the modern sense, wrote a century before Pater. Pater treats him with deep nostalgia, in full cognizance of the poignancy of a Renaissance figure who lived three centuries too late. The essay is a trip back from the ambiguities of the present to that "unperplexed youth of humanity," Hellenism, whose culture is one of intellectual light, characterized by "breadth, centrality, with blitheness and repose." Unlike many antecedents of contemporary thought that live an underground life, Hellenism alone is a conscious tradition to which culture is "drawn back to its source to be cherished and corrected." Sculpture is seen to be the quintessential art of the Greeks, with its clear presentation of form shorn of accident and of any tendency to subjective self-analysis. Indeed, the Greek genius lay in avoidance of excessive inwardness, never reaching for meanings beyond the realm of experience as it self-evidently manifests itself. This was the secret lost upon the modern world.

Winckelmann's accomplishment was to have made of himself a work of art that reflected the lucidity and balance of Hellenic culture, an anachronism in his own time, come into Italy and the world too late: "Certainly, for us of the modern world, with its conflicting claims, its entangled interest, distracted by many sorrows, with human preoccupations, so bewildering an experience, the problem of unity with ourselves, in blitheness and repose, is harder than it was for the Greek within the simpler terms of antique life. Yet not less than ever, the intellect demands completeness, centrality." And also: "The longer we contemplate that Hellenic ideal, in which man is a unity with himself, with his physical nature, with the outward world, the more we may be inclined to regret that we ever should have passed beyond it to contend for a perfection that makes the blood turbid and frets the flesh, and discredits the world about us."

Four pages from Pater's 1868 review of the poems of William Morris—which Pater later adapted for the conclusion of his book *The Renaissance*—lay out his understanding of the modern condition and the appropriate mode of living within it. Some, he writes, spend their lives in listlessness, "some in high passions, the wisest, at least among 'the children of this world,' in art and song." ... "Of such wisdom, the poetic passion, the desire of beauty, the love of art for its own sake," ... "For art comes to you proposing frankly to give nothing but the highest quality to your moments as they pass, and simply for those moments' sake." ... "To burn always with this hard, gem-like flame, to maintain this ecstasy, is success in life."

Such thoughts were immediately seized upon as evidence of Pater's hedonistic disposition, in which delectation through art was deemed the highest mode of being. While it would be disingenuous to deny this criticism altogether, it obfuscated Pater's serious concern with broader issues. In a striking parallel to contemporary scientific thought, Pater holds that bodies and the outer world are not as they seem to the eye but are in perpetual flux, as is the inner world of thought and feeling. Our sensations and cognition are merely "momentary acts of sight and passion and thought." Each of us is a highly subjective organ "dwarfed into the narrow chamber of the individual mind." Our impressions are divisible, limited in duration, and in constant flight.

It is on this scientifically founded exposition of the flux of being and cognition that Pater erects an aesthetic position, one that follows ineluctably his premises: "Every moment some form grows perfect in hand or face, some tone on the hills or the sea is choicer than the rest; some mood of passion or insight or intellectual excitement is irresistibly real and attractive to us—for that moment only." Not the fruit of experience, but experience itself is the end. The analogy of the flame, which Pater uses twice earlier in the essay, now becomes an exhortation to intense living, "to burn always with this hard, gem-like flame." Not to do so "is, on this short day of frost and sun, to sleep before evening."

Whereas the 1867 essay on Winckelmann is a dirge to the contemporary possibility of Hellenism, the pages that were to become the conclusion to Pater's book examine the conditions that made Hellenism a lamented memory and compelled new intellectual habits. It remained for Pater to describe the first modern man, and that he did in the Leonardo essay of 1869. Here the reader is urged to take Pater's essay in hand, for it would be folly to attempt to summarize or paraphrase one of the more seamless essays in the English language. The most I can do here is offer a thumbnail characterization of it and elaborate on a couple of aspects.

The essay on Leonardo and the essay on Winckelmann form a diptych whose two parts are painted in contrasting colors. Pater's Winckelmann is broad and serene, purged of the nonessential, at peace with himself and the palpability of the physical world, while Leonardo is conflicted, driven, never satisfied, discontented with outer appearances, overreaching the here-and-now to try and grasp the inward and unknown.

Unsatisfied with the surface of things, Leonardo reached for "a sanctified and secret wisdom," revealing in his work "something beyond the usual measure of great men." Because his desire outstripped his means, "it awoke in Leonardo some seed of discontent which lay in the secret places of his nature." No longer the cheerful objective painter, he learned "the art of going deep, of tracking the sources of expression to their subtlest retreats, the power of an intimate presence in the things he handled." Believer in mysteries, he "preferred always the more to the less remote."

"He was smitten with a love of the impossible" which churned in his "overwrought and laboring brain." To his contemporaries he seemed "the sorcerer and magician, possessed of curious secrets and a hidden knowledge." For Pater, and here lies the strongest contrast with Winckelmann, Leonardo was a mind that pushed too far: "Sometimes this curiosity came in conflict with the desire of beauty: it tended to make him go too far below that outside of things in which art really begins and ends." Unlike a pacific Hellene, Leonardo was afflicted with a struggle between reason and the senses, now no longer to be reconciled.

Leonardo, then, is anything but a delver in the face-value aspects of nature. "Out of the secret places of a unique temperament he brought strange blossoms and fruit hitherto unknown." Pater believed that Leonardo's fascination for us as an artist lies in part in the way in which his nominal subjects yield before their true content: while Leonardo "handles sacred paintings continually, he is the most profane of painters," their subjects but "the pretext for a kind of work which carries one altogether beyond the range of its conventional associations." In Pater's terms, how unthinkable this would be for a Greek sculptor of the gods.

Leonardo's modernity seems kaleidoscopic rather than linear, in constant movement, allusive, beyond the discourse of demonstrable argument, loathing closure. Small wonder that Pater habitually chose the essay as the genre best suited for evocations of indeterminacy and ambiguity. Within Pater's essays the points of emphasis are often a descriptive set piece, sometimes a landscape, usually a work of art through which the salient threads of a culture are seen large as if through a tailor's magnifying glass. Two important instances in the essay on Leonardo are the description of the peasant's shield near the beginning and that of the *Mona Lisa* toward the end.

Having evoked thoughts of strangeness and of discontent, a penchant for going deep and for the impossible, Pater discusses Leonardo's joining of the extremes of beauty and terror (compare Shelley), a vision that yields drawings both of gracious youths and of grotesques:

> All these swarming fancies unite in the *Medusa* of the Uffizi. Vasari's story of an earlier Medusa, painted on a wooden shield, is perhaps an invention; and yet, properly told, has more of the art of truth about it than anything else in the whole legend. For its real subject is not the serious work of a man, but the experiment of a child. The lizards and glowworms and other strange small creatures which haunt an Italian vineyard bring before one the whole picture of a child's life in a Tuscan dwelling—half castle, half farm—and are as true to nature as the pretended astonishment of the father for whom the boy has prepared a surprise. It was not in play that he painted that other Medusa, the one great picture which he left behind him in Florence. The subject has been treated in various ways; Leonardo alone cuts to this centre; he alone realizes it as the head of a corpse, exercising its powers through all the circumstances of death. What may be called the fascination of corruption penetrates in every touch its exquisitely finished beauty. About the dainty lines of the cheek the bat flits unheeded. The delicate snakes seem literally strangling each other in terrified struggle to escape from the Medusa brain. The hue which violent death always brings with it is in the features; features singularly massive and grand, as we catch them inverted, in a dexterous foreshortening, crown foremost, like a great calm stone against which the wave of serpents breaks.

Pater then characterizes the nature of Leonardo's investigations: "The science of that age was all divination, clairvoyance, unsubjected to our exact modern formulas, seeking in an instant of vision to concentrate a thousand experiences." To his contemporaries he seemed "the sorcerer or the magician, possessed of curious secrets and hidden knowledge, living in a world of which he alone possessed the key." The strange experimenter evoked by Vasari is joined to the Paterian dicta of flux and necessity to seize the moment, and by the close of the first third of the essay Leonardo's character is delineated, culminating in the following thought: "Curiosity and the desire of beauty—these are the two elementary forces in Leonardo's genius; curiosity often in conflict with the desire of beauty, but generating, in union with it, a type of subtle and curious grace."

It is above all that subtle and curious grace that marks *Mona Lisa* (see fig. 1), to which Pater devotes a brilliant passage toward the end of the essay:

La Gioconda is, in the truest sense, Leonardo's masterpiece, the revealing instance of his mode of thought and work. In suggestiveness, only the Melancholia of Dürer is comparable to it; and no crude symbolism disturbs the effect of its subdued and graceful mystery. We all know the face and hands of the figure, set in its marble chair, in that circle of fantastic rocks, as in some faint light under sea. Perhaps of all ancient pictures time has chilled it least. As often happens with works in which invention seems to reach its limit, there is an element in it given to, not invented by, the master. In that inestimable folio of drawings, once in the possession of Vasari, were certain designs by Verrocchio, faces of such impressive beauty that Leonardo in his boyhood copied them many times. It is hard not to connect with these designs of the elder, by-past master, as with its germinal principle, the unfathomable smile, always with a touch of something sinister in it, which plays over all Leonardo's work. Besides, the picture is a portrait. From childhood we see this image defining itself on the fabric of his dreams; and but for express historical testimony, we might fancy that this was but his ideal lady, embodied and beheld at last. What was the relationship of a living Florentine to this creature of his thought? By what strange affinities had the dream and the person grown up thus apart, and yet so closely together? Present from the first incorporeally in Leonardo's brain, dimly traced in the designs of Verrocchio, she is found present at last in *Il Giocondo*'s house. That there is much of mere portraiture in the picture is attested by the legend that by artificial means, the presence of mimes and flute-players, that subtle expression was protracted on the face. Again, was it in four years and by renewed labour never really completed, or in four months and as by stroke of magic, that the image was projected?

The presence that rose thus so strangely beside the waters, is expressive of what in the ways of a thousand years men had come to desire. Hers is the head upon which all "the ends of the world are come," and the eyelids are a little weary. It is a beauty wrought out from within upon the flesh, the deposit, little cell by cell, of strange thoughts and fantastic reveries and exquisite passions. Set it for a moment beside one of those white Greek goddesses or beautiful women of antiquity, and how would they be troubled by this beauty, into which the soul with all its maladies has passed! All the thoughts and experience of the world have etched and moulded there, in that which they have of power to refine and make expressive the outward form, the animalism of Greece, the lust of Rome, the mysticism of the middle age with its spiritual ambition and imaginative loves, the return of the Pagan world, the sins of the Borgias. She is older than the rocks among which she sits; like the vampire, she has been dead many times, and learned the secrets of the grave; and has been a diver in deep seas, and keeps their fallen day about her; and trafficked for strange webs with Eastern merchants: and as Leda, was the mother of Helen of Troy, and, as Saint Anne, the mother of Mary; and all this has been to her but as the sound of lyres and flutes, and lives only in the delicacy with which it has moulded the changing lineaments, and tinged the eyelids and the hands. The fancy of a perpetual life, sweeping together ten thousand experiences, is an old one; and modern philosophy has conceived the idea of humanity as wrought upon by, and summing up in itself, all modes of thought and life. Certainly Lady Lisa might stand as the embodiment of the old fancy, the symbol of the modern idea.

This unforgettable passage is often quoted as a paragon of "impressionistic criticism"—an extreme example of the projection of a writer's sensibility upon an aesthetic object. Less charitably, it has been deemed an exercise in writing about what is not to be seen in the picture itself. These views may well oversimplify Pater's purposes. The first paragraph is about cumulative memory—"From childhood we see this image defining itself on the fabric of his dreams"—a coming together at the picture's conception. The second paragraph broadens that notion to a panorama of the cultural landscape of the West. There is a continuity in metamorphosis in which new forms emerge, but nothing of value is ever forgotten. The painting is a crystallization of strangeness and newness, a validation of the historical road that we have traveled, a history perceived by the individual sensibility through the refracting lens of the work of art. The general idea of a Leonardo who sums up what came before is, as we have seen, French, as is the notion of using the work of art to embody that accumulated past.

Pater's 1873 *Studies in the History of the Renaissance,* in which the Leonardo essay was included, was criticized on publication as not being a work of history, which of course in any conventional sense it is not. Pater was sufficiently stung by the criticism that he changed the title of subsequent editions to simply *The Renaissance,* with the subtitle *Studies in Art and Poetry.* Yet, arguably, the microcosm that is the passage about the *Mona Lisa* characterizes the book as a whole, and suggests that Pater, beyond offering an aesthetic position, was a serious if unconventional historian.

The 1910 library edition of Pater's works runs to ten volumes. Much of it is fiction, along with some literary criticism, a smaller amount of art criticism, and hardly anything that one today would call straight history. Whatever the genre, however, Pater's work has an abiding theme, "the process of brain-building," described in his 1878 short story "The Child in the House." By "brain-building," Pater meant nothing less than the intellectual and spiritual pilgrimage of individuals, historical or imagined, undergoing constant change through the course of their lives, and, by wider extension, the intellectual odyssey of the West. This is what *Studies in the History of the Renaissance* is about, as is the long novel *Marius the Epicurean,* and those vignettes which Pater called imaginary portraits.

As the conclusion of *The Renaissance* intimated, in apparent contradiction to one's storehouse of memories, the individual mind is a closed chamber of fleeting sensations, of impressions of passing moments. This position, if taken to an extreme, precludes a shared tradition and hence a viable cultural community. Pater surely did not see things this way, for sensations in the sentient moment lack resonance unless played against the rich conundrums of cultural memories.

In Pater's 1893 *Plato and Platonism,* considered by him his best book, he describes a trait possessed by all people past and present as the "general consciousness." This general consciousness is our portal to the past, through which the historian must pass to evaluate the dead in the only way possible, by comparison to one's impressions of the present day. Indeed, the present is in part the synchronic presence of past vibrations. So it is in Pater that the pagan gods find employment in the new religion, and that Leda, Mary, Saint Anne, and Mona Lisa can exist in kaleidoscopic overlay. The momentary sensation evoked by a cloud, a cool breeze, or a sunset may constitute the present when the aesthete speaks, but for the historian, as the passage about the *Mona Lisa* reveals, the present is in part a newness arising from the evocative accumulation of memories. The past must in turn be reenacted by the living, or it is a dead issue, as is the present in extreme impoverishment without the constant nourishment of recollection. It follows that the historian is inevitably deeply implicated in the story that he or she tells.

So, I believe, emphasis should be shifted somewhat from Pater the aesthete to Pater the unconventional historian, invisibly and non-causally at the forefront of a recognizable historical tradition that includes Dilthey, Croce, and Collingwood, all of whom pointed to the inevitability of the historian's involvement in the object of study. If we are better to understand ourselves, which is ultimately the point of historical studies, we have to risk and indeed celebrate critical leaps of the imagination in an intellectual procedure that by its very nature is ambiguous.

Self-understanding surely was also at the heart of the enterprise of Michelet, that historian whom Pater names at the beginning of his essay on Leonardo, and the imagination was certainly no stranger to the Frenchman. Pater and Michelet shared similar ideas about the Renaissance: that it is a disposition of the spirit more than a chronological period; that continuity wearing different masks at different times is the glue of cultural history; that bellwether figures tend to be cultural rather than political; that a pagan-Christian reconciliation is the mediating role of these figures; and (in contrast to Nietzsche's beliefs) a viable future can be built only by weighing the significance of the past. But on this last point, separation begins to occur. In his most pessimistic moment, Michelet can still invoke the future, but Pater is always mired in the past, like his Winckelmann, a man born into the world too late. Both men are obsessed with death, but it is Michelet who points to the resurrection. Perhaps the main difference is in the matter of protest. At significant moments, Michelet's writing was a protest on behalf of women, children, the people. He was a seeker of general mentality, a listener to those without voice. Pater was an unbeliever, and it cost him in his Oxford career, but he protested nothing, confining his attention to the high culture of the West. While Michelet's life was a compelling drama, Pater coasted through an uneventful professor's career, which may be one reason that so far there is no wholly satisfying biography of him.

Despite the latent possibilities of Pater as historian, his reputation in the early twentieth century was constructed mainly as an aesthete propounding an extreme position of art-for-art's sake. This was in no small measure because of Oscar Wilde, who in his book *Intentions* of 1891 seized upon Pater as an example to deny vehemently Matthew Arnold's position that criticism is properly subordinate to the art of which it treats, and has as its end exposition of the object "as in itself it really is." For Wilde, Ruskin's "mighty and majestic prose" on the painter J. M. W. Turner surely overrides the banality as to whether the critics' views are historically sound or not, a point that Wilde brings home by considering Pater, critic of the *Mona Lisa:*

> Who, again, cares whether Mr. Pater has put into the portrait of Mona Lisa something that Leonardo never dreamed of? The painter may have been merely the slave of an archaic smile, as some have fancied, but whenever I pass into the cool galleries of the Palace of the Louvre, and stand before that strange figure "set in its marble chair in that cirque of fantastic rocks, as in some faint light under sea," I murmur to myself, "She is older than the rocks among which she sits; like the vampire, she has been dead many times, and learned the secrets of the grave; and has been a diver in deep seas, and keeps their fallen day about her; and trafficked for strange webs with

Eastern merchants; and, as Leda, was the mother of Helen of Troy, and as St. Anne, the mother of Mary; and all this has been to her but as the sound of lyres and flutes, and lives only in the delicacy with which it has moulded the changing lineaments, and tinted the eyelids and the hands." And I say to my friend, "The presence that thus so strangely rose beside the waters is expressive of what in the ways of a thousand years men had come to desire;" and he answers me, "Hers is the head upon which all the 'ends of the world are come,' and the eyelids are a little weary."

And so the picture becomes more wonderful to us than it really is, and reveals to us a secret of which, in truth, it knows nothing, and the music of the mystical prose is as sweet in our ears as was that flute-player's music that lent to the lips of La Gioconda those subtle and poisonous curves. Do you ask me what Leonardo would have said had anyone told him of this picture that "all the thoughts and experience of the world had etched and moulded therein that which they had of power to refine and make expressive the outward form, the animalism of Greece, the lust of Rome, the reverie of the Middle Age with its spiritual ambition and imaginative loves, the return of the Pagan world, the sins of the Borgias?" He would probably have answered that he had contemplated none of these things, but had concerned himself simply with certain arrangements of lines and masses, and with new and curious colour-harmonies of blue and green. And it is for this very reason that the criticism which I have quoted is criticism of the highest kind. It treats the work of art simply as a starting-point for a new creation. It does not confine itself—let us at least suppose so for the moment—to discovering the real intention of the artist and accepting that as final. And in this it is right, for the meaning of any beautiful created thing is, at least, as much in the soul of him who looks at it, as it was in his soul who wrought it. Nay, it is rather the beholder who lends to the beautiful thing its myriad meanings, and makes it marvellous for us, and sets it in some new relation to the age, so that it becomes a vital portion of our lives, and a symbol of what we pray for, or perhaps of what, having prayed for, we fear that we may receive.

This is heady stuff, an ancestor of critical attitudes that still exist today. No wonder that any thought of Pater as a historical thinker lay dormant for a long time.

So it was that Pater slipped from popular view in the earlier twentieth century, his deeper content ignored. The importance of his language was crucial, yet the Moderns remained largely silent about their staggering debt to him. This injustice has been rectified in numerous doctoral dissertations; but it was William Butler Yeats, in a passage in the introduction to his *Oxford Book of Modern Verse* of 1936, who intimated what is far more important about Pater than his basically unoriginal views on either Leonardo or the Renaissance:

> But one writer, almost unknown to the general public—I remember somebody saying at his death "no newspaper has given him an obituary notice"—had its entire uncritical admiration, Walter Pater. That is why I begin this book with the famous passage from his essay on Leonardo da Vinci. Only by printing it in *vers libre* can one show its revolutionary importance. Pater was accustomed to give each sentence a separate page of manuscript, isolating and analyzing its rhythm; Henley wrote certain "hospital poems," not included in this book, in *vers libre,* thinking of his dramatic, everyday material, in that an innovator, but did not permit a poem to arise out of its own rhythm as do Turner and Pound at their best and as, I contend, Pater did.

And so the very first poem in Yeats's anthology:

WALTER PATER

1839–1894

Mona Lisa

She is older than the rocks among which she sits;
  Like the Vampire,
She has been dead many times,
And learned the secrets of the grave;
And has been a diver in deep seas,
And keeps their fallen day about her;
And trafficked for strange webs with Eastern merchants;
And, as Leda

Was the mother of Helen of Troy,
And, as St. Anne,
Was the mother of Mary;
And all this has been to her but as the sound of lyres and flutes,
And lives
Only in the delicacy
With which it has moulded the changing lineaments
And tinged the eyelids and the hands.

CHAPTER 8

The Mind of the Maker

WRITERS FROM VASARI ON had contemplated the mind of Leonardo, and were badly hampered by scant knowledge of the master's writings. From Stendhal to Pater, given post-Neoclassical critical premises, such meditations had more to do with a mirroring of a given writer's own mind than it did with the mind of Leonardo. Finally in 1881 Leonardo's notebooks began to be published, and down to our own time a line of distinguished scholars created a more distinct and subtle portrait of Leonardo's mind than would have been possible earlier. The story of this scholarship is beyond the purposes of this book, but in its earlier phase it was complemented by two non-scholars who in radically divergent ways felt the need to come to grips with the phenomenon of Leonardo's mind: Paul Valéry and Sigmund Freud.

Not only did Valéry doubt the possibility of retrieving a specific mind from the grave—he was skeptical of the historical enterprise in general, believing history to be little more than work of the imagination based upon records. Yet there were metaphorical uses of the past as a gateway for understanding the present, and early on a Leonardo-like mind was the center of Valéry's attention.

The analyst Freud, on the other hand, was wont to generalize from specific clinical cases, and in a brilliant essay proposed that on the assumption that a Viennese mind in 1900 must approximate a Florentine mind of circa 1500, Leonardo was fit to be a dead analysand.

Valéry had begun to write poetry at the age of thirteen, and was first published in 1889, by which time he had composed some two hundred poems. In 1891 he met Mallarmé and Gide in Paris, and it seemed that a promising literary career had been launched. Yet the following year a personal crisis intervened—real, no doubt, but later magnified in Valéry's self-conscious cultivation of personal sagedom. He had fallen in love with a married woman, a relationship that was doomed, and during the "Night of Genoa," October 4–5, 1892, suffered an emotional episode that led to a renunciation of his art in favor of "the silence," a quarter-century hiatus in which in intellectual austerity he contemplated the possibilities of pure mind risen above the affective and quotidian concerns in which the usual run of humanity passes its life.

In 1894 Valéry began an intellectual notebook, writing several hours each day early in the morning a continuing meditation on the character, limitations, and potentiality of cerebration. By the time of his death these notebooks numbered some 29,000 pages. In their earliest form some of these pages look more than a little like sheets from Leonardo's hand, perhaps not surprising in that the master was now the focus of Valéry's attention.

It might be said that Valéry had succumbed to the particularly French malady of monstrous cerebration, already writ so large in Descartes. The early symptoms are two essays, "The Evening with Monsieur Teste," published in *Le Centaure* in 1896, and "Introduction to the Method of Leonardo da Vinci," which appeared in *La Nouvelle Revue* in 1895. These complementary essays were begun in mid–1894, and both were seminally important to Valéry's early development. Each initiated cycles of writing that extended through most of his life.

"The Evening with Monsieur Teste" is about a dozen pages long, without a wasted sentence or word. The essay is the portrait of a most ordinary-looking man who inhabits ordinary quarters and moves through daily life in a seemingly ordinary way. Teste's sole occupation is cultivation of enhanced intellectual power through developing self-awareness of mental processes. So concentrated is he on this task that he has given up reading and writing. Teste, it seems, is pure head (*tête,* in French).

The narrator begins the essay by observing of himself, "Stupidity is not my strong point." He, too, is an ordinary fellow who has strung together those experiences of persons, places, and books that constitute the conventional life as lived. But he is bothered; how is it that we tend to appraise our thought in the way that others express theirs? People who we regard as superior in fact dilute their powers by worrying about how they present themselves to others. Is it possible, he wonders, that the real connoisseurs of thought are uncompromising unknowns, authors of unwritten masterpieces, and "solitaires who know before all the rest"?

The narrator was beginning to think no more upon these matters when he met Edmonde Teste, an unobtrusive man to whom no one paid any heed. Behind that banal physical façade the narrator glimpses the "incomparable mental gymnastics" of a mind that "had managed to discover laws of the mind we know nothing of." Teste speaks: "I gave up books twenty years ago. I have burned my papers also. I scrape to the quick ... I keep what I want. But that is not the difficulty. *It is rather to keep what I shall want tomorrow.* I tried to invent a mechanical sieve."

One of Teste's great experiments was to plumb the nature of "duration, its distribution, and regulation," and his motto was *"maturare,"* to mature—the art of mentally becoming. He was a man who had become his own self-enclosed mental system, renouncing sensuous pleasures in search of the freedom of a disciplined mind. He is interested only in the ease or difficulty of knowing, meditated in pure detachment, a mind that "performed" what occurred to it.

Teste and the narrator go to the theater, a dazzling artificial setting of costumes, flickering lights, and shadows, evoked as if in a painting by Degas. The audience is classifiable by types, yet bonded by emotions that will culminate in the crescendo of the spectacle. But Teste looks not at this spectacle, but at the audience instead. He will not be pulled in: "Let them enjoy and obey! ... The supreme simplifies *them.* I wager they are thinking, more and more, *toward* the same thing. They will be equal at the climax or common limit. Yet the law is not so simple ... since it does not include me; and—here I am." Teste will not surrender. He renounces the spectacle and mentally stands aloof.

But pure cerebration is an ideal imperfectly realized in a mortal body. On leaving the theater, Teste complains of the chill night and of the onset of old pains. Asked by the narrator what is the harm of surrendering to the spectacle, Teste replies: "I am at home in MYSELF, I speak my own language. I hate extraordinary things. Only weak minds need them." *"Que peut un homme?"* (What is a man's potential?), asks Teste.

Back at Teste's apartment, over cigars and by the light of a candle,

Teste speaks of public tastes and passions, and recites a litany of stock market quotations, observing that "gold is somehow the mind of society." He slips into bed and asks the narrator to linger for a while. Children discover their physical selves bit by astonishing bit, but Teste knows himself by heart by now. In some pain, he evokes the stillness of death. Even in physical distress a person can always plunge into a problem or question, which, like suffering itself, requires supreme attention. Before Teste's illness was an actuality, he had already been able to pursue it in the form of an idea.

Teste begins to slip into sleep. "I am thinking, and that hinders nothing. I am alone. How comfortable solitude is. . . . Any man who talks to me, if he has no proof, is an enemy. I prefer the brilliance of the least thing that happens. I am being and seeing myself, and so forth. Let's think very closely. Rubbish! Any subject at all will put you to sleep. . . . Sleep will prolong any idea at all."

Teste now snoring, the narrator takes the candle and tiptoes out. So closes the brief portrait of a high priest of the intellect, a magician of worldly renunciation even in the face of intimations of death. A pure invention, Teste nevertheless seems to have been inspired by Valéry's friends the poet Mallarmé and the painter Degas. A new Leonardo was now invented to be Teste's activist brother.

The essay on Leonardo was commissioned by Madame Juliette Adam in 1894. The long essay that resulted is an inquiry into the potentialities of a Leonardo-like mind. Equally a hero of cerebration, Valéry's Leonardo differs from Teste in two respects: he has a historical rather than a fictional basis, and is a maker in addition to being a thinker.

Valéry is forthcoming about his qualifications and intentions: "Knowing very little about Leonardo, and in short being surprised by her request, I accepted for the reasons stated above, and invented a Leonardo of my own." And in a letter to his brother, probably of April 1895: "I don't give a hang for the erudite-aesthetic side. I rule out the known figure of a da Vinci mind, and the problems to me come down to this: 'People say he was a universal mind. What is the reality, the meaning of such a statement? Is there a method of making oneself universal?' "

It is then explicit that we will not be in the presence of a resurrected historical Leonardo, not surprising in the case of a man who wrote many years later that "the past is entirely a mental thing. It is nothing but images and beliefs." The uses of history, of this mental thing, serve, however, as suggestive material in the search for what Valéry would later call the *"moi pur"*—pure mental functioning unencumbered by autobiographical contingency.

Valéry begins the essay by observing, "What a man leaves after him are the dreams that his name inspires"—that in thinking about how he thought we tend to find a sort of thinking derived from ourselves that we then attribute to him. If he were an ordinary man, this would be easy, for commonplaces tend to unite us with our subject.

But if he were an exceptional man, then we must mentally stretch, for such a mind possesses a breadth whose continuities are difficult to grasp. Early on, Valéry introduces the concept of "continuity," borrowed from Edgar Allan Poe (who since Baudelaire translated him has been regarded as one of the most popular "French" writers of the second half of the nineteenth century). We need to understand, continues Valéry, for our desire is "to place a being in our likeness at the heart of the system we impose on ourselves, and in so doing win back our mental wholeness." As in "Monsieur Teste," the appeal is to the possibility of mind as an autonomous, closed system.

In order to explore this proposition, Valéry posits a man of such diversity that if a ruling idea could be found behind his activities, no mind could be considered more universal. Such a mind would not only study all things but scrutinize its own mental operations. Such a man, a creature of our thought, requires a name. None is more suitable than the name of Leonardo da Vinci. But, Valéry stresses, his intent despite that name is hypothetical rather than historical, the presentation of the model of the details of an intellectual order rather than dates, anecdotes, and catalogue entries of a life and oeuvre.

A model of this sort is won only with difficulty, for thinkers and inventors tend to suppress how they reached a given result, if indeed they understand the process of how they got there at all. The issue then is comprehension of the motions of the mind—swiftly moving, momentary, unresolved—rather than emphasis on the static form of a completed thought. As Valéry was to write later, the processes of thought are as much a work of art as the fulfilled work they yield.

For Valéry, mental activity is a drama in the mind, the actors mental images in flux, subject to "succession, frequency, periodicity, varying capacity for association, and finally their duration." Valéry's method is resolutely parallel to the scientific thought of his contemporaries, and, like such thinking, depends on the power of analogy to advance understanding. Only in studying mental movements can one hope to seize the web of continuity: "The secret—whether of Leonardo, or of Bonaparte, or that of the highest intelligence of a given time—lies and can only lie in the relations they found—and were compelled to find—*among the things of which we cannot grasp the law of continuity*. Only the keenest minds achieve such understanding." To this, Valéry adds the notion that mental emotion might be accelerated to a threshold after which nothing again would be the same.

But lest he be misunderstood, Valéry underscores the danger of seeing with the intellect at the expense of the eyes. To see through the dictionary, as it were, is to tend to see only conventional standpoints, while to see with the eye is to see unconventional perspectives, and leads to the desire to visualize the invisible whole to which apparently isolated visible parts are only the clue. To see without thinking is torpor, but to look fixedly is to find a nexus of multiple associations. The world is irregularly strewn with regular associations, such as the patterns of crystals or the forms of shells, yet regularity tends to get lost in the chaos of the apparently formless. Our intellectual goal should be the discovery of continuity: "It is certain, in any case, that the basis and aim of every speculation is the extension of continuity with the help of metaphor, abstractions, and special languages."

It is in the monumental attempt to span the lacunae that Valéry finds his intellectual hero and spiritual mentor, Leonardo da Vinci. Like a scientific hypothesis, Leonardo would have to be invented if in fact he did not already exist. But exist he does, in our minds as a symbolic mind, bursting with concepts and memories, and the power to arrange these in myriad combinations. For pages, Valéry lyrically evokes the many faces of Leonardo's investigations and inventions, brought into the desired connectedness by Leonardo's rich resources of metaphor.

Leonardo's mind itself is a regular combination, universal in its grasp of time and place, a *"system complete in itself,* or completing itself continually."* Such a mind is the despair of modern specialized men and women, whose competence is at the price of confinement to a narrow spectrum of thought and action. Specialism is a torpor of sorts, and more's the pity, for significant advances in a given specialized field often come via intrusions of ideas and methods from outside that field.

Valéry now moves to another subject, the joys of construction, again a harbinger of his later thought. Construction is a mediation between a concept and the materials that one uses. As in pure thought, so in construction success lies in seizing a single matter or law, thereby achieving continuity. This potential is seen in the art of ornament, where the opposition of art and nature come closest to being canceled out, with customary meaning and function giving way to a world of pure relations.

Painting judged as mimesis—imitation of nature—is a misguided exercise. Rather than inquiring after subject matter, the critic should make a series of inductions based on the form of the picture, rising from metaphor to metaphor, to gain the significance of the embodied constructive thought.

> No example I could give of the general attitude toward painting would be more amusing than the celebrated "smile of the Mona Lisa," to which the epithet "mysterious" seems irrevocably fixed. That dimpled face has evoked the sort of phraseology justified in all literatures, under the title of "Sensations" or "Impressions" of art. It is buried beneath a mass of words and disappears among the many paragraphs that start by calling it *disturbing* and end with a generally vague description of a state of *soul*. It might deserve less intoxicating studies. Leonardo had no use of inexact observations or arbitrary symbols, or Mona Lisa would never have been painted. He was guided by a perpetual sagacity.

So much, then, for the effusions of Michelet, Gautier, Pater, et al. Much later Valéry would write, "The idea, or rather the ridiculous and dangerous shadows of an idea of genius developed by the romantics (sparks, not sustained light) destructive of métier—of what made civilization."

Architecture for Valéry is the master metaphor for métier, whose highest form in richness and complexity is the city itself. And from architecture Valéry moves seamlessly to scientific thought, in which the problems of composition and analysis are equally reciprocal. This is the climax of the essay. He quotes Leonardo:

The air is full of infinite lines, straight and radiating, intercrossing and interweaving without ever coinciding with one another; and they *represent* for every object the true Form of their reason [or explanation].

Valéry allows that these words seem the first germ of the theory of light waves, but adds that he does not set much store in prophecies of the sort that this notion represents. Rather, the importance of Leonardo's words, which involve no scientific measurement, rests in postulating a mental image that no one had *seen* before. According to Valéry, Michael Faraday (1791–1867), the great English investigator and father of electrical science, introduced this idea to modern science. He believed that Faraday's concepts were a projection in the imagination of observed phenomena. The regular combinations of filings around a magnet were the outward sign of invisible transmissions of actions at a distance: "Like Leonardo he *saw* systems of lines uniting all bodies, filling the whole of space, and in this way *explained* electrical phenomena and even gravity; such lines of force can be regarded, for the purpose of this essay, as those of least resistance to the understanding." It was left to Clerk Maxwell to convert Faraday's essentially visual understanding into elegant mathematical formulations, and to Lord Kelvin to stress that natural processes must be expressed by mental images, leading to mechanical models.

Valéry closes by observing that his words may have disappointed art lovers, but that they, too, should be interested in the fundamental issues of composing and constructing. They need to cast out "the idols of the cave" and see afresh the work of art as "a machine designed to arouse and assemble the individual formation of minds." Much later, Valéry wrote: "A creator is one who makes others create."

Valéry's essay suffered the fate of most essays buried in journals, and even if it had received wide notice, its unclassifiable genre, far afield from both art history and the history of science, would have rendered it simply a brilliant curiosity. Nor did it help as far as the English-speaking world goes that the enormously influential Edmund Wilson in his book *Axel's Castle* painted Valéry as an intellectual poseur, a "super dilettante." But Valéry's intentions were gravely serious, and the subsequent publication of his early intellectual notebooks leaves no doubt of his thorough grounding in the mathematical and scientific thought of his contemporaries.

The nineteenth century is rife with monographs based on the assumption that knowledge of the life of a creator is the royal road to understanding his/her creations. Beyond doubting the efficacy of biography and history, Valéry countered with a proposed method based on the reciprocity of analysis and construction in examining works and the mental processes to which they are bound. In 1937 he wrote in a lecture on poetics: "A serious history of literature should then be conceived not as a history of authors and the incidents of their lives, not as a history of their works, but as a history of the mind in so far as it produces or consumes literature, and one might even write a history of this kind without so much as mentioning the name of any writer."

Was Valéry's Leonardo born of pure cogitation by a mind in dialogue with a Poe, a Mallarmé, a Faraday? It seems that he would like us to believe so, but that is unlikely. For centuries any clue to how Leonardo's mind functioned lay buried in his notebooks, with the exception of seventeenth-century exploration of his hydraulics, and the publication of the *Treatise on Painting*. Only in 1797 did Giovanni Battista Venturi lay out in brief form some of Leonardo's accomplishments, with excerpted illustrative examples from the notebooks that he had studied in Paris. In 1838 Guillaume Libri, infamous for vandalizing some of the notebooks, expanded on Venturi somewhat, and Alexander von Humboldt's immensely popular *Cosmos* (5 volumes, 1845–62) gave Leonardo a passing nod, as did the popularizing books of the Englishman William Whewell (1847–60). If there was a common thread in these various writings, it was the assessment of Leonardo as the harbinger of Galileo and his century. While Leonardo as scientist was commented on in most of the major European languages, it was a matter of bits and pieces, excerpts out of context.

That was to change in the 1870s and 1880s, in no small measure because of the first fruit of a project initiated by Charles Ravaisson-Mollien, and continued by him and others for more than twenty years, to present all of Leonardo's manuscripts, in facsimile and transcription. He introduced his project in several articles in the *Gazette des Beaux-Arts* in 1881, observing, "In the midst of all his hesitation, of all his tentative researches in art and science, Leonardo was inspired by thought constantly in accord with itself; in order to know it, one must not be content with isolated passages, in separating observations and reflections whose whole it is necessary to consider in order to penetrate the true sense of each of these passages." Therefore, Ravaisson-Mollien continued, the manuscripts needed to be available complete and unabridged, along with drawings that illuminate the written word, and vice versa.

From that moment, interest in and publication on the scientific-technological Leonardo accelerated, to culminate in the first decade of our century in the work of Pierre Duhem. Far from seeing Leonardo as the forerunner of modern science, Duhem fairly rooted him in the then-hitherto largely unexplored context of late medieval scholastic thought. Since Duhem, research has sought a balance in a Janus-like Leonardo, who faced both toward the future and back to the past.

Of the various publications between the proto-Galilean Leonardo and the scholastic-indebted Leonardo, possibly none is more interesting than an 1892 book by Gabriel Séailles, a professor of philosophy at the University of Paris. He called his book *Leonardo da Vinci, The Artist and Scholar: Essay in Psychological Biography.* No one until that time had attempted such a lengthy study dedicated to the proposition that Leonardo's oeuvre was the product of a mind in which art and science were seamlessly joined. For Séailles, art and science in Leonardo "seemed but two moments of the same activity" in which beauty and mental life were joined. The task was "to create the ideal, by thought, and by means of science of the real to enter the linkages of facts."

Séailles recognized the problem that Leonardo was perhaps better known through his legend than through his history. For Séailles, nothing was more real about Leonardo than his thought, and form represented only the projected images of the master's mind. Indeed, for Séailles the history of Leonardo's life is synonymous with the history of his thought.

At first glance, Séailles seems to have claimed for Leonardo the modern scientific approach a century before Galileo, but unlike his predecessors, Séailles goes on to spell out what he means. Leonardo's quest was a "perpetual effort toward unity." Leonardo recognized that "the universe is a sort of real mathematics, enveloped in appearances," and hence "the intelligible comes before the fact that it reveals, and is not with Leonardo an accidental idea, but his constant theory." "His greatest originality, in this order of knowledge, is perhaps to have seen universal applications." Séailles often comes back to the fundamental place of mathematics in Leonardo's thought: "The world, is it not but a sort of phenomenon linked according to a balance completely mathematical?"

While the Leonardo tradition had emphasized the acute observer and the arena of hands-on applications, Séailles emphasizes, in consonance with contemporary scientific thought, that deeper reality is invisible and consists of relationships most easily expressed by numbers. And relationships most readily yield themselves to analogy: "The imagination encompasses two powers that rarely are seen in one individual to such high degree: the one that of giving all intensity of the real to forms he evokes in his consciousness; the other that of combining representations in discovering the analogies that bind them one to the other." This Leonardo is austerely cerebral: "For sensation he substituted the idea, for unity of sentiment logical succession, for poetry science."

Séailles believed that Leonardo found the solution to life in the equilibrium of his soul and the harmonious unity of his diverse faculties: "living, possible men, not just the stock players in a machine." It was this balance that allowed him to create his paintings effortlessly.

The debt of Valéry to Séailles seems too obvious to point out, yet it is a relationship somewhat like that of Goethe to Bossi, a sympathetic and open transformation of scholarly insight into literature. Whatever the exact relationship, both men found a new Leonardo in the evolving world of the unseen that lay between the experimental science of Claude Bernard and the astounding theoretical propositions of Einstein.

For Valéry, the historical Leonardo could offer no more than an exploratory voyage in search of the highest potentiality of mind in general, while for Sigmund Freud the question was whether the techniques of psychoanalysis might not be capable of extension to a dead analysand. If so, a fruitful new approach to cultural history would be at hand.

Freud clearly had an affection for Leonardo and his works that predated work on his remarkable little book on Leonardo of 1910, *Leonardo da Vinci and a Memory of His Childhood*. As early as 1898, in a letter to Fliess on the subject of left-handedness, he invokes Leonardo. A decade later Freud had a patient whose characteristics strongly reminded him of Leonardo, and in reporting this in an October 1909 letter to Jung he suggests that he has penetrated the mystery of the master. In the following year he published *Leonardo da Vinci and a Memory of His Childhood,* a brilliant short work in which he claims neither an explanation of creativity nor any attempt to expose the dirty linen of a great man. Freud knew that the essay was a bold thrust at the margin of plausibility: in a letter to his painter-friend Hermann Struck he refers to his "half-fictional product" by which the soundness of his main body of work should not be judged.

What was Freud up to? Surely affection for Leonardo was involved, as well as the spark given off by a live patient, and Freud's initial interest in a possible rapprochement of psychoanalysis and cultural studies. But just as important may have been his interest in issues of sexuality, of parents and children, that may be more about Freud than they are about Leonardo. As is the case with much of the writing on Leonardo thus far, the root issue may have been an attempt at self-definition on the part of the author.

As with Pater's "Leonardo," it would do Freud's essay an injustice to attempt a summary. In reading it, two obvious points should be kept in mind: Freud's already developed premises that decisive mental processes operate in the realm of the unconscious, and that sexual impulses already active in the young child are central to understanding both mental illness and the development of social and cultural capabilities.

Freud begins by commenting on Leonardo's damped-down sexuality. The master's trajectory was sublimation, moving from infantile sexual repression to adult sublimation in intensive intellectual investigations. Obviously such a hypothesis renders it crucial to know something of Leonardo's childhood if the idea is to hold any water. In fact, all that is known is that Leonardo was born in 1452 in or near the town of Vinci in Tuscany, was the illegitimate son of Piero da Vinci and a peasant girl named Caterina, and that the boy was taken at some point into his father's household, to be joined by legitimate siblings (whom Leonardo later remembered in his will).

These facts are thin, yet Freud found all that he needed in one of Leonardo's notebook entries, apparently via Dimitri Merejekowski's highly popular turn-of-the-century Russian novel *The Romance of Leonardo da Vinci,* a book that was dependent on the French tradition of writing on Leonardo. The entry reads: "It seems to me that I was always destined to be so deeply concerned with vultures; for I recall as one of my very earliest memories that while I was in my cradle a vulture came down to me, and opened my mouth with its tail, and struck me many times with its tail between my lips." Memory or fantasy, the psychological content is in any event the same.

An image of infantile suckling, the dream/fantasy is also a powerful homoerotic evocation of fellatio. That the bird is a vulture is crucial to the argument, for in Egyptian mythology the goddess Mut (similar to *Mutter,* the German for mother) has the form of a vulture and conceived her young by being impregnated by the wind—lore used by the Fathers of the Church to argue the plausibility of the Virgin birth.

To Freud, the vulture dream/fantasy indicates that Leonardo thought of himself as a vulture-child without a father, i.e., illegitimate and separated from his father. Freud felt that the compelling lessons of psychoanalytic theory overrode the paucity of historical evidence: the argument had to hang on a presumed long separation between Leonardo and his father during his childhood years. Alone with his mother during those years, went the argument, Leonardo was showered with all the erotic attention that in an intact nuclear family a mother divides between her mate and her child. According to Freud, Leonardo was too intensely bound to her in a male-child/mother relationship often alleged to be typical of the youth of homosexuals. Freud reenforces the likelihood of Leonardo's homosexuality by reference to the slim evidence available, the 1476 anonymous accusation of sodomy, in which Leonardo was found not guilty, and his penchant for beautiful young male assistants. With his "normal" sexuality repressed, according to Freud, Leonardo's energy was channeled into his remarkable intellectual investigations.

This constructed account of Leonardo's early sexual profile is then brought to adulthood through evidence of the paintings, the same technique as had been used throughout the nineteenth century, and to which Valéry so strongly objected. *Mona Lisa*'s smile awakened memories of the affectionate smile of Leonardo's natural mother, Caterina, giving rise to the vulture dream/fantasy. The later *Madonna and Child and Saint Anne* (see fig. 27) represents two smiling women of the same age, pictorially layered one behind the other. In Freud's reading, the rear figure, Saint Anne, would be Caterina, while the active foreground figure, Mary, would be Ser Piero's new wife, Donna Albiera, who took care of the young Leonardo recently arrived in her household. The similarity of the two women reflects, of course, the probable similarity of their age in real life.

The story is a brilliant invention, and may have some validity: the vulture quotation is openly homoerotic, except to one who would deny the fruits of psychoanalytic theory altogether, and the cumulative evidence certainly suggests that Leonardo was homosexual, a surmise already mercilessly pursued in an (until recently) unpublished dialogue by Lomazzo. The success of Freud's story with later psychoanalysts—one even found a hidden vulture encoded in the drapery of Mary—is a symptom of the compelling suggestiveness of Freud's argument.

Yet on basic grounds of accuracy of translation, acceptable historical procedure, the history of style, and correct logic, the argument that Freud posits surely seems to fall to pieces. The identification of the bird as a vulture is a mistranslation from the Italian that Freud picked up from Merejekowski. The Italian word is *nibbio* (a kite, a pointed-wing raptor), a simple fact that guts one of the most intriguing cornerstones of Freud's argument. Evidence of prolonged separation of Leonardo and his father in childhood years is lacking, but because psychoanalytic theory predicates this necessity, Freud looks the other way. That Leonardo was taken into his father's house would seem to suggest the father's affection and attention from the beginning, unless there is evidence to the contrary. As for the smile that evoked memories of the mother and the stepmother, arguably it was none other than an artistic convention learned early in the Verrocchio studio, seen for instance in that master's bronze *David* from the 1470s. Here, Freud has succumbed to the fallacy that art copies life, whereas in fact more often than not it copies earlier art. The representation of figures as the same age when in fact they are a generation apart was a convention of the time; one need only think of the mother and son in Michelangelo's *Pietà* in Saint Peter's. These and additional arguments suggest that however intuitively correct Freud may have been, he chose to take his stand on fatally flawed grounds.

Freud's essay on Leonardo may be one of the last significant instances of Romantic fiction, steeped as it is in the Michelet-Pater tradition, an ending rather than a beginning whose premise is Pater's: "From child-hood we see this image [*Mona Lisa*] defining itself on the fabric of his dreams." But is the essay then worthless? Having read Freud's essay, it is not possible to look at Leonardo and his works in the same way again. Questions are opened, even if answers are not given. To what extent can or should personal biography be interpreted from works of art? Is sexual preference on the part of a creator manifest in such works in the way Freud would have us believe? How does one balance such consid-erations against the self-evident fact that works of art are to a large degree part of a history of evolving artistic conventions in which bi-ography may have little or no relevance? Try as they may, what might be called positivistic approaches always leave us short of the final mys-tery of creation. Like Dante's Saint Bernard, an art historian or a critic can only take us to the threshold of final mystery, at which point a leap of the imagination is required. Seen in this light, Freud's essay is not science but a work of the imagination, proposing that we visit a home we thought we knew so well and possibly see it for the first time. Its value is not in a truth-claim, but in an invitation to think about things we had not thought about before.

Be that as it may, in the early twentieth century people became tired of the mystifications and purple prose that characterize much of nineteenth-century writing on Leonardo. If Valéry tried to nail the lid on the coffin of this Leonardo, he failed, leaving the job to others.

In 1919 Marcel Duchamp, one of the most intellectually complex art-ists of our century, presented what he referred to as a Rectified Ready-made, a color postcard reproduction of the *Mona Lisa* adorned with a moustache and a goatee (fig. 40). It was inscribed with the acronym *L.H.O.O.Q.,* which is meant to be read phonetically as *"Elle a chaud au cul"* ("She's got a hot ass"). It was a magnificent slap at High Art and its High Priests that raised questions that have not been put to bed yet.

But then you always hurt the one you love. If Duchamp seemed to have rendered a body blow to Leonardo, it should not be forgotten that Duchamp was one of the most Leonardesque of artists. Both men held mathematics to be fundamentally important, and both supplemented their art by purely intellectual investigations. Both were vitally inter-ested in process as opposed to product, and took care to record their intellectual processes in annotated form (in Duchamp's case, his *Boxes*).

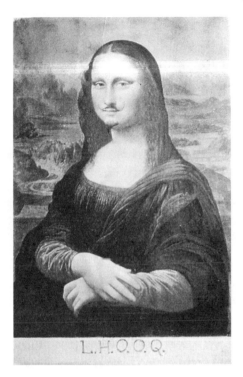

Fig. 40: Marcel Duchamp, *L.H.O.O.Q.*
Private collection, Paris

Finally both were secretive and enigmatic by temperament. Probably much more could be said on this comparison than has been to date.

If in Leonardo as in Duchamp much remains an enigma, the same cannot be said about the abrupt about-face of one of the most influential art historians of the twentieth century, Bernard Berenson. In his book *The Florentine Painters of the Renaissance* of 1896, Berenson wrote, "Leonardo is the one artist of whom it may be said with perfect literalness: Nothing that he touched but turned into a thing of eternal beauty. . . . No, let us not join in reproaches made to Leonardo for having painted so little; because he had much more to do than to paint, he has left us all heirs to one or two of the supremest works ever created," an opinion reiterated in his 1903 *The Drawings of the Florentine Painters*.

By 1916 all that had changed. In Berenson's *Study and Criticism of Italian Art* (Third Series), *The Last Supper* is seen as an object of repulsion, to a Northern sensibility an alarming agitation of people reminiscent of the vulgarisms of a Neapolitan marketplace. The *Mona Lisa* lies beyond the ken of his sympathies, unlike any woman he had ever known, filled with hostile superiority. The *Saint John* is a fleshy female, leering out of the darkness. Berenson objects to the "overmeanings" of Leonardo's pictures—those intimations of significance lying below the face-value subject matter of the painting, and hence below that surface where the expressive possibilities of painting begin and end.

Berenson's wrath falls equally on matters of form. Leonardo was the inventor and master of *chiaroscuro* (modeling in extremes of light and dark) and *contrapposto* (twisting of the body about its axis), which, according to Berenson, were facile means that any hack henceforth could use to smudge an outline and animate a body without need of solid artistic knowledge. Such was Berenson's wrath that he offered the astounding critical judgment that "no Tuscan painter born after Leonardo's death produced a single work with the faintest claim to any general interest."

In 1911 the *Mona Lisa* was stolen from the Louvre, but was later recovered—a notorious incident that probably received the greatest press coverage of any art incident before or since. Berenson declared that he would have had no regrets had it vanished forever. After Duchamp and Berenson, the Michelet-Pater Leonardo was a dormant volcano in the cultural life of the West, except for popularizing aftershocks felt to this day.

Valéry and Freud were the last to really need Leonardo, in the sense of coming to terms with who they themselves were at important junctures in their lives. Certainly later men and women studied Leonardo with passion and wrote eloquently about him, but self-definition does not seem to have been centrally at issue. Why? The reasons are doubtless many. In an era of increasingly narrow specialism, holistic interpretations have come to be regarded as amateurish and suspect. Accompanying this was a refinement of the protocols of connoisseurship and scholarship that tend to value the demonstrable over the persuasive. Increasingly the direction of scholarship had to do with learning *about* a picture or a book rather than learning *from* it. More facts, more documentation, more closely reasoned interpretations were preferred to learning from the transparent presence of the object itself. More recently, interpretations have claimed primacy over the objects of interpretation and shunted them to the periphery of discourse, the malevolent flowering of the seeds planted by Wilde. That is the condition today that has brought the fields subsumed under the humanities to be held in low esteem in some quarters, and their practitioners considered to be of questionable relevance. Such is the price exacted by the academic juggernaut in all its tenured maturity.

PART III

LEONARDO NOW

Being a meditation in four chapters on issues germane to Leonardo's age and ours: the status of the autonomy of the individual and the power of sight; how we possess the world; the body as ground of our experience; and the passion for order in the face of chaos and violence.

THE CLOSE of the last chapter could easily be read as an aversion to, or indeed a disdain for, specialized scholarship. But my concern lies not with the value of such work when directed toward larger ends—for it is almost always essential to the production of new understanding—but only with its too frequent place as a timid end in itself in the industry of academic advancement.

To borrow a book title of Frank Kermode's, the more varied the "forms of attention" lavished on an object or phenomenon, the greater the likelihood that there will be that production of new understanding. As surely as happy critical intuitions of the nineteenth century stood or fell on the basis of subsequent specialized scholarly inquiry, so most worthwhile generalizations in our day are stimulated and made possible only through the results of particularized inquiry.

That said, one does not want to fall into the trap of believing that the only questions worth posing are those that admit of "solutions" or accepting that the object of interpretation is definitive closure, the arrival of a false Nirvana where There Is Nothing More to Be Said.

The third part, or coda, of this book simply proposes general questions about Leonardo in relation to the concerns of our own time that I find intensely interesting, questions different from those a century ago, and doubtless different from those that might be posed a century hence. Their nature and generality however do not allow for formulations in terms of research problems that can be attacked and solved. They therefore remain posed in a ruminative and speculative plane, with all the pleasures and frustrations that such indeterminacy involves. I have chosen to end, not conclude, with four themes. They are of personal interest, beg no comparison with the matters considered in Part II, and probably would not be the same concerns as might engage another writer who has thought about Leonardo. The first of these involves the issues of the autonomy of the individual and the power of the sense of sight. The second is how we comprehend the physical world in which we live, how we possess it, make it our own. The third has to do with the body as cultural expression and object of science. And the last is a meditation on the imposition of order in a world whose natural state seems to be the disequilibrium of cataclysm and violence.

I ask not assent of the reader, but rather a questioning, a framing of the issues in a different way—indeed, the raising of questions I have not chosen to address. If Leonardo finally comes to be seen by the reader as a story with yet new chapters to be written, this book will have served its purpose.

CHAPTER 9

The Triumph of the Eye/I

I N 1855 JULES MICHELET, soon followed by Jacob Burckhardt, conceived a Renaissance whose center was the discovery of man and the
world. The potentiality of the autonomous individual, and the power
of sight to master the world, were celebrated. But was this world perhaps a lost one, if indeed it ever existed? Burckhardt wrote with a sense
of foreboding that the effects of mass society and modern industriali-
zation threatened the autonomy of the individual. To read him at a
distance of more than a century is to encounter a requiem for a heroic
age written in a day in which the shadows were lengthening.

Burckhardt was clairvoyant about the smothering effect of political
and economic collectives. The notion of the autonomous individual who
seeks excellence through the exercise of free choice today is often regarded as problematic, and indeed by many as a vestigial delusion in
the face of societal realities. At the worst, the autonomous individual
is viewed as the manipulative fabrication of a privileged class bent
on maintaining its traditional control over those without voice and
power.

Such views are often accompanied by a distrust of language as a re-
liable conveyor of intentional messages by an author to an audience
capable of consensually receiving those messages. According to such
thinking, claims to truth of written arguments, when analyzed, tend to
dissolve into conflicting possible meanings that ultimately cancel one
another out. A given "text," more than being an expression of authorial
intention, is rather part of a web of intertextual references through which
power flows, a power of which author and reader alike may be unaware.
While such a view implies a salutary warning that unexamined language
can injure us both by what is said and not said, it also tends to place in
doubt the authority of authors, whose words merely evoke an imper-

sonal verbal landscape of ambiguity, contingency, relativity, and constant flux. Taken to an extreme, this notion implies a total relativism of values in which authors are not to be held responsible for the words they write.

The combined failure of nerve concerning the autonomy of the individual, and of the intentionality of language itself, tends to yield an intellectual world of kaleidoscopic indeterminacies in grinding dissonance with the common sense of daily life. Small wonder that we at times seem sightseers at the Tower of Babel, with groups displacing individuals in a civic life whose power games create an unending flow of manipulated words.

If the ideal of the autonomous individual has become deeply disturbing, no less so is the status of the eye. "Seeing is believing" is a saying that sounds strangely quaint. As early as the late nineteenth century, nature became invisible, in the sense that mathematics displaced vision as the chief instrument in the advancement of knowledge. While Faraday "saw" his fields of force, Einstein posited equations.

The eye yields up pleasure as it always has in the past, but now we are wary of it: rather than being the generator of deep knowledge, more often it falls passive victim to deceptions. Television and the seductions of other mass media have come at a price—the dominance of visual surface abbreviation at the expense of sustained verbal argument, the prevalance of fragmentation and disconnectedness, a desensitizing passivity in the face of what is seen at a remove, and an abdication of will to sort out the possibly true from the merely entertaining. We have experienced a suspension of disbelief, as the eye has become the locus of sensual massage rather than a receptor of sharpened truths.

How far all this is from Leonardo's world, and how we feel nostalgia for that world without finally being able to surrender ourselves to it— that is the subject of this chapter.

IN 1487 the young humanist Pico della Mirandola wrote his *Oration on the Dignity of Man* as a counter to a traditional genre devoted to the chastising of humanity's fundamental abasement. It begins with God addressing Adam:

We have given you, Oh Adam, no visage proper to yourself, nor any endowment properly your own, in order that whatever the place, whatever form, whatever gifts you may, with premeditation, select, these same you may have and possess through your own judgement and decision. The nature of all other creatures is defined and restricted within laws which We have laid down; you, by contrast, impeded by no such restrictions, may, by your own free will, to whose custody We have assigned you, trace for yourself the lineaments of your own nature. I have placed you at the very center of the world, so that from that vantage point you may with greater ease glance round about you on all that the world contains. We have made you a creature neither of heaven nor of earth, neither mortal nor immortal, in order that you may, as the free and proud shaper of your own being, fashion yourself in the form you may prefer. It will be in your power to descend to the lower, brutish forms of life; you will be able, through your own decision, to rise again to the superior order whose life is divine.

It would be difficult to find within a Christian context a more powerful and optimistic challenge to humanity to forge its own destiny through conscious choice, the charge to the first man implicitly a charge to each and every one of his progeny. Only in self-realization of individual human potential can a life and world be purposefully shaped, an "I" realized.

To make one's active way in the world is first of all to use the senses, of which the sense of sight was primary for Leonardo in the quest for truths beyond those preserved in words:

Now do you not see that the eye embraces the beauty of the whole world? It is the lord of astronomy and the maker of cosmography; it counsels and corrects all the arts of mankind; it leads men to different parts of the world; it is the prince of mathematics, and the sciences founded on it are absolutely certain. It has measured the distances and sizes of the stars; it has found the elements and their locations; it divines the future from the course of the stars; it has given birth to architecture, and to perspective, and to the divine art of painting.

The divine art of painting: Leonardo's artist was both a recorder of actual worlds and creator of imagined ones, as evidenced in a passage headed "The Painter Is Lord of All Types of People and Things":

If the painter wishes to see beauties that charm him it lies in his power to create them, and if he wishes to see monstrosities that are frightful, buffoonish, or ridiculous, or pitiable, he can be lord and God thereof; and if he wishes to produce inhabited regions or deserts, or dark and shady retreats from the heat, or warm places for cold weather, he can do so. If he wants valleys likewise if he wants from high mountain tops to unfold a great plain extending down to the sea's horizon, he is lord to do so; and likewise if from low plains he wishes to see high mountains or from high mountains low plains and the sea shore. In fact, whatever exists in the universe, in essence, in appearance, in the imagination, the painter has first in his mind and then in his hands; and these are of such excellence that they are able to present a proportioned and harmonious view of the whole that can be seen simultaneously, at one glance, just as things in nature.

These two passages by Leonardo evoke the power of vision and the images derived from it in two different ways—sight as a yielder of descriptive and analytic understanding, and sight as the supplier of material for *fantasia,* or poetic synthesis. How did these two functions relate in Leonardo's work, and how may what he wrote be legitimately associated with things that he made? To appreciate the difficulty of these questions, one can turn to the earliest dated artifact from Leonardo's hand, a small sepia landscape drawing from 1473, done when the artist was twenty-one (see fig. 4).

Leonardo in fact or in his imagination has placed himself on the rim of a gorge. To the left the bluff is crowned by a castle, to the right is a wooded hillside. One looks down through the gorge to a river plain below, its fields lightly sketched and stretching away to distant hills. The castle and topography of the gorge are tightly sketched, in contrast to the quick and light parallel strokes that cause the trees to the right to fairly shimmer in the breeze. There is a freshness to the image that bespeaks spontaneous observation, a feeling reinforced by the writing in the upper left referring to a specific day, August 5, 1473.

The little drawing seems an illustration of the quotations just offered. Leonardo, the masterful I, has taken his place on "high mountain tops to unfold a great plain." He sees from a fixed position and in seeing commands a world, in this case seemingly born more from observation than the imagination.

The drawing is revolutionary, in the sense of being apparently conceived as an end in itself rather than as a study for the background of a painting. The genre of landscape painting as we understand it did not come into being until several decades later, and in 1473 representation of a landscape without a figural subject was all but unknown.

But just how original was Leonardo? Is the landscape to be understood as foretelling words written much later? Arguably, what Leonardo has drawn is quite within the bounds of a convention of rendering landscape from a high vantage point, first fully developed in northern Europe earlier in the century, and then imported to Italy, as for example in Baldovinetti's 1460 *Adoration of the Shepherds.* We are left with the question, then, of the degree of originality of Leonardo's vision, a question without closure in that it depends on one's subjective assessment of the visual evidence.

This raises a wider question as to just what the mind of the young Leonardo was like, how he developed the interests and competencies that would lead to a remarkable life's work. We know virtually nothing, and only by indirection can we probe what he might have been taught and what he learned, by examining some of the educational norms of his time.

Leonardo's father was a notary, and thus was verbally and mathematically literate. We may assume that he wanted the same for his son. The young Leonardo was probably placed with an elementary teacher, most likely a private schoolmaster, and there he would have had an opportunity that was available to about one-third of the boys of his time. It was assumed that a young student's mind was a *tabula rasa,* ready to be filled with information and knowledge imparted by rote repetition and memorization, be it reading or arithmetic. Elementary schooling might take four years or so, to age ten, at which time some students went on to abacus school to hone their business skills through the further acquisition of practical mathematics. While the primer was in both Latin and Italian (Latin still being the language of intellectual and bureaucratic culture), no mastery of Latin at an early age was required. The education described to this point was meant to prepare a youth for mercantile pursuits, and it cannot be stressed too much that there seems to have been scant encouragement of fresh observation or innovation.

In the early teens a person faced an educational and career crossroads, and the road taken was usually decisive for the activities of a lifetime. One might pursue a course that led through mastery of Latin, study of the liberal arts, and perhaps one of the three university degree subjects (law, medicine, theology), to be followed by a career in one of those fields, or in religious or secular administration. Or a young person might prepare for a trade, which presupposed mastery of vernacular Italian, some arithmetical capability, an apprenticeship of several years, and a career in active pursuit of practical applications and solutions. The choice that was made carried with it both a hierarchy of social prestige and different styles—intellectual and contemplative on the one hand, active and practical on the other.

In the case of Leonardo, the choice made was for the second track, and so meant apprenticeship in the workshop of an artisan. I purposely do not write "artist"—*artista*—a term at the time reserved for a university student of the liberal arts. The master chosen was Andrea del Verrocchio, whose shop Leonardo entered in about 1467. Leonardo arrived perhaps four or five years later than would have been normal, a possible clue that he may have attended an abacus school first.

What might Leonardo have learned in Verrocchio's shop? The particulars are unknown, but in general it must have been something like the course described in Cennino Cennini's circa-1400 *Book of Art*. The young boy would start with purely menial tasks such as sweeping up and grinding colors, and then slowly, through a process involving mastery of drawing based on good exemplars, achieve the capacity to assist his master with works of art in progress. As with elementary schooling, so in the workshop, it was through imitation, repetition, and mastery by memory that solid skills were won, for rarely it seems were notions of predisposed talent or precociousness recognized at the outset, despite Vasari's mid-sixteenth century contrived epiphanies of young geniuses. A boy of intelligence and good character could be trained to be a good painter as readily as a good leather craftsman.

Much has been written about the paintings and sculptures traceable to Verrocchio's studio, particularly Leonardo's possible participation. To empathize with what Leonardo may have learned, it pays to move beyond the connoisseur's concern with surviving objects and inquire about the wider activities of such a workshop.

Verrocchio was described by Vasari as "goldsmith, master of perspective, sculptor, master of intaglio, painter, musician." This variety of interests is paralleled by the documented instances of various sorts of activities undertaken by his shop between 1466 and 1476: a chapel at Orvieto, several bronze sculptures, preparation of metal for church doors and casting of a bronze bell for a monastery, a pennant for a tournament, pageant master for the visit of Galeazzo Sforza of Milan in 1471.

Probably the most challenging project of all was the construction and mounting of a sixteen-foot-diameter gilded ball atop the great dome of the Florentine cathedral (the current globe is a seventeenth-century replacement installed after lightning struck the original one). A sturdy armature would have to have been devised, plates possessing both durability and lightness created for the ball's skin, and crucial decisions made on work to be completed on the ground as opposed to on the top of the dome. The problem of hoisting materials would have involved the remembered or still-in-place technology of the dome's creator, Filippo Brunelleschi.

As the dome (built 1420–36) cast its shadow over the Tuscan people, so Brunelleschi cast his over all the engineer-technologists in the century following his death. Brunelleschi was called the New Daedelus, and hailed as a technical genius. While the lucid grace and proportions of his loggia and churches are what attract us to him, to his contemporaries his fascination lay as much or more in his technological accomplishments—designs of ships, clocks, military machines and architecture, stage productions, and, above all, the raising of the cathedral dome, a task only contemplated by the Florentines for more than a century in the absence of any certain means or man up to the job. Brunelleschi was a master of the eye and of pragmatic judgments, who communicated the concreteness of his solutions by constructing careful models. While most of the models and all of his drawings are gone, Brunelleschi's technological legacy survives in drawings by later men. The culmination of work on the ball came in 1468, and while Leonardo's first surviving (an important qualifier) technological drawings date from only a decade later, it is not difficult, given the way Leonardo's career unfolded, to imagine how deeply he must have been impressed by this undertaking.

For the Florentine of Leonardo's time, drawing—*disegno*—was the foundation of all the visual arts. Leonardo's education in draftsmanship would have been in the context of preparation for finished works of art, and probably learned in the sequence that he himself recommended to students much later: copying of the drawings of accomplished masters, followed by drawings of a three-dimensional model, culminating in drawing from an appropriate life model. In short, the emphasis was upon repeated imitation, not upon the imagination as the point of departure. The success of this training, supervised by the master, was a reciprocal process of making and judging.

In advocating that the twofold aim of painting was the rendering of the effect of relief where there is in fact none, and the depiction of figures in such a way that they reveal the mind of the figure who moves, Leonardo was simply echoing the earlier advice of Alberti and the advanced practice of the painters of his day. For the Florentines, picture-making to achieve these goals involved a methodical step-by-step process culminating in the coloring of a monochrome drawing on the surface to be painted. Various sorts of drawings were involved in these steps: An artist would begin with initial sketches probing the basic disposition of parts in a composition, followed by studies to work out particular parts. Yet other drawings would explore the perspectival disposition of space. Finally a cartoon, a 1:1 scale drawing, would allow transfer of the design to the surface to be painted. All of these drawings contributed to the methodical artistic synthesis. Given that the goal of painting was the imitation of nature as it appears to an observer's eye, many of the drawings convey accurately recorded information. As such, they are a natural bridge to Leonardo's drawings in which non-artistic drawing, be it of a machine or a part of anatomy, are a necessary and sufficient end.

The proposition that drawing might have as its primary purpose the recording of specific visual data was new in Leonardo's day. Although the notebook of the French architect Villard de' Honnecourt of about 1235 contains drawings of a variety of figures, both human and animal—including a lion, claimed to have been drawn from life (fig. 41)—to the modern eye these figures possess a schematic, non-specific quality. Their

Fig. 41: Villard de' Honnecourt,
Drawing of a lion. Bibliothèque
Nationale, Paris

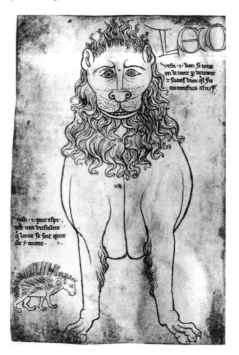

generality is underscored by the geometric configurations that determine their basic structure. This approach is understandable in a cathedral builder whose mode of planning was grounded in ratio, proportion, and geometry, but there is a deeper explanation. For the thinkers of Villard's age, particular visual appearances were accidental manifestations of ideal types emanating from the mind of God, a hidden reality that could be expressed through the visual metaphor of the figures of geometry. The drawing of a unique specimen at a particular place in a particular time simply did not correspond to fundamental reality.

But Villard declares in an accompanying note that he had drawn the lion from life. We may concede that perhaps he had a lion in front of him, but his mode of visualization was filtered through the orderly sweep of the compass arc. "From life," then, was an urge rather than a practice leading to a naturalistic image. That urge certainly was not unique at the time, but was acted out in the margins of artistic activity— for instance, in foliated capitals, or the marginal illustrations of Gothic manuscripts.

During the fourteenth century the desire to record specifics grew, but

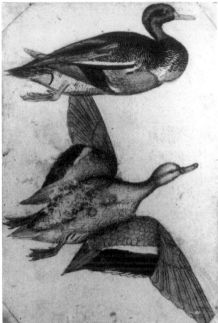

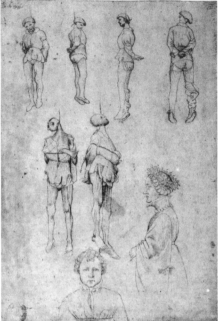

Fig. 42: Pisanello(?), Study of a duck.
Louvre, Paris

Fig. 43: Pisanello, *Hanged Men*. British
Museum, London

images still remained types, based on their rough similarity to things
observed rather than on the accurate recording of specific instances. If
an artist wished to record a mountain, copying a rock in the studio
would suffice, according to Cennini. If a bird was needed in a painting,
then a pattern book of birds kept in the studio could be consulted. To
be sure, someone had to draw the original bird by observing nature,
but once that was done there was no perceived need to "correct" the
image by returning to nature.

The hinge of change lies in northern Italy in the first part of the
fifteenth century, for instance in Pisanello. Some drawings of his circle
are probably derived from pattern books (fig. 42), but others by him
seem records of specific instances (fig. 43). Because Leonardo was part
of the continuing evolution of this change, his 1473 landscape drawing
(see fig. 4), even if it is based on a traditional landscape formula, has a
freshness and specificity about it that seem very modern. A triumph of
the eye, it is also a triumph of the I, of an individual who takes a view

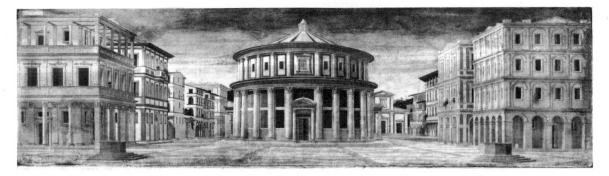

Fig. 44: Anonymous, Central Italian, late fifteenth century, *Ideal Cityscape*. Urbino

from a specific vantage point, and so in a sense possesses what he sees. Knowledge of linear perspective underlies the drawing, and was by Leonardo's time the accepted mode of organizing fictive pictorial space in a systematic way so that objects may be placed in that space in proper optical scale to one another.

In the 1420s, or possibly earlier, Brunelleschi created two lost demonstration panels, views, respectively, of the Florentine Baptistry and the Palazzo della Signoria. These panels were based on linear measurement and angular calculation, their apparent purpose to yield architectural renderings in exact scale to the architectural vistas represented. The humanist-architect-artist Leon Battista Alberti wrote down, perhaps as a codification of what his artist friends had worked out in practice during the preceding few years, how this method could be adapted to the creation of a fictive pictorial space when no actual scene to be copied was before the artist's eyes. He did this in his *De pictura* (*On Painting*) of 1435, which he translated into Italian for his artist friends the following year.

One of a series of architectural scenes, called *Ideal Cityscapes,* but possibly proposals for theater sets done by an anonymous painter around 1480, shows Albertian perspective in simple form (fig. 44). The space is ordered according to monocular vision, all lines receding into space and converging at one point on an imagined horizon, the so-called vanishing point. The painting represents a rectilinear pavement, any segment of which is in systematic optical relation to any other segment. Put another way, if the distance between two receding lines at the bottom of the painting is assigned a length, say twenty feet, each of the horizontal lines between those two receding lines as one moves back in space can also be assigned a span of twenty feet. So a grid formed by the pavement provides a scale whereby objects throughout the painting may be situated in proper optical relation to one another.

This may be clarified in diagrams that in oversimplified fashion explain Alberti's system (fig. 45). Take a square panel, then draw a horizontal line at the height of a person assumed to be six feet tall standing on the extreme foreground of the panel, and place in the center of it a dot, the vanishing point. Divide the baseline on a scale that would represent two feet (i.e., one-third of the assumed six-foot stature of a person standing on the baseline). Draw receding lines (orthogonals) from the points of division on the baseline to the vanishing point. Now the horizontal lines (transversal) of the grid must be established. Place the viewer at an assumed viewing distance from the picture to one side of the panel, then draw lines leading from the points on the baseline out to the eye of the viewer, which results in intersections on the edge of the panel. These points of intersection determine the proper rate of recession of the transversals. Thus a grid is established in which any segment of a transversal between two orthogonals is assumed to be two feet. So a person can be placed on any square grid in scale to the person on the baseline, or any objects whose dimensions are posited in relation to any other object whose dimensions are similarly posited.

It is one thing to draw an object, but quite another to place it in a constructed space where all the parts are in a systematic relation to one another. Leonardo gave great care to the perspective structure of space in the *Adoration* (see fig. 17), and it is of fundamental importance in the composition of *The Last Supper* (see fig. 23). He wrote extensively on all aspects of perspective, elaborating the ideas of Alberti and Piero della Francesca. Yet neither the Renaissance literature on perspective nor the free adaptations of that theory in practice (scrupulous application of Alberti's or anyone else's theory is the rare exception) do more than suggest its fundamental importance to the triumph of the eye as an investigative instrument.

The systematic structure of space in a painting as related to the monocular vision of an observer is, after all, a convention, no more or less true or valuable than the flattened planes of a Byzantine mosaic or the

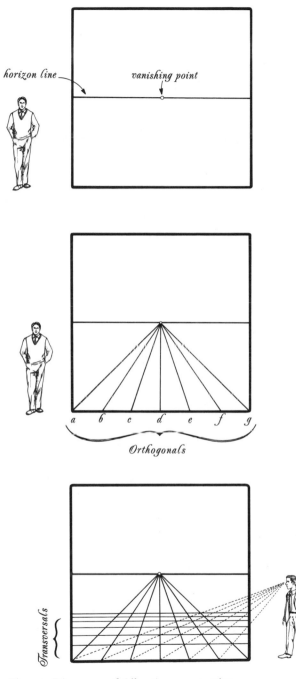

horizon line

vanishing point

a   b   c   d   e   f   g

Orthogonals

Transversals

Fig. 45: Diagrams of Albertian perspective

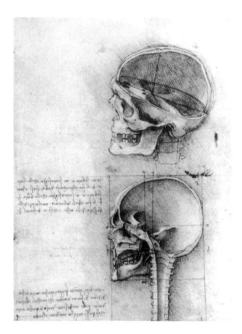

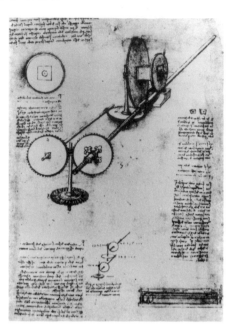

Fig. 46: Leonardo, *Two Views of Human Skull*. Royal Library, Windsor

Fig. 47: Leonardo, *Machine for Making Staves for a Gun Barrel*. Ambrosiana, Milan

spatial fragmentation of a Cubist painting. But as a visual explanation of how a complex three-dimensional object is structured, how its constituent parts relate to one another, perspective is an invaluable tool, making clear what words and/or diagrams can only suggest. In 1489 Leonardo did a series of studies of the human skull. The true nature of a surface enfolding a volume is hardly thinkable without a rendering of such a comparatively simple object in perspective (fig. 46). This is even more true of a complex artifact, such as a piece of machinery (fig. 47), the interrelation of whose parts would be impossible to describe visually in an adequate manner without application of perspective. When it came to constructing, perspective gave Leonardo and his contemporaries a new and powerful tool, whether on the small scale of design, or the vast scale of mapping the world.

What were the implications of that tool? Put most simply, it meant a distancing between an experiencing subject and an experienced object. In 1435 Alberti defined a painting as the world seen through a window.

According to this model, the picture's surface was an invisible plane cut through a visual pyramid that separated the space of the viewer on one side and a fictive space on the other. Paradoxically, perspective both subjectified and objectified vision—subjectified in the sense that objects are seen from the chosen viewpoint of a particular observer in a given place, but objectified in the sense that a multiplicity of perspectival views of the same object would yield something approaching a total visual understanding of that object, accessible to any individual who would step up to those various windows, assess the views, and synthesize the information thus gained.

Arguably, then, perspective is one of the first steps in the modern scientific outlook, in the sense that an object is no longer as it was in the Middle Ages, something loaded with symbolic qualities in which experienced subject and external object tend to fuse, but an entity to be held at arm's length and subjected to dispassionate optical scrutiny. It is the relationship between the mind and matter distinctly separate from that mind.

As we know, in late 1481 or early 1482 Leonardo left Florence for Milan, recommending himself in a letter to the Duke in which he vaunts his technological abilities, particularly in matters of war, mentioning only at the end his capabilities as an artist. By this point in his life the Eye/I had triumphed in Leonardo. He had learned to draw with exactitude, and had mastered perspective, that metaphor of space and time—time because it is often needful to suggest not only connections but the order in which things happen. The letter to the Duke suggests his unbounded personal confidence.

As recounted earlier, soon after his arrival in Milan, Leonardo began his notebooks. The chief characteristic of these sheets is the interaction of words and images in advancing his ideas, whether on hydrology, cosmology, anatomy, or myriad other subjects. While he was to remain an artist to the end of his life, it is clear that, in terms of time and energy expended, pure and applied investigation were now his passion. What was the relation of images and words in Leonardo's thought?

There can be no mistake about it; words were important to Leonardo. In about 1503 he owned 116 books, and claimed to have written 46 "books" (meaning arguments of varying length, not lengthy pieces of prose between two covers as we tend to think of the term "book"). In the 1490s he made a methodical list of some nine thousand Latin words, a poignant attempt to come to grips with the language of the learned, an enterprise that apparently was not very successful.

Contemptuously, and probably to a degree defensively, he declared himself an *"omo sanza lettere"*—a man without letters. For Leonardo, words are the inventions of humans, and inevitably require the interpretation of more words, while the phenomena of the world are unmediated experience directly grasped by the eye. Words are prey to the errors of tradition, while images record the truths of the present.

> Painting presents the works of nature to our understanding with more truth and accuracy than do words or letters; but letters represent words with more truth than does painting. But we affirm that a science representing the works of nature is more wonderful than one representing the works of a worker, that is to say, the works of man, such as works in poetry and the like, which are expressed by the human tongue.

While he knew that words and images proceed in tandem in the advancement of knowledge, when the chips were down Leonardo chose the side of images. His clearest expression on the matter comes on a sheet dedicated to study of the respiratory system:

> With what words, O writer, will you describe with like perfection the entire configuration which the drawing here does? Lacking knowledge, this you describe confusedly and leave little conception of the true shape of things which you, in self-deception, make believe that you can fully satisfy your auditors when you must speak of the configuration of some bodily structure bounded by surfaces. But I counsel you not to encumber yourself with words unless you are speaking for the blind. If, however, you wish to demonstrate in words to the ears and not to the eyes of men, speak of substantial or natural things and do not meddle with things appertaining to the eyes by making them enter through the ears, for you will be surpassed by the work of the painter.
>
> With what words will you describe this heart so as not to fill a book? The longer you write on the details, the more you will confuse the mind of the auditor. You will always be in need of com-

mentators or be required to return to experience, which in your case is very brief, and gives knowledge of but few things concerning the whole subject of which you desire an entire knowledge.

In another passage, in a study of the myology of the shoulder region, Leonardo expresses similar thoughts but comes to a less polemical conclusion that can well serve as the motto for the entire enterprise of the notebooks: "Therefore it is necessary to both illustrate and describe."

In the passage on the respiratory system, Leonardo wrote that "the longer you write on the details, the more you will confuse the mind of the auditor." And yet at the same time he had contempt for those he called abbreviators:

Abbreviators do harm to knowledge and to love, seeing that the love of something is the offspring of knowledge, the love being the more fervent in proportion as the knowledge is more certain. And this certainty is born of a complete knowledge of all the parts, which, when combined, compose the totality of the things which ought to be loved. . . . It is true that impatience, the mother of stupidity, praises brevity, as if such persons had not life long enough to serve them to acquire a complete knowledge of one single subject.

And so it was that Leonardo conducted himself, often giving multiple examples as he circled his intellectual prey, indulging in a copious variety of examples instead of seeking closure in one impregnable generalization or law. He is not the scientist in the modern sense who would craft a theory, but a naturalist with an unsatiated appetite for the bric-a-brac of visual phenomena. He seeks a control of his observations by constant evocation of correspondences by analogy: the human body is like a machine; swimming and flying are similar activities; the cardiovascular system is like a tree, the heart and its attendant vessels like a developing seed; the support of the skull by the neck like the rigging of a ship; the working of the digestive system like the action of springs in the mountains; sap oozing from a vine like blood spurting from a vein in a man's head; the obedience of nerves to the tendons like the obedience of soldiers to their captain, and so on. Some of these analogies are organic, others mechanistic, others loose figures of speech, but all of them taken together suggest Leonardo's place in an age straddling animistic and mechanistic explanations of the world.

To what degree did Leonardo realize that his fear of abbreviators, on the one hand, and concern, on the other, that overelaboration can confuse the reader, posed a dilemma? One cannot say, but consciously or otherwise this problem is at the heart of his insistence that the virtue of painting and drawing compared to other modes of knowledge is that they can present information all at once, with equal emphasis among the parts. In seeing and recording is possession of the world.

The triumph of the Eye/I in Leonardo's day was based on a solid assumption and two emerging notions. The assumption was that an autonomous individual, through the exercise of *virtù* (masterful excellence), could state an idea, perform a deed, or create an object whose intention and character were manifest to his audience. The first notion was that knowledge, beyond being the fuel to nurture understanding, was power in the hands of the person who used it. To be sure, a turn of fate might foil that power, but to avoid seeking such knowledge was an abdication of the God-given power of choice of which Pico della Mirandola had written. Second, the eye was the supreme instrument by which to acquire the knowledge to both criticize and move beyond the written tradition. To raise a great dome, to design a better cannon, to push across the expanse of the ocean, these were projects in which the eye, mind, and hand seamlessly joined to produce new knowledge and understanding.

While for the nineteenth century Leonardo was in various ways viewed as the heroic harbinger of the modern condition, our reading of him today is far different. He belongs to another age that seems increasingly distant from ours. As Pater nostalgically evoked a Winckelmann born out of his time, a vestigial survivor of past values, so it is with our Leonardo, who spoke in a code that—for better or for worse—in good measure we have left behind, in a world whose confidence in the autonomous I and beneficent Eye has been badly shaken.

CHAPTER 10

Possessing the World

THE TRIUMPH of the Eye/I was based in good part on the power of the naked eye to advance knowledge, before the invention of either the telescope or the microscope. Leonardo and his contemporaries were energized to comprehend and possess the world by harnessing its resources to human use, to investigate its smallest particulars, to attempt to tame the unknown by bringing it into the orbit of the known.

For centuries, from the familiar center Europeans had conjured in the imagination the unknown margins, be it the gold-sheathed palaces of Cipango (Japan) or the wonders and monstrosities of the distant Indies. The Catalan Atlas of about 1375 takes us from the familiar topography of the Mediterranean basin and adjacent lands on a voyage eastward to lands increasingly born of the imagination. One looks in vain for two continents that were the home of the Amerindians, isolated by two vast seas and so not yet a part of the European consciousness. In 1492 all that was about to change, when, on a Friday in August, Cristóbal Colón, that possessed servant of God, sailed west into the unknown, thus initiating the project of globalism as yet not wholly fulfilled in our own time.

In an important way, the nineteenth-century pairing of Columbus with Leonardo made sense, for the latter was equally an explorer of unknown worlds who in his quest, like Columbus, combined pragmatism with a rare reach of the imagination. Lest we jump to the conclusion that Leonardo's mode of thinking about nature is close to ours, we might ponder a brief fable that he penned around 1490:

The water finding itself in its element, the lordly ocean, was seized with a desire to rise above the air, and being encouraged by the

element of fire and rising as a very subtle vapour, it seemed as
though it were really as thin as air. But having risen very high, it
reached the air that was still more rare and cold, where the fire
forsook it, and the minute particles, being brought together united
and became heavy; whence its haughtiness deserting it, it betook
itself to flight and it fell from the sky, and was drunk up by the
dry earth, where, being imprisoned for a long time, it did penance
for its sin.

What should we make of this passage? It seems to combine the archetypical myth of vaunting ambition, the flight of Icarus, with the
notion of Christian penance, both presented in the form of a scientific
proposition. How are we to read it? As a moral statement? As a scientific
observation on the behavior of nature? What indeed is the relationship
between moral knowledge and natural knowledge in Leonardo?

If one reads other fables that Leonardo wrote during these same years,
the puzzle deepens. For instance:

An ass having gone to sleep on the ice over a deep lake, his heat
dissolved the ice and the ass awoke under water to his great grief,
and was forthwith drowned.

This may be taken as a simple fact, an unlikely suggestion, or as an
allegory of imprudence. But is that imprudence somehow a moral flaw?
The fables as a whole may be interpreted as addressing an imprudence
of quite another sort: bad things happen to he or she who fails to pay
attention to the necessary laws of nature. Leonardo's writings suggest a
man for whom knowledge of nature, on the one hand, and moral and
religious knowledge, on the other, had substantially parted ways. It
was not that he scorned the latter; it simply lay beyond the ken of his
interests.

Leonardo seems to stand between two world views—one that sees
the world as alive and spirit-endowed, the other that regards it as a
machine. The former, usefully called the animistic view, characterizes
cultures in most times and places in world history. The latter, the mechanistic view, is less than five hundred years old, characteristically Western, and now has spread through much of the world. This distinction
requires some elaboration before Leonardo's thought can be explored.

What does nature connote to us, if by that one means nature as understood by the person on the street, the tangible stuff "out there" to which the senses give access? In our time nature is above all resources, be it wood, oil, or wheat, by which we maintain our material life. Nature provides us the means of building, of producing, of generating energy. It is nature in the guise of commodity and exchange. We inhabit a world in which we humans are at center stage, all things animate and inanimate at our ready disposal and for our consumption. The things of nature are objectified and quantifiable, and hence only rarely do we see spots of sacredness in the world before us. We assume that the events of nature yield to causal explanation without recourse to supernatural powers. We possess the world, and in traveling its expanse only rarely experience an encounter between the known and the truly unknown. Wherever we go that is new, others have been there before, and have reported back through written word and recorded image.

I have just described some characteristics of a mechanistic conception of nature, a view that arose in the course of the sixteenth and seventeenth centuries, and that continues to hold sway in our own time. Some four centuries ago, Galileo turned his telescope on the celestial bodies, an act that was at once intimate—for distant objects were brought close—but also distancing, in the sense that only through a mediating instrument could something distinctly removed from the human body be apprehended at all. The philosopher Descartes proposed a cleavage between the mind and the body, conceiving the former as resident of a small gland hosted by the body-machine. Indeed, for him the universe as a whole was a machine—he compared it to a clock—whose marvelous workings could be explicated by mathematics.

And to what purpose was such thinking to be applied? Francis Bacon maintained that knowledge of nature had as its purpose the attainment of power over nature in the furtherance of human ends, and proposed a "priesthood" of scientists as the avatars of human progress. The method they advanced is a commonplace today—the positing of questions in the form of hypotheses, to which answers might be formulated on the basis of new information and experiment.

Isaac Newton pulled these threads together in the crystallization of classical physics. He saw nature as a vast system in constant motion whose workings could be quantified through mathematics. Newton was a believer, but, paradoxically, his work rendered God a supernumerary—simply the old gentleman who set the system in motion. Understanding lay in decoding the system, not in transcending it.

Such views are in striking contrast to animism, which has taken many forms in history. Its common characteristic is that nature is alive and infused with spirits. For the Greeks, a numinous world was filled with sacred places: groves, caves, mountains, springs, and grottoes. This living world was seen to be ordered and purposeful, as attested to by the turn of the heavens, the cycle of the seasons, the phenomena of birth, maturation, and death.

In the many centuries before Leonardo, the relation of order and matter was pondered. Matter was thought to be inert and without form, and only achieved form—say, as a human body or as a plant—by being invested with a soul. Soul was the process whereby an organism is born, takes mature shape, and eventually dies. Understanding of the world was not defined by considerations of cause and effect but through perceived correspondences between phenomena. The things of the world were seen to be symbol-laden, and the language of this world view is the language of myth rather than of quantification.

While such ideas lasted into the years after Leonardo's death, from the time of the Greeks and the Hebrews on there was little doubt that humans were the central actors in God's creation, as sanctioned, for instance, by the Book of Genesis, which gave humanity dominion over the creatures of the earth. On the whole, wild nature, particularly as embodied in forests and mountains, was abhorred. Good nature was nature subdued and turned to human purpose, such as cleared forests and cultivated fields. The last four centuries have seen the most minute details of this nature maniacally catalogued, and tamed so much that true wilderness is now a rarity on the face of the globe. The last remnants are national parks throughout the world—figuratively speaking, museums of nature where the traces of a vanished world are preserved.

Since the mid-nineteenth century the viability of this mechanistic view of nature and its attendant ideological baggage have been questioned, accelerating in our own time to a chorus of voices decrying the despoliation of the planet and the spiritual emptiness of the implications of a desacralized world. A bellwether of this concern is the postulating of the so-called Gaia theory by the iconoclastic scientist James Lovelock—

the proposition that all species and the total physical world are symbiotically fused in an overarching system, a self-regulating entity able to keep the planet healthy by constant adjustments of chemical and biological factors. The planet itself is regarded as being alive, with all individual manifestations of life subordinate to that fact, and with no organism intrinsically more or less important than any other. It is held that humankind's intervention in this system, on the grand scale now technologically possible, can do irreparable harm. True, Gaia theory appears to be on the outer margins of scientific credibility, but that is not the point. Rather, its significance is ultimately religious, demanding a radical reevaluation of the role and behavior of *Homo sapiens* in the thin and fragile layer of the biosphere. Most threatening of all, it implies that the mechanistic paradigm, fraught with the dominance, possession, and control that we Westerners have come so much to love, may not be a paradigm to live by.

What of Leonardo's world? There was still a fear of wild places, rarely represented in art except as the retreat for penitent, ascetic saints. In the mid-fourteenth century Petrarch climbed Mont Ventoux in Provence, either literally or in his imagination, and enjoyed the view, as reported in a letter. No sooner had he experienced that enjoyment than he opened his copy of Saint Augustine's *Confessions* at random to a passage that warned against such worldly vanities. Enjoyment of a more domesticated nature was permissible. The countryside was safer now, and the culture of the country villa had begun in tamed valleys and foothills. But to venture into the deep forest or climb the mountain heights was still an ambiguous undertaking, given the strictures against the sinful exercise of curiosity, which was inveighed against by thinkers stretching from Augustine to Aquinas. The probing natural history investigations of a Frederick II in the mid-thirteenth century are an anomaly, as is the nature mysticism of Saint Francis, who, had he lived in an age in which the Church was stronger, doubtless would have been tried as a heretic.

C. P. Snow wrote some years ago about the separate cultures of humanists and scientists, a problem that arguably can be laid at Petrarch's doorstep. The first great humanist sought the linguistic purity of ancient texts, but also found in these texts civic and personal models of how the good life might be lived. To Petrarch, investigation of the natural world was an inferior pursuit in that it gave no such guidance. Following his lead, later humanists paid scant attention to the natural world, although an occasional figure such as Enea Silvio Piccolomini or Lorenzo de' Medici could express genuine appreciation of natural scenery.

The preferred nature that writers and some artists celebrated was a soothing fiction, a picture of the Golden Age of humanity expressed in the genre of the pastoral, such as Sannazaro's *Arcadia* and the paintings of Giorgione, the young Titian, and their followers at the beginning of the sixteenth century. This was a static, unchanging world, knowing no turn of the seasons, no competition "red in tooth and claw." This was a world of forests, gently flowing brooks, and flower-bedecked greenswards where men and women lived in primal peace, knowing nothing of war, the burdens of materialism, or the deforming practices of advanced political structures. Arcadia was the invention of minds seeking release from the burdensome complications and violence of city life, a place in which a shepherd named Sincero (Sincere) roams a landscape where the days float by and nothing happens. It was the colored glass through which the Europeans preferred to view unfamiliar nature when possible, as Columbus did in his *Diario* when he first tried to make sense of the newfound inhabitants of the Caribbean.

What was the position of Leonardo among these various views of nature? The question is complicated. In his investigations of nature, Leonardo in some ways is quite unlike a modern scientist. The chief characteristic of modern (meaning mid-sixteenth-century onward) science is the trajectory from the asking of limited questions to the asking of general questions about the natural world. While Leonardo ruminates on such issues as movement and force, his sharpest focus is upon a diversity of particular issues. We find nothing in him that today would be recognized as a scientific theory, nor any strong inclination to experimentation. Indeed, the very notion of experimentation in Leonardo is in question, and some scholars even deny—incorrectly—that he carried out experiments at all. Discovery of things and particular relationships rather than the invention of theory is what drove him. The at times inchoate, fragmentary, and unsystematic nature of his writings, even when put in the best chronological order possible, seems to support this judgment. To an extent these points are irrelevant, for a hallmark of science as we know it is publication and peer review, and Leonardo never published his findings and seems not to have disseminated his work widely. Despite his magnificent work in anatomy, it remained largely unknown, and Andreas Vesalius (*De corporibus humanae,* 1543) holds the mantle as the father of modern anatomy, for he gave his work to the world in published form.

Nonetheless, in several aspects Leonardo *is* like a modern scientist. He preferred the quantifiable to the qualifiable in his investigations. His work consistently addresses operational rather than metaphysical questions, and he staunchly rejected the strains of alchemy and magic so prevalent in his day (*pace* Vasari and Pater). And he regarded "theory"— which in his terms should be defined as consistent reasoning—to be the underpinning of sound practice, writing several times that his investigations must pass the test of mathematics.

Although theory in the modern sense may be lacking in Leonardo's work, it certainly contains grand themes and compelling metaphors. Early on, his use of the ancient doctrine of the microcosm-macrocosm— which held that the structure of man reflects in miniature the structure of the world (e.g., the bones of man are the rocks of the earth, his blood its watercourses, etc.)—opened the way to innumerable correspondences and analogies in his thought. However, the microcosm-macrocosm notion seems at first organic, and belonging to an animistic world, whereas the specifics of how the elements of the earth operate on one another are understood in mechanistic terms, formulated in the 1490s in the doctrine of the Four Powers: Motion, Force, Weight, and Percussion. As Leonardo's thought evolved, his faith in the microcosm-macrocosm waned in favor of a growing interest in dynamic processes, which culminated in his studies of the heart. Throughout his years of investigation, he believed the works of nature to be perfect, in the sense that they displayed an economy of means, neither under- nor overelaborated in relation to their functions.

As both a draftsman and describer in words, Leonardo had in mind two quite different senses of nature, also inherited from antiquity and his immediate predecessors: the distinction between *natura naturata* and *natura naturans*. *Natura naturata* is passive nature, nature created—for instance, a lovingly drawn botanical specimen. *Natura naturans* is active nature, nature creating—as symptomatically indicated in drawings of water flowing around obstacles. In practice, in Leonardo's work these two ideas are usually fused—for instance, in the vegetation in the *Virgin of the Rocks,* which beyond being studies of inert specimens are given a life that suggests that Leonardo at this early date already clearly understood the heliotropic nature of plants.

Naturally, there is an irresistible tendency to see Leonardo as a systematic thinker, to recast him in the proto-Galilean role so dear to the nineteenth century. But as one pores over the drawings and thousands of pages of notes, the overwhelming impression received is of acute visual recordings of specific instances. To be an aesthetically motivated observer is one thing; to be an impassioned recorder is quite another. It is this impassioned recording that makes Leonardo in one sense a forerunner of modern science, and different from those that went before.

Perhaps it is fair to describe Leonardo as more the naturalist than scientist, drawing on the distinction made by the Harvard biologist William Morton Wheeler earlier in our own century:

> The naturalist is mentally oriented toward and controlled by objective, concrete reality, and probably because his senses, especially those of sight and touch, are highly developed, is powerfully affected by the aesthetic appeal of natural objects. He is little interested in and may even be quite blind to abstract or theoretical considerations. He is primarily an observer and fond of outdoor life, a collector, a classifier, deeply impressed by the overwhelming abundance of natural phenomena and revelling in their very complexity. . . .
>
> The biologist *sensu stricto,* on the other hand, is oriented towards and dominated by ideas, and rather terrified or oppressed by the intricate hurly-burly of concrete, sensuous reality and its multiform and multicolored individual manifestations. He often belongs to the motor rather than the visual type and obtains his aesthetic satisfaction from all kinds of analytical procedures and the cold desiccated beauty of logical and mathematical demonstration. His will to power takes the form of experimentation and the controlling of phenomena by capturing them in a net of abstract formulas and laws. He is a denizen of the laboratory. His besetting sin is oversimplification and the tendency to undue isolation of the organisms he studies from their natural environment.

When Leonardo traveled to his new life in Milan in the early 1480s, it was to present himself primarily as a technologist. Milan, unlike most great cities, was neither on the sea or by a large river, so major canal systems had to be developed over the course of several centuries. Leonardo arrived there to find a wealth of prior experience and work. It is reasonable to suppose that at first he was more student than master of waterworks. Probably it is less apt to think of his projects in terms of inventions than it is as work in refinement and development of pre-existing technology. But as an inevitable consequence, his thoughts turned to issues of hydrostatics and hydrodynamics in thinking that had to be mainly intuitive, for the mathematical knowledge necessary to secure hydraulic knowledge still lay a century in the future.

As his thinking in various technological fields developed, it took on aspects of the grandiose in projects ranging from a plan to raise the Florentine Baptistry to casting the huge equestrian monument to Francesco Sforza. From about 1488 onward he turned his attention to a proposal that had been around for a century, to make the Arno navigable between Florence and Pisa. Early in the new century his thinking came to fruition. On leaving Florence, the river was to be diverted into a canal toward the plain of Prato and Pistoia, where it would offer irrigation, would then cross the Apennine streams on viaducts, after which, to accommodate differences in altitude, it would be sent through a tunnel or trench at the pass at Seravalle, finally to be passed through the now-drained marshes of Fucecchio to the sea south of Pisa. However, even had this been accomplished, the primary purpose of navigability would have been frustrated by the meager flow of the Arno during the summer months. So Leonardo proposed an ancillary project that would have linked the watersheds of the Arno and the Tiber. The marshy valley of the Chiana was to be transformed into a large reservoir, fed by waters of the Tiber diverted below Perugia, and then passed through a tunnel between Mugnano and San Savino to the Arno. Lake Trasimeno was to be transformed into a large artificial body of water, with locks to control the amount of water transferred. The whole system was a project worthy of a modern mechanized corps of engineers, and came to nothing, as did the concurrent military project to cut Pisa off from the sea.

But Leonardo's reputation as a manipulator of land and water was secure, as evidenced by a call from the Venetians at the turn of the

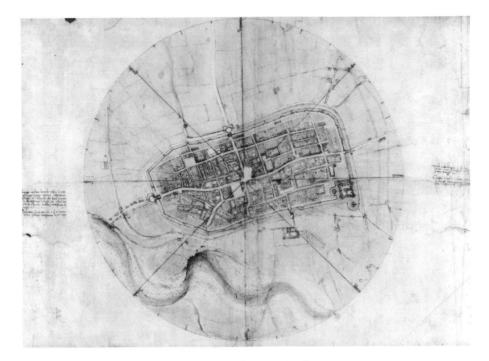

Fig. 48: Leonardo, *Map of Imola*. Royal Library, Windsor

century to develop a plan to flood the Isonzo plain below Gorzia as a
defense against the encroaching Turks. Later, under the French rulers of
Milan, Leonardo studied the feasibility of a bypass for the Adda at Tre
Corni; and it was partly his hydraulic expertise that led him to Rome,
and finally to France.

These projects required technological strategies, topographical studies, and—for large-scale solutions—maps. Leonardo executed what
might be called bird's-eye views, as well as maps in the modern sense.
The most remarkable of the latter, made in conjunction with his military
work for Cesare Borgia, is a map of the town of Imola (fig. 48), based
on the use of a horizontal surveying disk combined with accurate survey
measurements. The outcome is an absolutely accurate reduction of spatial dimensions of topography onto a sheet, a possession of the world
in microcosm. This sort of thinking complements the control manifested
in the painter's constructs of perspective; and, indeed, perspective may
be seen as the prologue to mapping the world.

Thus far, we have seen Leonardo as a manipulator and dominator of the physical face of the land for improved human use, following a tradition that goes back to the monks who cleared the lands around their monasteries, and to various projects of antiquity. The major difference is the grandiosity of Leonardo's plans. Yet it would be wrong to see Leonardo as the kind of prototypical leveler and dominator of the land all too familiar in our own day. Leonardo was also the mountain man who scaled the heights to gain information, some of which offered little practical value, and contravened medieval injunctions against idle curiosity.

From the beginning Leonardo ascended to high places, and continued to do so, making observations in which the purposes of art and investigation fuse. "Mountains are made by the currents of rivers. Mountains are destroyed by rains and rivers." For him mountains were the bones of the earth laid bare, carved by the incessant workings of water.

> There is to be seen, in the mountains of Parma and Piacenza, a multitude of shells and corals full of holes, still sticking to the rocks, and when I was at work on the great horse for Milan, a large sackful of them, which were found thereabout, was brought to me in my workshop by certain peasants.

He ponders fossils at length, their forms, their positions on the mountains, their layering, and rejects the biblical flood as the causal agent, glimpsing instead an immense past where mountains and water interacted.

> In this work you have first to prove that the shells, at a thousand braccia of elevation were not carried there by the deluge, because they are seen all to be at one level, and many mountains are seen to be above that level; and to inquire whether the deluge was caused by rain or by the swelling of the sea; and then you must show how, neither by rain which makes the rivers swell, nor by the overflow of this sea, could the shells—being heavy objects—be floated up the mountain by the sea, nor have been carried there by the rivers against the course of their waters.

Around 1506 he made a list of subjects for books that would detail the interaction of water and earth:

A book of the ordering of rivers so as to preserve their banks.

A book of the mountains, which level down and become land, if our hemisphere were to be uncovered by water.

A book of the earth carried down by the waters to fill up the great abyss of the seas.

A book of the ways in which a tempest may of itself clear out filled-up sea-ports.

A book of the shores of rivers and of their permanency.

A book of how to deal with rivers, so that they may keep their bottom scoured by their own flow near the cities they pass.

A book of how to make or repair the foundations for bridges over the rivers.

A book of repairs which ought to be made in walls and banks of rivers where the water strikes them.

A book of the formation of hills of sand or gravel at great depths in water.

These notes reveal the intimate tie in Leonardo's thinking between hydraulic phenomena in general and the need to put such information to practical use.

Leonardo's observations from the heights of mountains reveal secrets of water and earth, and also of the atmosphere that envelops them:

And this may be seen, as I saw it, by any one going up Monbroso, a peak of the Alps which divide France from Italy. The base of this mountain gives birth to the 4 rivers which flow in four different directions through the whole of Europe. And no mountain has at its base so great a height as this, which lifts itself above almost all the clouds; and snow seldom falls there, but only hail in the summer, when the clouds are highest. And this hail lies [unmelted] there, so that if it were not for the absorption of the rising and falling clouds, which does not happen more than twice in a lifetime, an enormous mass of ice would be piled up there by the layers of hail, and in the middle of July I found it very dark, and the sun as it fell on the mountain was far brighter here than in the plains below, because a smaller extent of atmosphere lay between the summit of the mountain and the sun.

This observation has the ring of true reporting, yet is fidelity to observed phenomena always to be assumed in Leonardo? Apparently not, because like others of his time he needed to move beyond direct experience to possess a wider world in his imagination.

Around 1508, at the height of his empirical powers, Leonardo wrote this description:

> From the shore of the southern coast of Cilicia may be seen to the south the beautiful island of Cyprus, which was the realm of the goddess Venus, and many navigators, being attracted there by her beauty, had their ships and rigging broken amidst the reefs, surrounded by the swirling waters. Here the beauty of delightful hills tempts wandering mariners to refresh themselves amidst their flowery verdure, where the winds are tempered and fill the island and the surrounding seas with fragrant odours. Ah! how many a ship has here been sunk. Ah! how many a vessel broken on these rocks. Here might be seen barks without number, some half wrecked and half covered by the sand, others showing the poop and another the prow, here a keel and there the ribs, and it seems like a day of judgment when there should be a resurrection of dead ships, so great is the number of them covering all the northern shore; and while the north gale makes various and fearful noises there.

In prose finely polished for Leonardo, this passage invokes the realm of Venus, Odyssean echoes of shipwreck, and the motif of Christian resurrection. It is a landscape of the mind, in contrast to topographical inventories in which Leonardo writes of 300 rivers flowing into the Mediterranean, a sea of 40,200 ports. The Cilicia passage—not surprisingly given its literary pretensions—is based on work of contemporary writers, appropriated by Leonardo to travel geographically outward and temporally back in time. While in this case it is hardly difficult to guess that there are literary sources, a caution should be sounded, for other passages that seem to be straightforward and factual may be derivative or may stem from the imagination.

If real landscapes such as that of Cyprus are evoked in Leonardo's writings, what of those rocky settings in his major paintings, the *Saint Jerome,* the *Virgin of the Rocks,* the *Madonna and Child and Saint Anne,* the

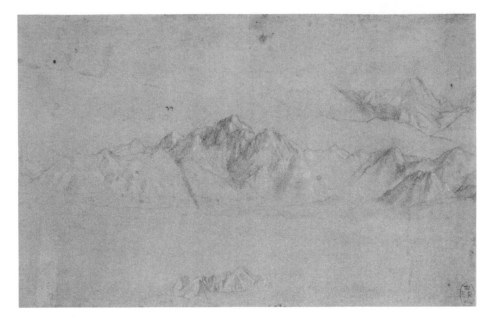

Fig. 49: Leonardo, *Mountain Landscape*. Royal Library, Windsor

Lady on a Balcony (see figs. 18, 19, 27, and 1)? Leonardo's topographical drawings leave no doubt that these visions, if visions they be, are well founded on observation (fig. 49). But what is involved in the passage from empirical observation to what look like the products of a synthesizing imagination? In the case of each painting, scholars have adduced a textual basis that justifies Leonardo's inclusion of a rocky landscape, yet these proposals usually overlook the fact that Leonardo's interest in this topography is a constant, whether in a Christian altarpiece or a secular portrait. The effect of these landscapes certainly speaks to fantasy more than it does to observation, and it almost seems as if the figural subjects of these pictures are merely changing actors in a primordial world whose meaning to Leonardo lies deeper than the iconographer can probe.

The *Virgin of the Rocks* presents the quintessential Leonardesque bones of the earth shaped by underground waters. At roughly the same time he painted it, Leonardo wrote the following, which at first glance would seem to presume a trip to Sicily:

Like a whirling wind which rushes down a sandy and hollow valley, and which, in its hasty course, drives to its centre everything that opposes its furious course . . .

Nor otherwise does the northern blast whirl round in its tempestuous progress . . .

Nor does the tempestuous sea bellow so loud, when the northern blast dashes it, with its foaming waves, between Scylla and Charybdis; nor Stromboli, nor Mount Etna, when their sulphurous flames, having been forcibly confined, rend and burst open the mountain, fulminating stones and earth through the air together with the flames they vomit . . .

Nor where the inflamed caverns of Mount Etna, rejecting the ill-restrained element, vomit it forth, back to its own region, driving furiously before it every obstacle that comes in the way of its impetuous rage . . .

Unable to resist my eager desire and wanting to see the great multitude of the various and strange shapes made by formative nature, and having wandered some distance among gloomy rocks, I came to the entrance of a great cavern, in front of which I stood some time, astonished and unaware of such a thing. Bending my back into an arch I rested my tired hand on my knee and held my right hand over my downcast and contracted eyebrows: often bending first one way and then the other, to see whether I could discover anything inside, and this being forbidden by the deep darkness within, and after having remained there for some time, two contrary emotions arose in me, fear and desire—fear of the threatening large cavern, and desire to see whether there were any marvelous thing within it.

Did Leonardo travel to Sicily in these years? It is of course possible, but both undocumented and unlikely. To fret over this unanswerable question would be to miss the obvious, that the passage is a literary tour de force evoking the immense powers of nature. Whatever the contribution of actual experience to either this passage or the topography of the *Virgin of the Rocks,* both the writing and painted landscape are poetic syntheses, travels in the imagination to the margins beyond the familiar and known.

Leonardo was a traveler, both literally and in his imagination. As suggested earlier, from antiquity onward travel accounts and maps grow more fantastic as one moves from the known center to the fantasized: men with tails, dog-headed people, a birdlike creature capable of lifting an elephant, people with feet so large that they could use them as parasols, and the like. Leonardo plays with this tradition in an early letter to Benedetto Dei, in which he reports on a giant born on Mount Atlas who roamed the desert, wreaking havoc among the people. The word "play" should be stressed, for again Leonardo seems to have been trying his hand at a literary conceit.

Rarely did Leonardo resort to the tradition of wonders of the East in his explorations in the imagination. Instead, he would possess the world by projecting the empirical data of the world before him onto the imagined canvas of distant worlds. If this surmise is correct, then one should not expect to find dramatic differences between the directly observed and inventions of the imagination. For instance, the following has all the earmarks of apprehended experience:

> I have once seen such a conglomeration of clouds. And lately over Milan towards Lago Maggiore I saw a cloud in the form of an immense mountain full of rifts of glowing light, because the rays of the sun, which was already close to the horizon and red, tinged the cloud with their own hue. And this cloud attracted to it all the little clouds that were near while the large one did not move from its place; thus it retained on its summit the reflection of the sunlight till an hour and a half after sunset, so immensely large was it.

Compare this to a letter allegedly written by Leonardo to the Defterdar of Syrea, Lieutenant to the Sacred Sultan of Babylon. In it, Leonardo recounts the woes of his and his compatriot's suffering as they were buffeted by mountain fury of avalanche, flood, and fire. The bulk of the letter is devoted to establishing the geographical particulars of Mount Taurus:

> . . . the side, which faces the wind is always full of clouds and mists, because the wind, which is parted in beating the rock closes again on the farther side of that rock, and in its motion carries with it the clouds from all quarters and leaves them where it strikes. And it is

always full of thunderbolts from the great quantity of clouds which accumulate there, whence the rock is all riven and full of huge debris. This mountain, at its base, is inhabited by a very rich population and is full of most beautiful springs and rivers, and is fertile and abounding in all good produce, particularly in those parts which face to the south. But after counting about three miles we begin to find the forests of great fir-trees, and beech and other similar trees; after this, for a space of three more miles, there are meadows and vast pastures; and all the rest, as far as the beginning of the Taurus, is eternal snows which never disappear at any time, and extend to a height of about fourteen miles in all. From this beginning of the Taurus up to the height of a mile the clouds never pass away; thus we have fifteen miles, that is a height of about five miles in a straight line; and the summit of the peaks of the Taurus are as much, or about that. There, half-way up, we begin to find a scorching air and never feel a breath of wind; but nothing can live long there; there is nothing brought forth save a few birds of prey which breed in the high fissures of the Taurus and descend below the clouds to seek their prey on the wooded hills; there all is bare rock, that is, from the clouds upwards; and the rock is purest white. And it is impossible to walk to the summit on account of the rough and perilous ascent.

This account has all the specificity of the passage on the cloud over Lago Maggiore, yet there is not a shred of evidence that Leonardo went to the Near East; in fact, the preponderance of evidence all but rules out such a trip. It has been shown that the passage depends heavily on the spurious fourteenth-century armchair travel writer John de Mandeville, from whom, incidentally, Columbus got the assurance that the globe could be circumnavigated. The Mount Taurus description is undoubtedly vivid, but its eyewitnesslike freshness is due to Leonardo's reading and his quite extraordinary inner eye.

Thus, medieval marvels and monsters are replaced in Leonardo's work by projecting known natural phenomena onto the unknown, a way of extending his mastery of the world. Whereas for earlier writers the unknown was at the horizontal margins, for Leonardo the mountain man the progression away from home is vertical, from abundant fertile valleys to the unreachable wind-strafed summits of the bones of the earth. That unknown could descend in avalanche and deluge to crush the order of domesticity and annihilate our very bodies, bodies that are our center of reference, our opening metaphor for comprehending the world. While Cristóbal Colón ventured across the vast expanse of the ocean into the unknown, it was left to Leonardo to be the greatest explorer of something closer at hand, the human body itself.

CHAPTER II

The Body as Nature and Culture

AN IDEAL HISTORY of the world would be based squarely upon our bodies and our emotions, matters often all but inaccessible to words. The body is our master metaphor, the vehicle by which we compare ourselves to others, to sense who they are and, in turn, who we are. We go through life at times in ecstasy, at others in pain. We know love, ponder birth and death, feel happiness, hatred, jealousy, and fear. This is the real stuff of the human story, and the history of each one of us, but it is not the sort of history that we read in schoolbooks.

Rarely has the body been so unattuned to the rest of nature as in our time. We usually do not rise with the sun or cease to work when it sets; we can shield ourselves from the changing climate of the seasons, take our nourishment from containers packaged hundreds or thousands of miles from us, and travel at speeds far faster than the fastest-known animal; and, except for the superstitious among us, we no longer think that the fate of our bodies is somehow sealed to the movements of the stars. While the mysteries of the brain have not fully yielded to our understanding, the body, like the world we inhabit, has been thoroughly explored. We assume that this body of ours can be repaired when necessary, and are affronted by mortal disorders, on which we declare wars and pledge that one day they will be eradicated in what presumably is to be a disease-free world. In short, we fervently hope against all evidence to the contrary that our bodies may be free of contingency and fate.

We experience the body in a number of different ways. Above all, the body is our corporeal, visceral self. We can feel a clear head on awakening, the pain of arthritis in the joints, the exhilaration of exercise, the sting of a scrape. On occasion we reflect upon these things, but their reality always seems to revert to mute personal feeling, to the truth that the felt body and our emotions are inexorably linked.

There is then our visual assessment of static images of the body, from Michelangelo's Adam about to be imbued with spirit to the enticements of modern advertising. In early childhood our eyes help us to learn the distinction between self and other, and we compare images of other bodies to our own, something done in the mind's eye except when we stand before a full-length mirror.

And then there is the very different body seen in terms of science and medicine, a body measured, analyzed, probed, treated, incised, dissected. It is the body as object of physical investigation and explanation, a body that we understand well enough in our minds, but a body wholly alien to the particular one that we experience in our personal life.

Finally, there is what might be called a kinesthetic body, where to a degree these various notions of the body come together. By our motions we initiate and react, touch, define the space that is ours, measuring these things against the action of other bodies in the community of bodies. This sense of the body is deeply implicated in notions of body language, invoked by the movements of rappers, rockers, and modern dance, which remind us in a word-centered culture of another sort of language of which we know far too little.

In Leonardo's day the physical body was of course the same as ours, but the thinking about it radically different. The body was seen to be the microcosm of the world, a tribute to its centrality, but at the same time bearing the possible burden of deep involvement in cosmic processes. Above all, the body was the seat of fundamental mysteries divine in origin, and to physically violate a body could be a transgression of divine intentions. For the average person, the body experienced unrelieved pain sooner rather than later, and it was normal that its life would end in disease about which little or nothing could be done.

We may well wonder, then, what was in Leonardo's mind when in the final decade of his life he painted a *Saint John the Baptist* and drew a study of the myology of the shoulder region, the one evocative in its penumbral smokiness, the other a rigorously incisive, linear demonstration (figs. 32 and 50). Both are surely images of the body, yet in drastically different senses.

Leonardo's unfinished 1481 *Adoration of the Magi* (see fig. 14) is a dem-

Fig. 50: Leonardo, *Myology of the Upper Torso*. Royal Library, Windsor

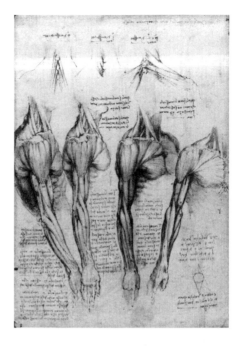

onstration of his belief that a major task of painting is to reveal the mind of a figure through its movements. Leonardo was committed to this proposition as few artists before him had been, and he is arguably the first great master of body language as it is rendered in the static images of art. He saw the depiction of such movement as a profound task, a quest like philosophy: "Painting is proved to be philosophy because it treats of the motion of bodies and the rapidity of their actions, and philosophy also includes motion."

The *Adoration of the Magi* abounds in a variety of figures, their energy suggested through posture, gesture, and facial expression. He sought variety and appropriateness of motion for each figure, as if through contrast the compelling qualities of every figure would be enhanced. To the Madonna's left, straining to behold the wondrous epiphany, are several male figures, the older ones boldly three-dimensional in the definition of their craniums, their eye sockets and cheekbones roughly brushed in deep shadow (see fig. 15). A bearded man shades his eyes, and directly behind him a second figure cocks his head to one side, less a head than a skull, the eyes lost in pools of shadow. Had Leonardo carried the painting to a finished state by applying colors, these effects surely would have been moderated. As it is, the unfinished product is testimony to Leonardo's habit of thinking of bodies from the core outward.

Here, as in *The Last Supper,* the source for the bodily expression of mental movement lies in the narrative of the painting itself. The *Treatise on Painting* later makes clear that the mental-physical motion should be understood in terms of generic states of mind: "The most important things that can be found in the analysis of painting are the movements appropriate to the states of mind of each living creature, such as desire, contempt, anger, pity, and the like."

The Last Supper (see fig. 23) is the *locus classicus* of the power of painting's mute testimony to challenge the effectiveness of verbal narrative. Whatever the niceties of theological interpretation, the painting immediately proclaims the theme of betrayal: twelve men variously react in posture, gesture, and facial expression to the announcement of Jesus that one of them will betray him. The scene is a conversation of hands, as if Leonardo unconsciously or otherwise were aware of the ancient rhetorician Quintilian's reflections on the potency of speaking hands.

In his writing, Leonardo urges the painter to understand these things before dwelling on beauty: "Therefore, painter, compose the parts of your figures arbitrarily, then attend first to the movements representative of the mental attitudes of the creatures composing your narrative painting, rather than to the beauty and goodness of the parts of their bodies." He suggests that an effective way to reach this understanding is to observe the dumb, who must rely on gesture far more than other persons, or, in the case of a group of speakers, to see how their gestures relate to what they say. In all this, he says, the painter will be served well by making quick sketches in a little notebook which he should carry with him at all times.

The effectiveness of painting finally depends upon an equivalency of reaction between the protagonists within a represented narrative and the reaction of a spectator to that narrative: "The elements of narrative paintings ought to move those who look at or contemplate them in the same way as he who the narrative painting represents."

Although I wrote earlier that perspective posits a separation between the viewer and objects in a fictive space beyond the picture plane, that statement now needs to be qualified. While images of inanimate objects hold their spatial placement in the grid laid down by perspective, it is not as simple with depictions of living beings, for the psychological exchange between these represented figures, and between them and the viewer, may well violate their relative importance or lack of it as defined only by the logic of optical scale relations. Viewers are deeply psychologically implicated in the work of art, as suggested by the example Leonardo gives of the lover who will speak to or kiss the portrait of his or her beloved. And the painter likewise can be implicated, to his possible peril: "For the soul, the master of your body, is that which is your own judgment, and readily delights in things made like that which he created in composing your body. Thence it happens that there is no figure of a woman so ugly as not to find a lover, if she is not monstrous. By all means remember the defects that are in your person, and defend yourself against them in the figures that you compose."

The step from the craniums in the 1481 *Adoration* to the series of skull drawings of 1489 seems a natural and easy one, as if Leonardo's observations on what lay on the surface impelled him to look inside as the next logical move. But, far more to the point, Leonardo was moving from the cultural body image to the scientific body image, a bold and difficult step, given the context of his times.

We are apprehensive about having our bodies become the bodies of medicine and science, yet when this happens we do not feel it to be any sort of violation of the order of things. Indeed, we welcome it when the alternative is continuing pain or possible death. In our medical schools the scientific body, the cadaver, is prepared, in a procedure that is antiseptic and orderly. Flesh is incised and viscera revealed so that the young may see and understand, and in understanding take their place one day with confidence at the bedside or operating table. In the laboratory, the pathologist looking inside the body seeks to answer why suddenly the rhythm of life has given way to death. Far more often it is the living who are probed, so that morbid pathology might be halted or diverted in its course. All that has been made easy now: orifices may be examined with lens and light, while X rays can penetrate living lay-

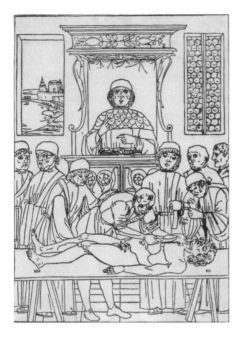

Fig. 51: *Mondino de Luzzi Directing Dissections*. Woodcut, Bibliothéque Nationale, Paris

ers, with CAT scan, NMR, Mag-scan, tracer, and sonogram giving access to what for centuries was forbidden knowledge. Only after all this is the scalpel the revealer.

In Leonardo's day, and in the long centuries before his birth, it was different. Often the pain of the living was without remission until the final hour was up. One spoke of the balance of humors, the flow of animal and vital spirits. Blood was let, potions drunk, and one waited and prayed, even as intestines tightened and eyes grew dim. And what of the cold flesh of the recently dead? Victims of accident or war might be examined hastily en route to the grave, the bones of dead crusaders boiled to their pristine whiteness on return from the East, until in 1299 Pope Boniface forbade the practice. Material for anatomical demonstrations was provided by the fresh carcass of the recently executed criminal, here quartered, there mutilated, in the last spasm of torture. His body—for it was almost always a male—was opened on a table by a barber in the winter, whose chill for a brief time slowed the bodily putrefaction (fig. 51). The barber, a so-called demonstrator, revealed the moist waves of viscera, while, at a lectern above, the professor read aloud from the anatomical texts of the ancients, which by the fourteenth century consisted of a confused aggregate of Greek and Arabic thought. No matter that the words read and the evidence of the flesh might suggest radically different things: the point of the exercise was not fresh investigation, but the confirmation of received tradition.

Such anatomical demonstrations apparently did not begin until the fourteenth century. They were sporadic, not public, and apparently undertaken with studied formality. Cutting open a body was fraught with deep taboos. The idea that the body is the cosmos in miniature carried with it the possibility that intervention in the body could constitute interference in the perfect workings of God's creation. The body was under the rule of the planets, and such medical treatment as existed was subject to favorable or unfavorable celestial configurations. To cut open a body was to draw blood both sacred and profane—the blood of Christ, but also the blood of menstrual flow. No wonder that incision and dissection were considered ominous enterprises, a quest for forbidden knowledge inviting the same deadly fate as Dante's Ulysses, who dared venture beyond the pillars of Hercules. And no wonder that among the anathematized were executioners, butchers, and surgeons. Cutting open a body was something to be done under the most controlled of circumstances, and only then to confirm tradition rather than to advance knowledge. Such ambiguities persisted in Leonardo's day, as shown by the scant number of specimens at his disposal and the papal refusal of anatomical material during his years in Rome.

Why then in 1489 did Leonardo turn to anatomy in earnest? Certainly it was not for occult or magical reasons, for he is outspoken against such practices. And while he does mention anatomy as a means of understanding wounds, his opinion of doctors was low, and thus medical reasons would have been at best tertiary. Nor does the correction of received authority seem to have been an initial stimulus, for he takes on his predecessors by name only in his later anatomical work. One is left with the likelihood that his motivation was pure investigation, and probably only to a degree a direct extension of his activity as an artist.

What seems clear is that Leonardo's developed thought on the body conceives it in mechanistic terms, and grows out of his concern with machines. After the turn of the century, he begins an entry, "We shall demonstrate the mechanical structure of man," and later, "O speculator on this machine of ours." Around 1510 he writes on a sheet dedicated to the study of the musculature of the upper extremities, "Arrange it so that the book on the elements of mechanics with its practice comes prior to the demonstration of movement and force of man and the other animals, and by means of these [examples] you will be able to prove all your propositions." And several years earlier, "On Machines. Why Nature cannot give motion to animals without mechanical instruments is shown by me in this book On Motive Agents Made by Nature in Animals." Notes on his anatomical drawings abound in mechanistic concepts—levers, counter levers, cords, and so forth, and it is clear in the *Treatise on Painting* that the painter should understand the human machine: "The painter who knows well the sinews, muscles, and tendons, will know very well when a limb moves how many and which sinews are the reason for it, and which muscle, by swelling, is the reason for the contraction of the sinew, and which sinews, changed into very thin cartilage, surround and contain the muscle." Despite this and similar passages pertaining to art, Leonardo's view of the body as machine probably has as much or more to do with his technological investigations of the 1480s and '90s.

Leonardo's mechanistic view of the body—"this machine of ours"—carries with it certain implications. Like a machine, the body serves some functional purpose(s). Like a machine, it is a unity consisting of subordinate parts, each of which is specific and distinct from the others. These parts interrelate, and to understand the machine-body, or to repair it when it malfunctions, one must have an unequivocal grasp of the causal relations among the parts. Finally, like a machine, a live body requires an energy source to drive it. Lack of energy means a machine not in operation; lack of energy means a body that has become a corpse. What is missing in this view is the nature of the immune system, the composition of the blood, the systematic collapse brought about by stress—in short, the mystery of an entity that is an organism, not a machine.

By 1489 Leonardo had come into possession of a human skull and neck, probably the remains of an executed criminal. It was a precious acquisition, for, contrary to what Leonardo claimed, his dissection material was most incomplete and sporadically obtained. He had this skull and neck and, in Florence early in the new century, the cadavers of a hundred-year-old man and a two-year-old child. A little later he dissected a seven-month fetus. Beyond that there are hints of the availability of an elderly man, perhaps a young person, and a dismembered leg. With this scant material, supplemented by reading and animal parts, Leonardo probed his human machine.

What must Leonardo have thought as he cut into the skull? Although we cannot know, a hint appears in a note on a sheet of drawings done some twenty years later: "And you, O Man, who will discern in this work of mine the marvellous works of Nature, if you think it would be a criminal thing to destroy it, reflect how much more criminal it is to take the life of a man; and if this, his external form, appears to thee marvellously constructed, remember that it is nothing compared with the soul that dwells in this structure; for that, indeed, be it what it may, is a divine thing. Leave it then to dwell in its work at its good pleasure, and let not your rage or malice destroy a life—for indeed, he who does not value it, does not himself deserve it."

As his thinking evolved, Leonardo became staunchly anti-speculative concerning issues not accessible to the senses, such as the soul, heaven, God. While Vasari's 1550 intimations of Leonardo's lack of Christian faith are exaggerated, it was a good intuitive insight, in that Leonardo simply did not concern himself often with mysteries to which the senses could not give access. This may have allowed him to look inside the body with far less trepidation than most of his contemporaries.

The double drawing of the skulls (see fig. 46) the one above bisected in medial sagittal section, the one below shown in complete section to reveal the nasal cavity, sinuses, and cranial fossae—is among the most exquisite of all Leonardo's drawings. I use an adjective appropriate to a description of a work of art, and purposely so, for the scientific intent of the drawing is not immediately obvious. Whatever the intent, certain skills are revealed that are crucial to the clarity of the image: control of perspective as rigorous as would be exercised in a painting, use of light and shade to define mass and volume as nuanced as the head of an angel in an altarpiece, and a controlled hatching in brown ink over black chalk that yields a crystalline clarity. It reveals the eye and hand of an artist at work, here as surely interested in mimetic representation as he is when drawing a domed church or an angel's head.

The grid of lines on the lower drawing, and the accompanying inscription, reveal the intent of the cranial demonstration—to locate compartments of the brain in which various mental functions take place, such as sense reception, cognition, fantasy, imagination, judgment, and memory. Leonardo's views varied over time on these unseen matters, finally settling on three: a receptor area in the front of the brain for the gathering of sense impressions (of which sight was paramount); a mental processing area called the common sense; and an area in the back of the brain for memory. A drawing of about 1490 elaborates these ideas in diagrammatic form, with these three cranial areas seen from above at the foot of the page.

The skull drawings show, on the one hand, the observed beauty of a precious object and, on the other, speculation upon the unfathomable mysteries that it enfolded—the centers of perception, cognition, and memory. These are mysteries that no anatomist could lay bare, and no artist could see with his eyes. At this point Leonardo was the consummate describer of volumes and surfaces, a speculator on unseen things that lay inside, a habit of mind that he would increasingly abandon. But the heart of his anatomical explorations still lay ahead.

In the 1490s Leonardo's thinking moved toward principles marked by necessity, for he believed that observed phenomena were not correctly understood until seen in the light of controlling principles. It was during these years that he developed the idea of the Four Powers—Motion, Force, Weight, and Percussion. Machines and bodies alike were to be analyzed in terms of the interaction of these phenomena. The significance of thinking for Leonardo's understanding of human anatomy lay in his realization that the human machine had to be considered as a totality, seeing the component parts and their functional relationships. This was hardly a matter of simple observation, for the various systems—osteological, myological, cardiovascular, nervous, respiratory, genito-urinary, and alimentary—lay intertwined and over one another, offering potentially chaotic confusion to the eye and mind of an observer. There had to be a system to anatomical study, and this Leonardo developed over the years.

It was necessary to understand each anatomical system, and the nature and relationship of its constituent parts. So Leonardo drew the vertebral column, and in an "exploded" view demonstrated the individual vertebrae (fig. 52), much as he did with machinery. An arm is a hoisting device and must be explicated. The support of the head on the trunk of

Fig. 52: Leonardo, *Vertebral Column.*
Royal Library, Windsor

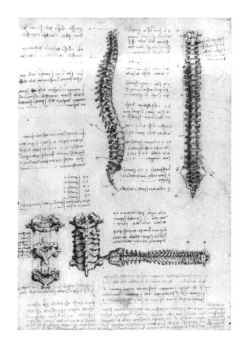

the body must be understood, and to do so Leonardo reverts to the analogy of the rigging of a ship. He realized that a single view of an anatomical passage offered only partial information, and so in a study of the musculature of the shoulder he offers several views (see fig. 50). He codified this procedure in the dictum that any adequate exposition of the body would have to involve consideration of eleven demonstrations, each seen from four points of view. At times, diagrammatic devices needed to be used if proper understanding were to be gained. Another study of the musculature of the shoulder includes at the upper right a visual explanation created by the use of stretched wires, and, in like manner, copper wires are utilized to indicate the lines of force in the muscles of the leg. All these preludes to understanding underlie one of Leonardo's most lucid anatomical drawings, of the muscles of the lower leg (fig. 53). Everything is verbally and visually observed with rigorous acuity, something that is possible only after gaining a thorough understanding of the significance of what is seen.

To represent musculature, cardiovascular phenomena, and the like separately is one thing, but to see them together something else again.

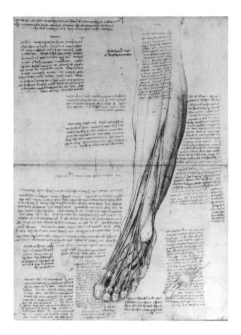

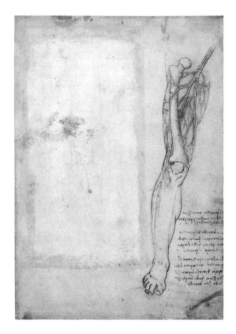

Fig. 53: Leonardo, *Anatomy of Lower Leg and Foot*. Royal Library, Windsor

Fig. 54: Leonardo, *Femoral Vessels and the Femur*. Royal Library, Windsor

In order to do this, Leonardo developed the transparency drawing, as seen in a study of the leg where blood vessels and bone are seen in juxtaposition (fig. 54). The most famous of Leonardo's anatomical drawings, the so-called Great Lady Anatomy (fig. 57), is his boldest venture in this type of representation. Essentially the drawing focuses on the genito-urinary system, yet much else is also included. Leonardo sought total understanding, but even here he had to stop short in the interests of clarity: inclusion of the bones and nerves would have created an impossible visual overload.

Anatomical demonstration, then, was a symbiotic play between observation and knowledge, and no small part of that knowledge came from the writings of others, notably the great second-century Greek physician Galen, who had been court doctor to the Roman emperor Marcus Aurelius. In his later years, Leonardo increasingly came to grips with Galen's contributions, but the writings of Galen and others led Leonardo into a number of errors. Such was the pervasive power of tradition, even for this *"omo sanza lettere"* who possessed the consummate eye.

The drawings that we have been considering lack the nuanced sfumato of the early skull drawings, instead marked by a dry precision that is in stark contrast. The drawings are impersonal, in the sense of revealing nothing of an artist's individual expressive marks. While an artist studies anatomy to capture the particular look of things at a moment in time, the anatomist seeks system and clear order in rendering the murky and viscous layers of membranes and complexities of myological articulation in multiple views and clear transparencies. He will resort to an impersonal style of drawing, subordinating his autobiographical marks on the page to the clarity of the parts presented, and suppressing any emotiveness such as might be engendered by the active play of light and shade. Were the anatomist and the artist in Leonardo now separate beings? Before speculating on that possibility, it is necessary to turn to what can only be called the anatomical drama of Leonardo's late investigations.

The last six years of Leonardo's life were spent in Rome and then in France, where he died. If painting still occupied him, we have little indication of it. What few glimpses we have are of the unfulfilled tinkerer, the dabbler in trifles, if Vasari is to be believed, and of a hand that has slowed, probably because of a stroke. His last anatomical drawings were done around 1513, studies of the heart of an ox (fig. 55). These are mostly on blue paper, and rougher in handling than earlier drawings. The heart baffled Leonardo, and his alternative explanations of the cardiovascular system were complex and contradictory over the years. He was denied access to cadavers at the Hospital of the Holy Spirit in Rome, which reduced the remote possibility of his making the momentous discovery of the circulation of the blood, a riddle that the Englishman William Harvey solved a little more than a century later. Leonardo cannot have doubted that the blood and its movement lay at the core of the mystery of life, but the analogies provided by the microcosm-macrocosm hypothesis offered no practical furtherance of understanding. Nor could the motion of waters, a passionate subject of Leonardo's research through several decades, provide the needed clues, although some of his descriptions of blood have the implied violence of raging torrents. From an early date, Leonardo appealed to mathematics as the

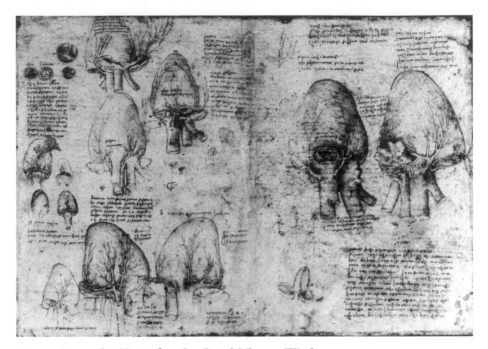

Fig. 55: Leonardo, *Heart of an Ox*. Royal Library, Windsor

key to controlling the disparate chaos of appearances, but it is ironic that his strongest encomiums to mathematics are written on these late drawings of the heart, where the discipline could be of no help in breaking the code of fluid dynamics.

Finally the body as machine needs an energy source. Matter was believed—in Leonardo's time as it had been in the Middle Ages—to be composed of four elements and to be in itself inert. Life, and hence motion, can be explained only by resorting to an incorporeal and invisible energy, what Leonardo called among other designations a *"virtù spirituale."* This force is the "first motor," and "motion the cause of every life." Without being moved, force is capable of moving, and is thus a prime mover. The cosmic force of the universe is invested in the soul, and invisible spiritual movement in turn activates the material movement of the muscles, the visible matter that Leonardo explores in his anatomical drawings. Material motion—life—is the subject of the artist who confronts the body, while the scientific body, the subject of the anatomist, is a residual symptom of departed life. Hence the complementarity of art and investigation in Leonardo, but from first to last in him the overwhelming importance of painting as a species of philosophy.

Finally force is a mystery, and Leonardo speaks of it allusively and poetically, something beyond his scientific understanding:

> Force is the same throughout and the whole is in every part of it.
>
> Force is a spiritual power, an invisible energy which is imparted by violence from without to all bodies out of their natural balance.
>
> Force is nothing but a spiritual power, an invisible energy which is created and communicated, through violence from without, by animated bodies to inanimated bodies, giving to these the similarity of life, and this life works in a marvelous way, compelling all created things from their places, and changing their shapes.
>
> It speeds in fury to its undoing, and continues to modify according to the occasion.
>
> Retardation strengthens, and speed weakens it.
>
> It lives by violence, and dies through liberty.
>
> It transmutes and compels all bodies to a change of form and place.
>
> Great power gives it great desire for death.
>
> It drives away in its fury whatever stands in the way to its ruin.
>
> Transmuter of various forms.
>
> Wherever it is held, it is always ill at ease.
>
> It is always opposing forces of nature.
>
> It grows slowly from small beginnings, to terrible and marvelous energy, and by compression of itself, compels all things.
>
> —it lives in bodies which are out of their natural course and state.
>
> —it likes to consume itself.
>
> Force is the same throughout, and the whole of it is in the body where it is generated.
>
> Force is but a desire to flight.
>
> It always wants to weaken and extinguish itself.
>
> —when compressed it compels all bodies.
>
> Without it nothing moves.
>
> No sound or voice is heard from it.

Its true source is in living bodies.

Weight is transmitted to the full by perpendicular resistance, and it is all in every part of the resistance.

If an oblique resistance opposed to the weight be loosened and freed, it will make no resistance to the weight; on the contrary it will descend with it in ruin.

It is in the nature of weight to transmit itself of its own accord to the desired place.

Every part of force contains the whole—contrary to weight.

Often they are victors over the other.

They are of similar nature as regards pressure and the stronger overpowers the weaker.

Weight does not change of its own accord, while force is always fugitive.

Weight has body, force has none.

One desires flight and death, the other seeks stability and permanence.

Often one generates the other.

If weight creates force, force is weight.

If weight conquers force, force is weight.

And if they are of equal strength they will keep company for a long time.

If one is eternal, the other is mortal.

This passage is unusually allusive and poetic for Leonardo, and yet in other ways characteristic of him: it contains sharp observation joined to redundancy, and a tendency to stalk phenomena from a number of different angles. In this, even if he was a seeker after principles, Leonardo differs sharply from a modern scientist, who will seek the simplest formulation that will cover all cases. A Leonardo will posit dozens of explanations of weight, whereas a Galileo will try for one.

To return to this chapter's starting point, the painting of *Saint John the Baptist* and the drawing of the musculature of the shoulder (see figs. 32 and 50): while the relationship of art and science in Leonardo seemed clear enough at the outset, how did they relate at the end?

Many tentative answers have been offered, and clearly the temptation to find a compelling unity is very strong. The lost painting of *Leda and*

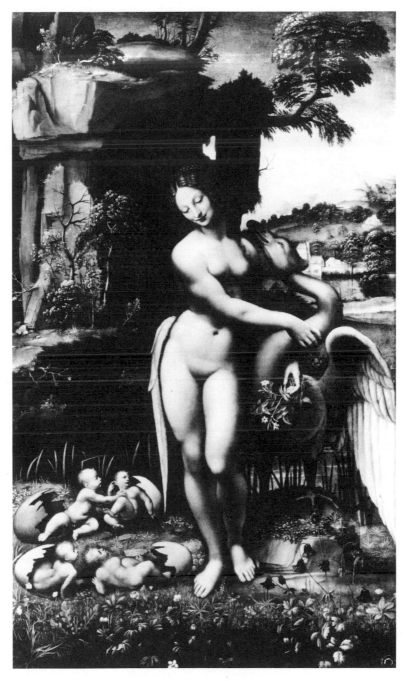

Fig. 56: Follower of Leonardo, *Leda*. Uffizi, Florence

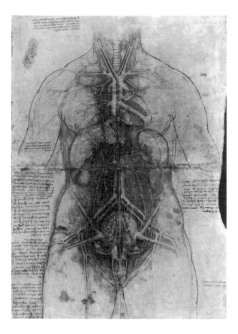

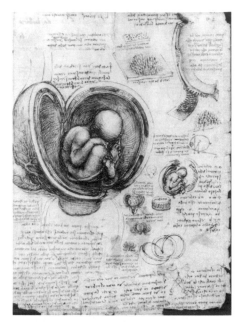

Fig. 57: Leonardo, So-called Great Lady
Anatomy. Royal Library, Windsor

Fig. 58: Leonardo, *Fetus in the Womb.*
Royal Library, Windsor

the Swan (fig. 56), kneeling and standing versions of which occupied
Leonardo during the first decade of the century, testifies to his fascination with life processes. It represents the strange ancient myth of generation of life between human and animal, one of the overtly classical
themes in Leonardo's oeuvre. Zeus in the form of a swan cohabited
with Leda by the river Eurotas, and from the eggs of that union hatched
Castor and Pollux, and Clytemnestra and Helen, pairs, respectively, of
harmony and discord in human affairs. Why Leonardo chose such a
subject is not known, but perhaps the reasons had to do with his abiding
love of contrasting opposites and his long fascination with comparative
zoology. Should one take things a step further, and say that the *Leda*
was the product of the same curiosity that led Leonardo in these same
years to explore coition and the mysteries of the womb (fig. 58)? Possibly, but it is a free leap of the imagination.

    And what of the *Lady on a Balcony,* which Leonardo probably com-
pleted at about the same time that he drew the so-called Great Lady
Anatomy (see figs. 1 and 57)? Did his X-ray eye look within her fluid

curves to penetrate her inner mysteries? Perhaps, but do we risk drifting back to sorts of mystifications perpetuated by Michelet and Pater?

Rather, it may be that the incisive linearity of the study of the shoulder and the velvet evanescence of the *Saint John the Baptist* speak to worlds that had grown apart for Leonardo, which is not necessarily to say that they were contradictory.

"Nature is full of infinite causes that have never occurred in experience." Probably these words are properly taken in the context of Leonardo's various thoughts on cause and effect. But is it not possible that the *Saint John,* at face value a supreme study in light and shade, alludes to intimated mysteries central to human experience, but beyond the grasp of science?

The scientist rationally explains, the artist in an act of faith proclaims. That, I suggest, is the point at which Leonardo finally arrived. Different though they may be, art and science are opposite ends of the keyboard of human experience, but the same keyboard nonetheless, in whose playing are revealed the harmonies of the universe.

CHAPTER 12

A Blessed Rage for Order

ORDER STANDS at the center of the received character of the Italian Renaissance. The circle is the image of divine perfection, the five Platonic solids the building blocks of the cosmos, and the human figure the microcosm of that universe, a figure whose extensions are encompassed by the circumscribed shapes of the circle and the square (fig. 59). This may have been the ideal, but it was an affirmation in the face of difficult and disquieting realities. Against *virtù*, the possession of powers to act efficaciously and with excellence, stood *fortuna*, the blind hand of chance that could foil the best-laid plans in a world often disfigured by violence and disease.

Our age is no less concerned with issues of order and disorder, but metaphors of order are harder to come by in a world grown older. Our science of chaos probes the apparent randomness of aperiodic phenomena, and a president of the United States calls for a "new world order." These concerns with order are wholly different, of course—order ascribed to the structure of natural phenomena and human artifacts versus order embodied in willed human actions.

Artists are the arbiters and proclaimers of order, be it the lucid circular complementarities of a Raphael composition, the precise form of the Shakespearean sonnet, the intricate structures of a Beethoven string quartet, or the geometry of the cathedral builders. Leonardo was from first to last an artist, whatever else he may have been, and the compositional principles of his images are the fountainhead of the classical tradition in post-medieval painting. Yet Leonardo was also a military engineer and purveyor of designs for machines of destruction. How were these activities reconciled in him? How did his myriad investigations color his notions of an ordered world?

His brief late notes written on cardiovascular studies leave no doubt that Leonardo saw a perfect efficacy and economy in the products of nature. "Nothing is superfluous and nothing lacking any species of animal or product of Nature unless the defect comes from the means which produce it." "It has been stated that Nature always accomplishes her effects in the easiest way and shortest time possible." Few now dispute the concept of evolution (a concept unknown to Leonardo), nor that it is a process in which the efficient functionality of organisms is the driving force. While Leonardo did not divine the process, he grasped that the marvels of nature are a parade of masterpieces of design, understandable in comparison to one another, and rich in suggestiveness for enterprises in human design. If Leonardo held God responsible as a consummate artificer, he does not tell us so. But that is not the important point. The refusal to see randomness rather than efficacy and efficiency in nature is the clear testimony to belief in an ordered world, whatever its ultimate cause.

For an artist who holds mimesis as a high value, the danger is that disparate facts of nature in which he/she delights may overwhelm the needed organizational clarity of a composition whose inevitable quality rests on simplification and generalization. This danger is already present in the *Virgin of the Rocks* (see fig. 19), where the rich specificity of floral and topographical detail is in tension with the four idealized figures arranged in a triangle in the foreground of the painting. Leonardo used geometry, proportion, and perspective to control his detailed observations, and extended these tools to the control of other phenomena, such as the dispersion of sound waves or the measure of heavenly bodies.

Mathematics was his controlling grid upon the material world: "He who blames the supreme certainty of mathematics feeds on confusion and can never silence the contradictions of the sophistical sciences which occasion an everlasting clamor." "There is no certainty in sciences where one of the mathematical sciences cannot be applied, or which are not in relation with these mathematics."

But what sort of mathematics did he have in mind? There was first the mathematics of the abacus school, practical mathematics to gauge volumes and quantities in a world of unstandardized measures. But there was also the mathematics of divine geometry and divine proportion (the latter the title of a book by his friend Luca Pacioli, to which Leonardo contributed designs of the Platonic solids), the geometry of the cathedral

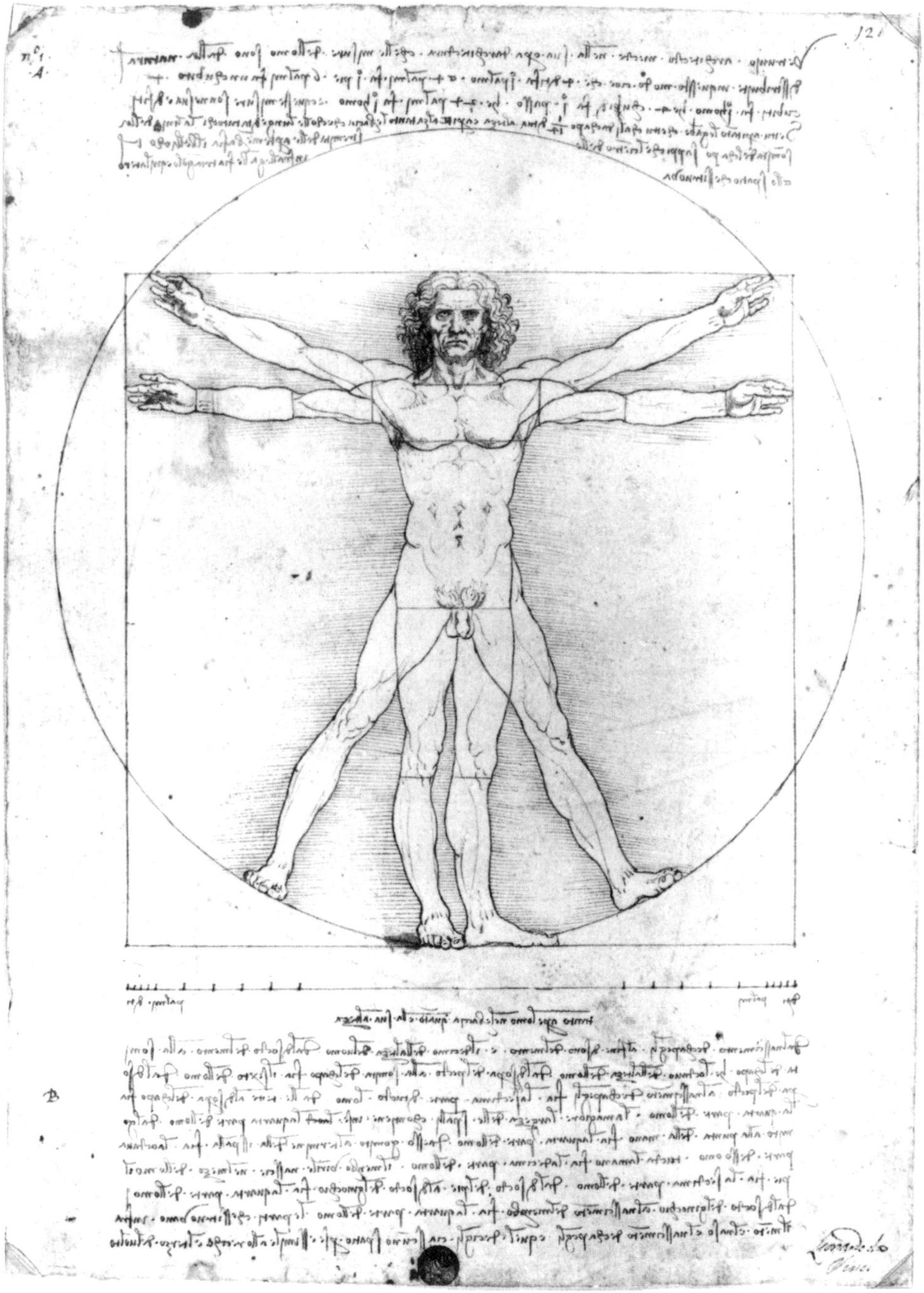

Fig. 59: Leonardo, *Vitruvian Man*. Accademia, Venice

builders and the architects of Leonardo's own time, from Alberti to Palladio. This was a mathematics that celebrated the transparent clarity and order of the First Artificer's grand design.

Leonardo used both in *The Last Supper* (see fig. 23). Perspective, with liberal departures from the Albertian formula, is used to structure a coherent space in which objects can be placed in systematic optical relation to one another. But there is use of another sort of mathematics in structuring the mural that escaped notice until recently—a formula based on relations of 12:6:4:3. The mural is 6 by 12 units in dimension, with the back wall equal to 4 units, the windows 3, and the recession of the tapestries as widths on the mural's surface 12:6:4:3. These are the harmonic proportions of music, 3:4 equaling the interval of a fourth, 4:6 the fifth, and 6:12 the octave, as already noted by Alberti. Leonardo himself commented on the resonance between visual and aural harmonies, and in making use of it offered praise to the harmonies of the universe.

The ordered geometry of his major pictures, the *Adoration,* the *Virgin of the Rocks,* the *Madonna and Child and Saint Anne,* may be only pleasing visual solutions to problems of achieving clarity and balance, but it seems likely that they bore a further meaning: the power of geometry to suggest the inherent order of creation. In like manner, drawing on the earlier prescriptions of Alberti concerning the ideal church, Leonardo concentrated on the perfection of the circle and geometric forms allied to it as the generating forms for the house of God.

If these are some of the manifestations of Leonardo's quest for ideal order in art, we must also remember his manifold practical projects to rearrange God's creation in a way useful to humans—the Florence–Pisa canal, the Milanese canalization projects, the draining of the Pontine Marshes, to name but a few.

Quite different is Leonardo the fascinated observer of ultimate disorder and cataclysmic destruction, whether seen, imagined, or proposed—the collapse of mountains, the inundations of armies, the extraordinary late series of the deluge drawings in which the end of the world seems to be contemplated. These things may be better understood in the light of another kind of disorder: the peculiarly human propensity for violence, by which I mean human action coercive and/or harmful to others, against their will.

The evidence is slight but suggestive concerning the relationship between two connoisseurs of violence, Leonardo and Machiavelli. The
latter entered public life in Florence in 1498. It was probably Machiavelli
who dispatched Leonardo to assist Cesare Borgia, and who was present
with Leonardo in the Romagna; Machiavelli who sent Leonardo to Piombino to plan fortifications for Jacopo Appiani; Machiavelli who was
behind the commission for *The Battle of Anghiari* in the Great Council
Hall of the Palazzo della Signoria (the description of the *Battle* in the
Codex Atlanticus is generally agreed to be in the hand of Machiavelli's
secretary); and possibly Machiavelli who lay behind the aborted scheme
to cut Pisa off from the Arno. In any case, in a town the size of Florence
it is implausible to imagine that the two men did not know each other
well.

Machiavelli's writings, notably *The Prince,* speak to a pessimistic view
of a humanity finally unable to serve anything other than self-interest.
His prescriptions for the conduct of civic life based on this dismal premise are too familiar to warrant summary here. At the close of his play
The Ass, Machiavelli has the pig of Circe address a man:

> Nature gave you hands and speech, and with them she gave you
> also ambition and avarice, with which her beauty is canceled. To
> how many ills nature subjects you at starting! and afterwards for-
> tune—how much good she promises you without fulfillment!
>
> Yours are ambition, licentiousness, lamentation and avarice,
> which bring on mange in the life you reckon so high. No animal
> can be found which has a frailer life, and has for living a stronger
> desire, more disordered fear or greater madness. One hog to an-
> other causes no pain, one stag to another; man by another is slain,
> crucified, and plundered. Consider now how you ask that I again
> become a man, being exempt from all the miseries that I endured
> as long as I was a man. And if any among you seems a god, happy
> and rejoicing, do not believe him such, because in this mud I live
> more happily.

How different from Pico della Mirandola's radically optimistic view
of humankind, or Leonardo's encomium to the divine painter who can
conjure wonderful worlds! But there was another side of Leonardo,

expressed around 1500 in one of his *profetie* (prophecies), "Of the Cruelty of Man":

> Animals will be seen on earth who will always be fighting against each other with the greatest loss and frequent deaths on each side. And there will be no end to their malice; by their strong limbs we shall see a great portion of the trees of the vast forests laid low throughout the universe; and when they are filled with food, the satisfaction of their desires will be to deal death and grief and labour and fears and flight to every living thing; and from their immoderate pride they will desire to rise towards heaven, but the excessive weight of their limbs will keep them down. Nothing will remain on earth, or under the earth, or in the waters, which will not be persecuted, disturbed and spoiled, and those of one country removed into another. And their bodies will become the tomb and the means of transit of all the living beings they have killed.
>
> O Earth, why dost thou not open and engulf them in the fissures of thy vast abyss and caverns, and no longer display in the sight of heaven so cruel and horrible a monster?

Humans, then, are the violence-prone animals, their capacities in this respect nowhere more magnified than in that undertaking with which Machiavelli and Leonardo were all too familiar, war. War may be defined as organized institutional violence, and around 1500 few would have questioned war as a normal and acceptable fact of life. But not many would have recognized the full implications of the development in those years of effective chemically powered guns, the most momentous change in the destructive potential of warfare before Hiroshima and Nagasaki. To appreciate Leonardo's place at this juncture in the history of warfare, a look both forward and backward is needed.

The look forward is to an incident of April 5, 1585, during the uprising of the Lowlands against Spain. The Spaniards were manning a pontoon bridge at Antwerp, when the Dutch set adrift a ship ironically named the *Hope,* which had been rigged as a huge floating time-bomb. When it reached the bridge it exploded, reportedly killing about two thousand men and sending debris for a half mile in all directions. This horrifying incident has many of the fingerprints of modern war—action directed at a group rather than an individual, a killing zone where the nature and the number of casualties is to a degree random, ingenuity producing a technological intermediary that relieves the need for physical prowess on the part of the aggressor, and a detachment between any specific act of an aggressor and the consequences for any particular victim.

The *Hope* represented an ugly new face of war, made possible by the socioeconomic and technological changes in Leonardo's day. How different this face was is suggested by a sketch showing that medieval attitudes toward war were radically different. The teachings of the Gospels and the legitimacy of the violence of war were blatantly at odds until someone could come up with an acceptable rationalization, which was provided by Saint Augustine, who saw war as God's design for punishing sin. A just war might be waged by legitimate authority, with good intent, for a just cause. While legitimate authority and just cause could be argued vigorously, how was one to define, let alone know, inner disposition, which is finally a matter of the heart? The ways of the heart are known only to God, so human conduct must be content to be guided by the laws of the state, crafted so that they are perceived not to grossly contravene divine law. In the thirteenth century, Thomas Aquinas added an important corollary to Augustine: that while the latter's criteria could be met in full, there remained the possibility that war could yield unintended bad results.

Whatever the nuances of the just war argument, the important thing is that it sanctioned war in a religious context. In practice, late medieval war was conducted by knights, gentlemen against gentlemen, according to agreed-upon legal and moral codes, for a specific purpose. In modern terms, bloodshed was light, with a preference for a symmetrical battle, in the sense that numbers and weapons on each side were similar. The ideal centerpiece of a battle was individual combat, a tradition as old as the *Iliad,* alive and well in the *chansons de geste.* The sense of fairness, limits of violence, and assumption that likes should battle likes in some situation of parity—those were the rules.

From the early thirteenth century onward the towns grew in economic power, and with this growth came a gradual change in attitudes toward war. As notions of mercantile profit took hold, the feudal system of lord and vassal bound in mutual obligation in the rural landscape became an economic anachronism, and the knight thereby lost his raison d'être. While it was clear that war remained a fact of life, there was money to be made, and those who would make it found it more profitable to leave the waging of war to others.

At first those others were *compagnie di ventura,* unruly bands of social outcasts tempted by that primal motivation for war, theft of the goods and property of others. They came to be replaced in the fourteenth century with a system that flourished into Leonardo's time, featuring the *condotta* (contract) whose executant was a professional soldier, the *condottiere.* A contract was drawn up between a *condottiere* and his employer for a specific purpose, to be undertaken in a set period of time for an agreed-upon price. While the use of the *condottiere* entrusted war to the competence of specialized hands, relations between employer and employee were usually wary, for under the right circumstances the professional soldier could seize power, as happened with Francesco Sforza in Milan. Whatever the arrangement in a given city, it was general practice for the burghers to buy their way out of war by hiring mercenaries, a practice that Machiavelli was to deplore in calling for a citizen militia. While his reasons were various, he was certainly right that when healthy men and healthy horses constitute the basis of one's living, devotion to a cause and risk-taking are likely to be minimal. War continued to be a somewhat ritualized affair in which comparatively few lives were lost until guns came into their own at the end of the fifteenth century.

If socioeconomic changes spurred new directions in the pursuit of war, what of technological changes, of which the first to come to mind are gunpowder and guns? Realization of the implications of the gun came slowly, for then, as in almost all times, war remained one of the most ritualized and tradition-bound of activities, intimately connected, as Machiavelli astutely recognized in the beginning of his *Art of War,* to the mores and conduct of society in general. Early writings on war, such as Roberto Valturio's *De re militari* (1472), are heavily based upon ancient sources, and bound to strategies and weapons often useless in practice. Even Machiavelli's thoughts on war, as expressed in *The Art of War, The Prince,* and the *Discourses,* are much more tied to the advice of antiquity than they are to the imperatives of the battlefield in his own time.

Change in war comes when a psychological shift accompanies major technological change. Take the case of the English longbow, used with deadly effectiveness in several mid-fourteenth-century battles, and then at Agincourt in 1415. The longbow had nothing like the destructive potential of guns, but did anticipate a battlefield situation different from what had gone before. The longbow required a powerful draw, and could launch arrows for a distance of well over 200 yards. With alternate lines of archers shooting and restringing their arrows, an almost nonstop hail of missiles was possible. Horse and rider were helpless before such a barrage, and its effect was to establish a killing zone in which the arrows fell. The damage was impersonal, in the sense that a rain of arrows did the work rather than a given archer targeting a specific individual, and hence no distinction of social rank could be made between combatants, which enabled a commoner to kill any noble who might get in the way. Of the old ideals of combat between social equals, all that now remained was physical prowess: it took skill and training to shoot arrows a maximum distance in quick succession, even if the specific results of that action were rarely immediately seen.

With the advent of the gun, even physical prowess was mostly removed. Guns and gunpowder appeared in Italy between about 1290 and 1320, at first highly ineffective and best used as a means of intimidation. By the mid-fifteenth century, stone projectiles had been replaced by metal balls, accurate artillery pieces decisive in Burgundian battles of the 1470s. The triumph of artillery culminated in 1494 when Charles VIII passed through Italy to Naples unopposed, his portable small-bore cannon reducing the walls of the fortress of Monte San Giovanni to rubble in a matter of hours. By 1550 weapons based on chemical propulsion had advanced as far as they would until the mid-nineteenth century.

Strangely, in the face of undeniable evidence, many failed to see that the nature of war was about to change drastically. Machiavelli himself put good men above good arms, praising the formidable Swiss phalanx *all'antica,* a tempting gunner's target if ever there was one. Ariosto in the first canto of *Orlando Furioso* lamented the arrival of firearms mainly as a threat to the knight and his noble ideals. In reality, guns were the portent of a new world of violence, perfect for the mercenary who could kill from a distance under the illusion of comparative safety.

Reports from the field of battle were clear early in the sixteenth century, registering the effect of cannon fire upon infantry. Despite this, bizarre incidents testify to the powerful hold of one-to-one combat between social equals. In 1503 at Barletta, a battle was decided by a combat between thirteen Frenchmen and thirteen Spaniards. At Ravenna the brilliant leader Gaston de Foix and a group of gentlemen pursued a group of Spaniards, to be gunned down for their efforts. In 1525 Francis I personally led repeated charges at the imperial lines, had his horse shot out from under him, and was captured in what was the greatest slaughter since Agincourt. And in 1536 the Emperor Charles V challenged the French king to a duel, an event prevented only by the intervention of Pope Paul III. Whatever these gestures to the ideals of the past, the gun had arrived, and in the gruesome Thirty Years' War (1618–48) was in part responsible for the decimation of the population of Germany, in the hands of drilled armies in which individuals were but cogs in a well-oiled machine.

And what of Leonardo? At the beginning of the 1480s his bellicose interests are clear enough, even if not yet put to the test. As we have seen, his letter to the Duke of Milan promises the means to destroy fortresses, to invent naval weapons, mines, chariots, various sorts of guns, catapults, and the like. Several of his prophecies leave no doubt that he appreciated the deadly effects of gunpowder. One telling passage written near the end of his life concedes far more than Machiavelli would have been willing to: "If any man could have discovered the utmost powers of the cannon, in all its various forms, and have given such a secret to the Romans, with what rapidity they would have conquered every country and vanquished every army, and what award would have been great enough for such a service!"

How much of Leonardo's interest in the mechanics of war was simply in a day's work? After all, during that period anyone who possessed architectural and/or engineering capabilities was expected to contribute to the ongoing business of war. Around 1490 Leonardo called war a *"bestialissima pazzia"* (a beastly madness), and in a curious note of almost twenty years later he wrote:

> How by a means of a certain machine many people may stay some time under water. How and why I do not describe my method of remaining under water, or how long I can remain under water, or how long I can stay without eating, and I do not publish or divulge, by reason of the evil nature of men, who would use them as means

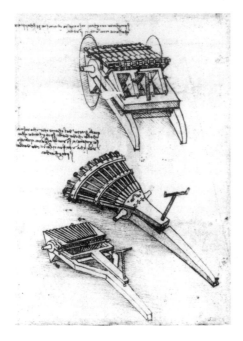

Fig. 60: Leonardo, *Multiple Barrel Gun.*
Ambrosiana, Milan

of destruction at the bottom of the sea, by piercing a hole in the bottom, and sinking them with the men in them.

Like so many observations by Leonardo, this one lacks sufficient context for us to be at all certain about his attitudes. It would be skating on thin ice to postulate either a closet pacifist or premature arms controller. What is certain is that in words and images he trafficked in arms through the years, and the evidence that remains only allows for speculation.

Leonardo's interest in the machines of war is manifest in the years around his departure for Milan, as shown in his devices for scaling walls, and around 1481, in a drawing for a couple of types of caisson guns with multiple barrels (fig. 60), a visual complement to the letter to the Duke in which he promises unusual weapons. At first glance these proposals look practicable in terms of the technology and needs of the day. The middle rank of the drawing shows a rakelike arrangement of ten barrels that could be raised or lowered by turning a large vertical screw, the whole apparatus mounted on wheels, of which only the axle is represented in the drawing. The presumed target would be infantry, and the method much the same as the longbow, with a targeted killing zone where the spray shot does its random work.

The top and bottom representations elaborate the idea: multiple barrels on three sides of a revolving triangular structure, again based on the method of the longbow, in the sense that one rank of barrels could be fired, as with a rank of archers, a second rank brought up as the spent barrels are cleaned and reloaded, and so forth. Positive judgment of the practicality of such an arrangement, however, may lie more in our confidence in modern technology than in the actual technological capabilities of Leonardo's day. The many barrels multiply the chance of the malfunction of one or more of them, their close packing promising deadly results should a barrel rupture on firing. Arguably, Leonardo flirts here with irrational technology, neither the first nor the last to do so, as witness the failed weapon systems of our own day.

In the late 1480s he turned in earnest to instruments of war, now in the thrall of antiquity and some seemingly irrational schemes. We find a drawing of various instruments—mainly bows, swords, slings, maces, and the heads of pikes—and the appearance of a visual catalogue of weapon types, in large part ancient in origin, and relying on Pliny, Vitruvius, and his contemporary Valturio, who was in turn indebted to antiquity. His interest here seems more a catalogue of types than a statement about function.

Another drawing of the same years represents a huge horse-driven scythe above, and a sort of proto-tank below (fig. 61). The former is again an idea ancient in origin, and described in a related sheet in the past tense, with emphasis on the power of the weapon to intimidate friend and foe. The ungainliness of the instrument, its problematic relation to its source of power—the horse—and its obvious need for firm, level terrain attest to its status as a meditation rather than as a practical proposal. The proto-tank visually fulfills one of the promises made in the letter to Ludovico. It was to be manned by eight men, some of whom presumably were to propel it, others to man guns in the multiple ports. Once again the deficiency of the power source to adequately move such a contraption seems obvious, as does its vulnerability in the absence of fast-repeater guns.

A third drawing, perhaps done a few years earlier, combines the plau-

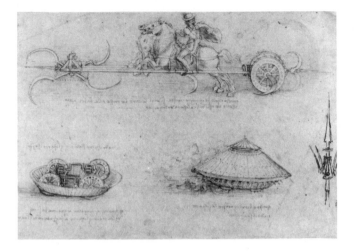

Fig. 61: Leonardo, *Scythe Machine and "Tank."* British Museum, London

sible with the fanciful (fig. 62). At the top a mortar with its multiple shot is accompanied by a note indicating that its major purpose is to cause fear and confusion, seemingly a leitmotif in Leonardo's thinking about weapons. The middle rank of the drawing proposes among other things a double-barreled cannon that would move on a central horizon-

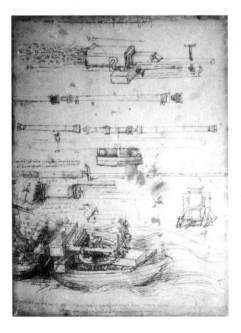

Fig. 62: Leonardo, Studies of weaponry. Royal Library, Windsor

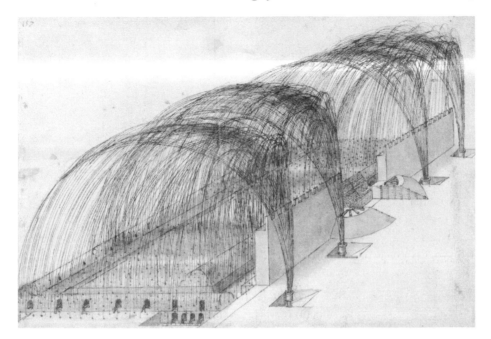

Fig. 63: Leonardo, *Mortars Firing into a Courtyard.* Royal Library, Windsor

tal support, allowing an artilleryman to fire one of the barrels while the other was being loaded. An unsolved problem is how recoil would be absorbed in such an arrangement. If this is a dubious proposal, the bottom drawing of a mortarlike device mounted on a small boat is simply ludicrous, the whole arrangement perilously top-heavy, with inadequate friction between hull surface and water to allow proper propulsion of the missile.

A picture emerges of a highly imaginative Leonardo, in the tradition of such contemporaries and predecessors as the Sienese Francesco di Giorgio and Taccola, who proposed preliminary ideas in sketches but did not follow them up with the much harder work of step-by-step development. There is not any evidence of any of these designs by Leonardo having been actually constructed, and reason to doubt that few, if any, found their way to the battlefield. Was it perhaps that he wanted it that way?

Indeed some of Leonardo's schemes seem abstractions of considerable beauty, far from the business of killing—for instance, the drawing of

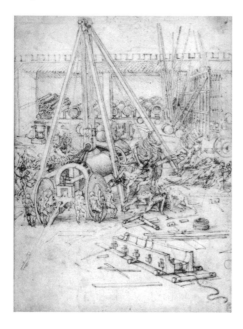

Fig. 64: Leonardo, *Weapon Yard*. Royal Library, Windsor

four vertical mortars firing from the upper terrace of a fortification into its lower courtyard (fig. 63). The arc of the shot respects Leonardo's earlier parabolic studies, but the completely orderly saturation of the courtyard bears little relation to the probable erratic pattern of projectiles emitted from the wide mouths of mortars.

The hallucinatory quality of war, in which humans are engulfed in a horrific enterprise that degrades the stature of individuals, is evoked in a late 1480s drawing of a weapon yard (fig. 64). A huge gun barrel (echoed in the enormous and, significantly, never fired monster in the Kremlin) is being lowered from a four-legged hoist onto its carriage. Mortars, cannon barrels, and huge cannonballs are stacked about the yard, dwarfing the tiny nude workers, whose exertion seems frail in contrast to the ponderousness of the weapons of destruction.

It is well known that in war few soldiers are disposed to kill except in self-defense, and that more of them than we might imagine do not discharge their weapons at all. Was Leonardo psychologically one of these? Was his practical work limited to refinements of individual projects in the Milanese arms establishment, such as the improved boring of cannon barrels, while the drawings that we have considered were an

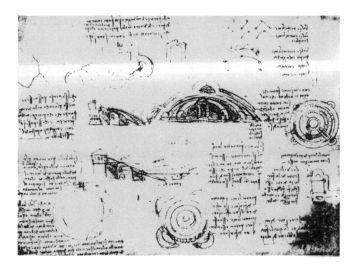

Fig. 65: Leonardo,
Circular Fortress.
Ambrosiana, Milan

imaginative outlet for himself and for his patron's delectation? These questions are ultimately unanswerable, but the evidence of the images suggests that it may have been so.

If Leonardo's offensive weapons were more imaginative exercises than practical proposals, it was quite otherwise with plans for defensive fortifications. The chief result of the development of effective artillery was to change war from a pitched battle to sieges, with the need for defensive structures to withstand those sieges. The traditional fifteenth-century and earlier fortress had close-to-vertical walls, a perfect target for the direct impact of cannonballs. As one scholar has put it, the need to rethink fortifications in the light of the capabilities of cannon turned Italy into a virtual public works enterprise during the first quarter of the sixteenth century. Earthworks were built to absorb the masonry-shattering projectiles, with walls shaped and kept low to deflect cannon shot rather than absorbing the full brunt of a frontal hit; and other new arrangements were worked out, with concentric walls and star-shaped configurations whose bastions could command every possible angle of enemy attack.

One of Leonardo's remarkable proposals was for the fortification of Piombino in 1504. Among many defensive designs, he conceived a circular fortress of three concentric ring-tunnels, each apparently slightly higher as one moves toward the center (figs. 65 and 66). Each ring with

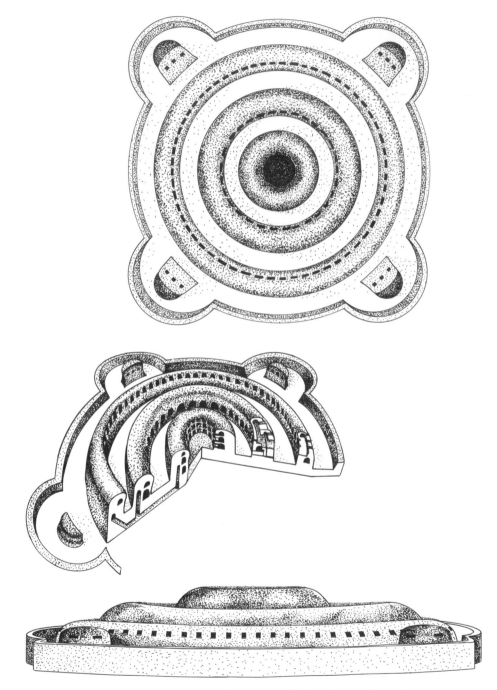

Fig. 66: Reconstruction based on *Circular Fortress* (fig. 65)

its gun ports was curved to deflect incoming fire, the whole protected by an outer quatrefoil moat with four pillboxes in the circular projections to provide cross fire. Should the need arise, the two depressed inner circles separating the ring-tunnels could be flooded to inhibit any invader who might breach the outer wall. Better than any written words, this never-executed design shows Leonardo's grasp of the challenge presented by powerful and accurate artillery.

One can only speculate on the importance Leonardo gave to the ebb and flow of human violence as represented in his ideas concerning fortifications and weapons of war, as opposed to his fascination with the incomparable power of the forces of nature to change human affairs and the face of the earth. The evidence of the notebooks suggests that history as the record of willed human action and the ways of politics were of scant interest to him compared to the motion of great waters and the force of *tempo consumatore*—time that consumes all. It was nature rather than men alone that could participate in the undoing of armies. Hence: "A book of driving back armies by the force of a flood made by releasing water. A book about inundating valleys by closing the mouths of valleys."

To Leonardo, human violence seems to have been trivial in the face of cataclysmic natural forces. Toward the end of his life—or so it is generally agreed—he did sixteen drawings of unleashed torrential energy, nine of them a closely related group in black chalk, though whether they constitute a series in the sense of having a temporal narrative order is not clear. The whole group is usually called the deluge drawings, an unfortunate name in that the word "deluge" evokes a probably unwarranted specific association with the biblical flood.

One of the black chalk drawings shows vortices of water filled with matter that swirl with spring-taut energy about a dwarfed town below (fig. 67). As in a hurricane, distinctions of solid and void are obliterated, one's sense of scale evaporates, and the loss of the horizon becomes utterly disorienting. A second drawing in chalk and yellow ink has a more architectonic quality, a combined explosion-implosion of rock and water over a landscape with tiny, swaying trees, to a modern eye reminiscent of nuclear holocaust (fig. 68). One of the most riveting drawings, in its immense scale and dissolution of spatial orientation, represents a writhing mass of swirls and tight curls above a wind-racked landscape

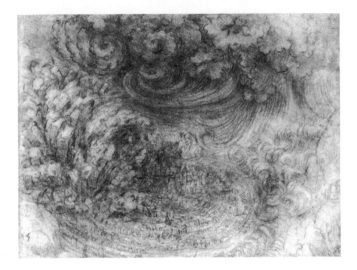

Fig. 67: Leonardo, *The Deluge*. Royal Library, Windsor

with minute human figures and horses thrown asunder, presided over by a wind god in the upper-left-hand corner.

What is to be made of these extraordinary drawings? Are they apocalyptic visions of the end of the world, somehow akin to the fulminations of divine wrath preached by Savonarola, to Dürer's vision in 1525 of an inundation from heaven, or Columbus's belief in Armaggedon? It

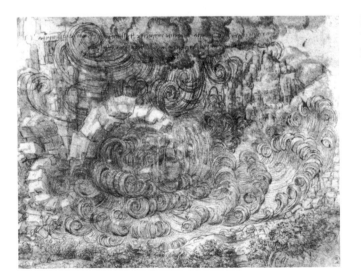

Fig. 68: Leonardo, *The Deluge*. Royal Library, Windsor

is a tempting romantic scenario, of a Leonardo the artist who has run beyond the far reaches of reason in contemplating ultimate mysteries. Such an interpretation carries a certain psychological interest in that someone seeking final personal freedom might delight in seeing all constraints of existing structures swept away in chaos. However, the evidence of the images themselves, the writing accompanying them, and chronologically associated writings collectively offer little evidence for this, and indeed speak to the contrary.

Consider Leonardo's description of how to represent a deluge:

> The air was darkened with heavy rain whose oblique descent, driven aslant by the rush of the winds, flew in drifts through the air not otherwise than as we see dust, varied only by the straight lines of the heavy drops of falling water. But it was tinged with the colour of fire kindled by thunderbolts by which the clouds were rent and shattered; and whose flashes revealed the broad waters of the inundated valleys, in the depths of which were seen the bending tree-tops. Neptune will be seen in the midst of the water with his trident, and let Aeolus with his winds be shown entangling the trees floating uprooted, and whirling in the huge waves. The horizon and the whole hemisphere were obscure, but lurid from flashes of the incessant lightening. Men and birds might be seen crowded on the tall trees which remained uncovered by the swirling waters, originators of the mountains which surround the great abyss.

The introduction of mythological figures plus the (for Leonardo) unusual stylistic pretensions of the passage place it firmly in a literary tradition that asks for a suspension of disbelief. We contemplate the distancing power of art more than the shudder of existential angst. In an earlier chapter I suggested Leonardo's penchant to move to the margins of the unknown in his imagination, be it on Mount Etna or imagined Armenia, where he contemplated a similar cataclysmic happening. I also suggested that these imaginings were firmly rooted in direct experiences that Leonardo had had or that were recounted to him (for instance, a rockfall in the Dolomites). This sort of experience is reflected in writings on or associated with the deluge drawings, where a coolly analytical approach converts hydrological studies to imaginative use.

Another passage begins in an evocative vein:

Let the dark and gloomy air be seen buffeted by the rush of contrary winds and dense from the continued rain mingled with hail
and bearing hither and thither an infinite number of branches torn
from the trees and mixed with numberless leaves. All around
may be seen venerable trees, uprooted and stripped by the fury
of the winds; and fragments of mountains, already scoured bare
by the torrents, falling into those torrents and choking their valleys
till the swollen rivers over flow and submerge the wide lands and
their inhabitants.

There then follows a long narrative of the subject, closing with the
thought "that you may reproach me with having represented the currents made through the air by the motion of the wind notwithstanding
that the wind itself is not visible in the air. To this I must answer that
it is not the motion of the wind but only the motion of things carried
along by it which is seen in the air." This is hardly the observation of
a writer either caught up in poetic evocation or consumed by fright of
his subject.

In a related passage he turns dispassionately analytical:

. . . and let the mountains, as they are scoured bare, reveal the profound fissures made by great earthquakes. . . . Round these again
are formed the beginnings of waves which increase the more in
circumference as they acquire more this movement; and this movement rises less high in proportion as they acquire a broader base
and thus they are less conspicuous as they die away. But if these
waves rebound from various objects they then return in direct opposition to the others following them, observing the same law of
increase in their curve as they already have acquired in the movement they started with. . . . And if the heavy masses of ruin of large
mountains or grand buildings fall into the vast pools of water, a great
quantity of water will rebound in the air and its course will be in a
contrary direction to that of the object which struck the water; that is
to say: the angle of reflection will be equal to the angle of incidence.

Still other passages refer to the curvature of the movement of water,
impetus, and percussion, leaving no doubt of the hydrological basis of

Fig. 69: Studies of obstructed and falling water. Royal Library, Windsor

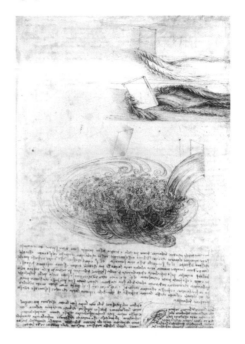

Leonardo's vision, as for instance in an earlier drawing of a flow of water interrupted by vertical obstacles and water issuing from an opening into a pool (fig. 69). The language of the accompanying note on this drawing bears comparison to the passage just quoted, and, more compellingly, the view of turbulence is the same, only on a vastly different scale.

Possible literary associations and close observation of empirical data do not, it should be stressed, invalidate the possibilities of awe, foreboding, and even revulsion that may have led Leonardo to such studies. To be sure, the push from the real to the imagined can hardly be denied, and the tension is palpable in the imposition of artistic order on potential chaotic dissolution. But it would be dishonest to choose whether Leonardo conceived his images in personal anxiety, or rather in equanimity saw the shuddering of the bones of the old earth as a necessity to which in the nature of things human beings must bend.

As mentioned earlier, an insistent theme of Leonardo's fables, maxims, and prophecies is that harm comes to him/her who fails to observe the rules of nature. Recall the fate of the donkey who went to sleep on the ice, melting it into water, in which the beast drowns. Leonardo knew that water was the shaper of mountains and their eventual undoing, and that while humans could control water to a degree, finally water could overwhelm any and all human enterprise. On the theme of control achieved and fate not to be resisted, note the following passage from Machiavelli's *Prince*:

> Nonetheless, so as not to rule out our free will, I believe that it is probably true that fortune is the arbiter of half the things we do, leaving the other half or so to be controlled by ourselves. I compare fortune to one of those violent rivers which, when they are enraged, flood the plains, tear down trees and buildings, wash soil from one place to deposit it in another. Everyone flees before them, everybody yields to their impetus, there is no possibility of resistance. Yet although such is their nature, it does not follow that when they are flowing quietly one cannot take precautions, constructing dykes and embankments so that when the river is in flood they would keep to one channel or their impetus be less wild and dangerous. So it is with fortune. She shows her potency where there is no well regulated power to resist her, and her impetus is felt where she knows there are no embankments and dykes built to restrain her. If you consider Italy, the theatre of those changes and variations I mentioned, which first appeared here, you will see that she is a country without embankments and without dykes: for if Italy had been adequately reinforced, like Germany, Spain and France, either this flood would not have caused the great changes it has, or it would not have swept in at all.

This sort of thought was probably arrived at independently by the two men, which does not lessen the fascination that for both of them the image of water stood at the center of meditations on order and disorder, on the controlled and uncontrollable in the world.

But let us close by returning to the notion of violence as I have defined it, and contemplate one of Leonardo's great unfinished works, the 1503–5 *Battle of Anghiari*. Anghiari was a 1440 victory of the Florentines over the Milanese, a fit symbol of patriotism for the new Great Council Hall of the Palazzo della Signoria. The only reasonable certainty about the unexecuted project is the appearance of the central portion, preserved in several copies, of which the drawing by Peter Paul Rubens is the most evocative (fig. 28).

There are no eyewitness diary accounts of battle that I know of before revolutionary Europe, but those from the last two centuries leave little doubt about the actual face of battle, the inability of an individual participant to grasp the whole, his confusion, fear, and intense focus on a highly localized corner of the action in which one is bonded but to a handful of one's fellows. The order of battle, whether or not it unfolds in some rational design, may only be evident to the general who observes it from a height, or in our time a view pieced together from electronic intelligence. Thus a battle in its reality is one of the most intractable of subjects for an artist, who must distill its disorder and broad sprawl, and crystallize its temporal ebb and flow into some sort of a significant moment.

Leonardo's centerpiece is usually called *The Battle for the Standard,* a compact group of four horsemen locked in ferocious battle, with three fallen infantrymen below them. Monumentally explosive in energy, a harbinger of Baroque visual dynamics, the image poses a paradox: the conversion of quintessential violent chaos into an ineluctable order in which the displacement of any part would distress the composition as a whole. This is aesthetic order taming the violence of real life, and as such the image has little to do with a particular battle that happened in 1440.

Leonardo the artist-scientist had "a blessed rage for order," sought to find it in nature, to impose it on the world in his projects and art, to ponder its limits in the face of overwhelming forces of *natura naturans.* As Leonardo was beginning to paint the never-completed mural, he recorded the following note:

> On June 6, 1505, a Friday at the stroke of one, I began to paint in the palace; at the moment of picking up the brush the weather turned bad and the bell began to toll to summon men to their duty. The cartoon tore, the water ran down and the jug broke that held the water; suddenly the weather deteriorated and it poured rain until evening, the day as dark as night.

The great mural was never realized, just as the equestrian monument had not been finished, the movement of the blood never comprehended.

In the end, cosmic forces of the deluge are explored on an artist's terms, based on years of scientific observation and cogitation, that is, a proclamation of form in the face of the formless. Leonardo's thought, projects, and works of art were largely unfinished stories, as are—and doubtless will continue to be—the reinventions of Leonardo da Vinci. To borrow Wordsworth's words about Sir Isaac Newton, "A mind forever voyaging through strange seas of thought alone."

Epilogue: 1492–2019

ANNIVERSARIES OF MEMORABLE EVENTS and persons, whatever the hype and commercialism surrounding them, usually manage to produce valuable new insights. Such is happening in 1992, when these words are written, with the observance of the anniversary of Columbus's Enterprise of the Indies. Leonardo, in contrast, has no such luck, becalmed as he is in the anniversarial doldrums between 1952 and 2019. The Columbian observance leads to an unanswerable question: What will Leonardo look like on the quincentennial of his death in 2019? A brief juxtaposition of the posthumous fortunes of Columbus and Leonardo may make my speculative question worth asking, for at the least it focuses on the issue of the public versus private cultural afterlife of great historical figures.

If one takes a look at the events surrounding the 1919 and 1952 Leonardo celebrations, they seem not to have meshed with the passionate public issues of their day. The collected essays, books, and articles published on these occasions tell a primarily scholarly story of deepened old investigations and invented new ones. Given the private character of Leonardo, this is hardly surprising.

No one can have failed to note that the Columbus quincentennial is wholly different. We remember not a man but an event—the landfall on October 12, 1492, at an unknown island in the Bahamas. Nor is it the relative banality of that landfall that we observe, but rather the momentous subsequent events, many of which rattle in the chambers of our hopes and guilt down to the present. Just what is this 1492–1992 Columbian affair about? We walk on eggshells: the benighted "celebrate" it, the alleged victims and those in solidarity with them "protest" it, and the rest of us, if we're smart, take the neutral ground and "observe" it. The only certainty, and it is a stark one, is that in 1992 Christopher Columbus is a wholly public man in a virulently political arena.

It was simpler in 1892. A minority report notwithstanding, Columbus was a hero. It was he who had launched the paternal benevolence of colonialism, carried across the sea the torch of material progress, and gave new hope in the form of a new, unspoiled world.

In 1992 times have changed. Colonialism is largely gone from the map, today only memories of different hues in the heads of colonized and colonizers alike. The old world order is gone, replaced by a new one to which the word "order" hardly applies, a fractious contention of ethnic groups who when not engaged in actual violence are ideologically polyglot tourists at the Tower of Babel. With this sea change, Columbus—the pride of Italy, the equivocal figure of Hispanic thought, the devil of the Amerindians—has been reborn as the prime mover of the sins of the West: imperialism, colonialism, sexism, eco-despoliation, white supremacy—you name it, the malevolent handiwork of the archetypical oppressing Dead White European Male.

Did Columbus have a private side? Of course. We all do. It centrally involved the self-fashioning visions of a man who thought himself a providential agent in the Lord's design, an agent who would lead the people to the threshold of the Earthly Paradise, and hence to the Last Days. Strange and alien stuff, this, but beside the point, for Columbus's own actions and those of his handlers assured that the only Columbus who mattered was one of public actions.

Above all, he was a public man because it was he, not Vikings, Portuguese, or even possibly hypothetical Africans, who discovered what was soon to be called America. Discovery requires an acknowledging audience, and this alone Columbus had. With potent political and economic support he went, returned, published what he had found, made the trip three times again, and so showed the way. In the process, colonial abuses and one more dark chapter in the long book of slavery can be laid at his feet, as can the horrific if inadvertent devastation caused by microbes carried to the Amerindians. Whoever the private Columbus was, it is the physical head and shoulders of the man of action that tower above the crowd in 1492.

And what does all of this have to do with Leonardo? If Columbus is the center of tumultuous public events that continue to have an active public life in 1992, he is the foil that sharply focuses Leonardo's role as the consummate private man. Leonardo's notes reveal little of his inner life, and none of them were published in his own day, despite the flourishing of the new technology of movable-type printing. He was not a participant in the great public passions of his time, and seems to have entered the public light only as required by the task assigned by his employers. Intellectually absorbed, he seems rarely to have played the hand of flattery.

To be sure, the posthumous Leonardo was kidnapped a couple of times to be a major player on a public stage—Milan around 1800, and Paris around 1850, but these are exceptions. Leonardo's legacy has lived in its most nuanced form in a series of intimate dialogues—including Leonardo–Pater, Leonardo–Valéry, Leonardo–Freud—and will probably continue to do so.

And the quincentennial of 2019? It's hard to imagine circumstances in which this private man could be caught up in the sort of public and political issues that currently embroil the Columbian observance, or that his scientific and technological writings will emerge again from their current storage in an arcane corner of the history of science. That leaves many other writings—tales, fables, prophecies, works of the imagination in various forms—and the endlessly provocative drawings and paintings. It is these that will surely resonate in new ways among private sensibilities in cultural conditions now unknown and perhaps vastly different from ours.

The one thing that seems certain is that there are new Leonardos yet to be born, for undefinable contingencies and impenetrable silences spur the ongoing project of interpretation. It is safe to say that there will be no interpretive closure, for that would be both an affront to the needs of the imagination and a denial of the truism that with new times inevitably come new questions.

Bibliography

INTRODUCTION

On Leonardo as the New Apelles: K. Posner, *Leonardo and Central Italian Art: 1515–1550* (New York, 1974). For thoughts on the nature of masterpieces: W. Cahn, *Masterpieces: Chapters on the History of an Idea* (Princeton, 1979).

PART I: *A Working Life*

This is a selective bibliography of writings on Leonardo's age, and writings on Leonardo himself.

History: The book that is the fountainhead of modern definitions of the Renaissance is J. Burckhardt, *The Civilization of the Renaissance in Italy,* first published in German in 1860, and available in a number of English translations. The changing interpretations of the Renaissance are reviewed in W. Ferguson, *The Renaissance in Historical Thought* (Cambridge, Mass., 1948). There are numerous general histories of the Italian Renaissance, of which one of the more recent and best is L. Martines, *Power and Imagination: City-States in the Italian Renaissance* (New York, 1979). Also recommended: M. Gilmore, *The World of Humanism 1453–1517* (New York, 1952). J. Hale, *Renaissance Europe: Individual and Society* (London, 1971) is topically organized, and gives a particularly good feel for the fabric of daily life. D. Hay, *The Renaissance in its Historical Background* (Cambridge Eng., 1961) is an excellent short introduction that makes the case that rather than being the beginning of the modern world, the Renaissance is a transition between medieval times and the age that we consider distinctively our own. Of particular interest to readers of this book will be P. Burke, *Culture and Society in Renaissance Italy 1420–1540* (Princeton, 1986), a work combining historical and sociological methods to illuminate the social standing, education, and work patterns of the creative élite of those years. G. Brucker has written several books on Renaissance Florence, of which the broadest introduction to the life and culture of the city is *Renaissance Florence* (New York, 1969). Unfortunately there is no comparable recent literature in English on Milan, but there is a concise introduction in Italian: E. Garin, "La cultura a Milano alla fine del Quattrocento," in his *Umanisti artisti scienzati* (Rome, 1989).

Letters and Humanist Learning: A superb overview of the Renaissance debt to classical learning and letters is given in R. Bolgar, *The Classical Heritage and its Beneficiaries,* (Cambridge, Eng., 1958). Three books by the dean of Renaissance studies are especially recommended: P. Kristeller, *Renaissance Thought: The Classic, Scholastic, and Humanist Strains* (New York, 1961); *Renaissance Thought II: Papers on Humanism and the Arts* (New York, 1965); and *Eight Philosophers of the Italian Renaissance* (Stanford, 1964), which includes translations of important works. In the same vein, see E. Cassirer, P. Kristeller, and J. Randall, Jr., *The Renaissance Philosophy of Man* (Chicago, 1948). A somewhat different approach to the differing strains of Renaissance thought is found in E. Garin, *Italian Humanism: Philosophy and Civic Life in the Renaissance* (New York, 1965). For the philosophically hearty, there is the recent lengthy C. Schmitt and Q. Skinner, eds., *The Cambridge History of Renaissance Philosophy* (Cambridge, Eng., 1988). For a sound survey of literature, see E. Wilkins, *A History of Italian Literature* (Cambridge, Mass., 1954). For the important question of the invention of printing and the dissemination of the printed book, see L. Febvre and H. Martin, *The Coming of the Book: The Impact of Printing 1450–1800* (London, 1984), and T. Eisenstein, *The Printing Revolution in Early Europe* (Cambridge, Eng., 1983).

Art and Architecture: The classic definition of the style of art in Leonardo's time was provided by Burckhardt's student H. Wölfflin in his 1899 *Classic Art* (London, 1952). The best textbook survey of the arts of the Italian Renaissance is F. Hartt, *History of Italian Renaissance Art* (New York, 1987). The most complete and abundantly illustrated work on the art of Renaissance Florence is G. Andres, J. Hunisak, and A. Turner, *The Art of Florence,* 2 vols. (New York, 1988). An old but still generally useful introduction to the art theory of the period is A. Blunt, *Artistic Theory in Italy 1450–1600* (Oxford, 1940). Several surveys of Renaissance art, all with bibliographies, are listed in alphabetical order:

L. Benevolo, *The Architecture of the Renaissance* (Boulder, Colo., 1978).
S. Freedberg, *Painting of the High Renaissance in Florence and Rome,* 2 vols. (Cambridge, Mass., 1961).
————, *Painting in Italy 1500–1600* (Harmondsworth, Eng., 1979).
L. Heydenreich and W. Lotz, *Architecture in Italy 1400–1600* (Harmondsworth, Eng., 1974).
P. Murray, *The Architecture of the Italian Renaissance* (London, 1978).
J. Pope-Hennessy, *Italian High Renaissance and Baroque Sculpture,* 3 vols. (London, 1963).
————, *Italian Renaissance Sculpture* (New York, 1971).
C. Seymour, *Sculpture in Italy 1400–1500* (Harmondsworth, Eng., 1966).

Finally, a miscellany of books can be suggested for various topics. For Renaissance writings on art in translation: R. Klein and H. Zerner, *Italian Art 1500–1600: Sources and*

Documents (Englewood Cliffs, N.J., 1966). For the iconography of art in Laurentian Florence: A. Chastel, *Art et humanisme à Florence au temps de Laurent le magnifique* (Paris, 1971). (See also additional books by Chastel that are in English translation.) Anyone interested in Leonardo should be familiar with the work of his great predecessor Alberti. For the best translation of Alberti, *On Painting,* see C. Grayson (ed. and trans.), *Alberti on Painting and Sculpture* (London, 1972). For a recent work on Alberti: M. Jarzombek, *On Leon Battista Alberti: His Literary and Aesthetic Theories* (Cambridge, Mass., and London, 1989). Issues of patronage and working conditions are discussed in M. Wackernagel, *The World of the Florentine Renaissance Artist,* trans. A. Luchi (Princeton, 1981; originally published in 1938). As a background to Leonardo's interest in landscape, see A. Turner, *The Vision of Landscape in Renaissance Italy* (Princeton, 1966). A magisterial treatment of the thought underlying Renaissance architecture is in R. Wittkower, *Architectural Principles in the Age of Humanism* (London, 1952).

Science and Technology: Leonardo's position as a transitional figure who did not disseminate his results is perhaps symbolized by the fact that his name does not appear in one of the most important works by one of the greatest of historians of science, A. Koyré, *From the Closed World to the Infinite Universe* (Baltimore, 1957). An excellent concise introduction to the various sciences in the Renaissance is to be found in A. Debus, *Man and Nature: The Renaissance* (Cambridge, Eng., 1978). Highly readable is G. Sarton, *Six Wings: Men of Science in the Renaissance* (Bloomington, Ind., 1957). M. Boas offers a sensible, clear survey in *The Scientific Renaissance 1450–1630* (New York, 1962). One of the best inquiries into aspects of scientific method in Leonardo's day is in J. Randall, Jr., "The Development of Scientific Method in the School of Padua," in *Renaissance Essays,* eds. P. Kristeller and D. Weiner (New York, 1968). B. Gille, *Engineers of the Renaissance* (Cambridge, Mass., 1966) is a good survey, but excessively harsh on the subject of Leonardo's alleged lack of originality. See below in the Leonardo bibliography, and the bibliography to chapter 9, for more on this general subject.

Selected bibliography on Leonardo
The bibliography on Leonardo is immense, and all that can be done here is to offer a small selection in four sections: a core bibliography, bibliographical tools, Leonardo's writings in translation, and a wider miscellany.

Core bibliography: Any scholar's list of essential books on Leonardo would differ somewhat, and with that caveat, here is mine. K. Clark, *Leonardo da Vinci,* intro. M. Kemp (New York, 1988) is still far and away the most readable account of Leonardo as an artist. It was first published in 1939, and revised in 1958; the 1988 edition is the best illustrated and has an essay by Kemp that puts Clark and his book into historical perspective. P. Galluzzi (ed.), *Leonardo Engineer and Architect* (Montreal, 1987) is the catalogue of an exhibition held in Montreal, and has strong, informed essays on these aspects of Leonardo's activity. To my mind the most rounded book on the many aspects of Leonardo's activity is M. Kemp, *Leonardo da Vinci: The Marvelous Works of Nature and Man* (Cambridge, Mass., 1981). K. Keele, *Leonardo da Vinci's Elements of the Sciences of Man* (New York, 1983) is a detailed and lucid exposition of Leonardo's thought, with emphasis on the relation of mechanistic concepts to the understanding of the human body. M. Kemp, J. Roberts, et al., *Leonardo da Vinci* is a catalogue of a show held at the Hayward Gallery in London. It has short, informed essays, a basic bibliography, and a selection of works, heavily illustrated in color. Given the low price and the fact that as of this writing Kemp's monograph is out of print, this is a book for the student to own. The best survey of the anatomical work is C. O'Malley and J. Saunders, *Leonardo da Vinci on the Human Body* (New York, 1952; subsequently available in Dover paperback). A collection of uniformly excellent essays on a variety of topics is in C. O'Malley, *Leonardo's Legacy: An International Symposium* (Berkeley and Los Angeles, 1969). A. Popham, *The Drawings of Leonardo da Vinci* (London, 1973) is the fullest selection of drawings between two covers (many editions). M. Philipson, *Leonardo da Vinci: Aspects of the Renaissance Genius* (New York, 1966) gathers important classic and new essays on Leonardo.

Leonardo's own writings: Leonardo's manuscripts have been published in facsimile and transcription, and many works on Leonardo include the bibliography of these works—such as Kemp and Roberts mentioned above—so it is not given here. There are many anthologies in various languages, but I confine myself here to important ones in English. The first full anthology was published in 1883 with facing Italian and English: J. P. Richter, ed., *The Literary Works of Leonardo da Vinci,* 2 vols. (London, 1970; available in later paperback editions with the title *The Notebooks of ——*). It is topically organized by the editor, and so has the inevitable disadvantage of obfuscating questions of context and chronology. These problems have been greatly ameliorated by the work of C. Pedretti, *The Literary Works of Leonardo da Vinci—Commentary by Carlo Pedretti* (Berkeley and Los Angeles, 1977). This work should be used in tandem with Richter, for it clarifies innumerable problems of context, dating, and interpretation. E. MacCurdy, trans., *The Notebooks of Leonardo da Vinci* (New York, 1939) is an anthology which, unlike Richter, does not give the Italian. While it happens that almost all the quotations in this book are drawn from Richter, the reader should bear in mind that Richter and MacCurdy are complementary, not redundant. Leonardo's *Treatise on Painting,* assembled from the master's notes by his pupil Melzi, and today in manuscript in the Vatican Library, is published in facsimile and translation, A. McMahon, ed., *Treatise on Painting by Leonardo da Vinci,* 2 vols. (Princeton, 1956). The clearest presentation of Leonardo's thought on this subject is the translation and editing by M. Kemp and M. Walker, *Leonardo da Vinci on Painting* (New Haven and London, 1989).

Bibliographical tools: A chronological author and subject-matter bibliography, the culmination of years of work, unfortunately is only likely to be found in major libraries: M. Guerrini, *Biblioteca Leonardiana 1493–1989,* 3 vols. (Milan, 1990). See also A. Lorenzi and P. Marani, *Bibliografia Vinciana 1964–1979* (Florence, 1982). C. Pedretti has begun an annual, *Achademia Leonardo da Vinci: Journal of Leonardo Studies and Bibliography,* of which five, published in Florence, have appeared as of this writing. The chapters of Part II of this book are covered in an annotated bibliography first published in 1931: E. Verga, *Bibliografia Vinciana,* 2 vols. (New York, 1970).

Additional bibliography on Leonardo: These items are listed alphabetically by author, with some commentary where needed.

L. Arano, *Leonardo: Disegni di Leonardo e della sua Cerchia alle Gallerie dell' Accademia* (Milan, 1980).

L. Batkin, *Leonardo da Vinci* (Rome and Bari, 1988). Sees variety and discursiveness as the key to understanding Leonardo.

E. Bellone and P. Rossi, eds., *Leonardo e l'età della ragione* (Milan, 1982). A group of important essays in several languages on Leonardo the scientist-technologist.

L. Beltrami, *Documenti e memorie riguardanti la vita e le opere di Leonardo da Vinci in ordine cronologico* (Milan, 1919). The fundamental work on the documents.

G. Calvi and A. Marinoni, *I manoscritti di Leonardo da Vinci* (Busto Arsizio, 1982). The manuscripts and their chronology.

K. Clark and C. Pedretti, *The Drawings of Leonardo da Vinci in the Collection of Her Majesty the Queen at Windsor Castle,* 3 vols. (London, 1968).

W. Emboden, *Leonardo da Vinci on Plants and Gardens* (Portland, Ore., 1987).

E. Franziosi, *Il mito di Leonardo: sulla fenomenologia della creazione artistica* (Milan, 1987). An abstruse and difficult book in which contemporary critical theory meets Leonardo.

L. Goldschneider, *Leonardo da Vinci: Life and Work. Paintings and Drawings* (London, 1959). A good photographic compilation, with relevant documentation, including a translation of the early brief life of Leonardo by Paolo Giovio.

E. Gombrich, "The Grotesque Heads," in *The Heritage of Apelles* (London, 1966).

———, "Leonardo's Method for Working Out Compositions," in *Norm and Form: Studies in the Art of the Renaissance* (London, 1966).

C. Gould, *Leonardo the Artist and Non-Artist* (Boston, 1975). Despite the title, biased toward the artist.

C. Hart, *The Prehistory of Flight* (Berkeley, Los Angeles, and London, 1985). The most lucid account of Leonardo's study of this subject.

I. Hart, *The Mechanical Investigations of Leonardo da Vinci* (Berkeley and Los Angeles, 1963).

L. Heydenreich, *Leonardo da Vinci,* 2 vols. (New York, 1954). One of the best books on the relation of art and science in Leonardo.

———, *Leonardo. The Last Supper* (New York, 1974). A short monograph on the famous work, written, however, before the cleaning now in progress (for which see Brown in the bibliography for chapter 6). Contains an abridged version of Goethe's essay.

C. Luporini, *La Mente di Leonardo* (Florence, 1952). A brilliant and subsequently contested book on Leonardo's thought.

Leonardo da Vinci (New York and Novara, 1956). A richly illustrated mammoth tome, with qualitatively uneven essays by various authors on many aspects of Leonardo.

Leonardo nella scienza e nella technica (Florence, 1976). Important essays in various languages on Leonardo's science and technology growing out of a conference held in 1969.

Leonardo da Vinci: Intuizione della natura (Milan, 1982). Catalogue of an exhibition of Leonardo's studies of nature.

P. Marani, *Leonardo: Catalogo completo dei dipinti* (Florence, 1989). Up-to-date bibliography.

A. Marinoni and L. Arano, *Leonardo all'Ambrosiana. Il Codice Atlantico. Disegni di Leonardo e della sua Cerchia* (Milan, 1982).

E. Müntz, *Léonard de Vinci: l'artiste, le penseur, le savant* (Paris, 1899). Richly detailed book that remains valuable for placing Leonardo in his historical setting.

C. Pedretti, *Studi vinciani* (Geneva, 1957). Includes an important essay on the *Lady on a Balcony* (the *Mona Lisa*).

———, *Leonardo da Vinci on Painting: A Lost Book (Libro A.,* Berkeley and Los Angeles, 1964). A very important book on the genesis and structure of the *Treatise on Painting.*

———, *Leonardo: A Study in Chronology and Style* (London, 1973). An interesting gathering of observations by the dean of Leonardo studies that does not jell as well as a synthesis as do the studies of Clark, Heydenreich, Kemp, and others.

———, *Disegni di Leonardo da Vinci della sua scuola alla Biblioteca Reale di Torino* (Florence, 1975).

———, *Landscape, Plants and Water Studies in the Collection of Her Majesty the Queen at Windsor Castle* (London and New York, 1982).

———, *I Disegni di Leonardo da Vinci e della sua Cerchia nel Gabinetto disegni e stampe della Galleria degli Uffizi a Firenze* (Florence, 1985).

———, *Leonardo Architect,* trans. S. Brill (New York, 1985).

———, *Horses and Other Animal Drawings by Leonardo da Vinci in the Collection of Her Majesty the Queen at Windsor Castle* (London and New York, 1987).

C. Pedretti and K. Keele, *Leonardo da Vinci: Corpus of Anatomical Drawings in the Collection of Her Majesty the Queen at Windsor Castle,* 3 vols. (New York, 1979–80).

A. Popham and P. Pouncey, *Italian Drawings of the 14th and 15th Centuries in the British Museum,* 2 vols. (London, 1950).

L. Reti, ed., *The Unknown Leonardo* (London, 1974). Essays by various scholars motivated by rediscovery in the late 1960s of two Leonardo manuscripts in Madrid.

L. Venturi, *La critica e l'arte di Leonardo da Vinci* (Bologna, 1919). A review of the critical fortune of Leonardo on the four hundredth anniversary of his death.

J. Wasserman, *Leonardo* (New York, 1975). A colorplate book with some interesting and at times iconoclastic observations.

V. Zubov, *Leonardo da Vinci,* trans. D. Kraus (Cambridge, Mass., 1968). Leonardo the scientist-technologist; useful if read in conjunction with Pedretti and Keele.

PART II: *The Anatomy of a Legend*

CHAPTER 4: *Giorgio Vasari Invents Leonardo*

S. Alpers, "Ekphrasis and Aesthetic Attitudes in Vasari's Lives," *Journal of the Warburg and Courtauld Institutes* 23, (1966), p. 190ff. Vasari's debt to ancient literary conventions.

M. Baxandall, "Doing Justice to Vasari," *Times Literary Supplement* (Feb. 1, 1980), p. 111ff. Important exposition of the major issues concerning the *Lives.*

T. Boase, *Giorgio Vasari: The Man and the Book* (Princeton, 1979). A solid if somewhat old-fashioned account. See Baxandall's review listed directly above.

B. Cellini, "Della architettura," in *Opere di Baldassare Castiglione, Giovanni della Casa, Benvenuto Cellini* (Milan, 1960).

E. Cochrane, *Historians and Historiography in the Italian Renaissance* (Chicago, 1981). Vasari in the wider context of Renaissance historiography.

P. Giovio, *Life of Leonardo.* I have used the translation in Goldschneider, listed in the last part of the bibliography to Part I.

Paolo Giovio: Il Rinascimento e la Memoria (Como, 1985).

Leonardo e l'incisione: Stampe derivate da Leonardo e Bramante dal XV al XIX secolo (Milan, 1984). Prints after Leonardo.

P. Murray, *An Index of Attributions Made in Tuscan Sources Before Vasari* (Florence, 1959).

G. Vasari, *Vasari on Technique,* trans. L. Maclehose, intro. G. Baldwin (New York, 1960). The quotation of Vasari on *disegno* is from this translation.

———, *Lives of the Artist,* trans. G. Bull (Harmondsworth, Eng., 1965). Aside from the Vasari quotation cited above, all quotations from Vasari in this book are in Bull's translation.

———, *Vite de' piu eccellenti pittori, scultori e architetti nelle redazione del 1550 e 1568,* comm. P. Barocchi, 6 vols. (1966–87).

———, *Il Vasari Storiografo e Artista: Atti del Congresso Internazionale nel IV Centenario della Morte* (Florence, 1976).

———, *Le Vite . . . nell'edizione per i tipi di Lorenzo torrentino Firenze 1550,* ed. L. Bellosi and A. Rossi, presentation by G. Previtali (Turin, 1986). Scholarly edition of the 1550 Vasari.

R. Whittemore, *Pure Lives: The Early Biographers* (Baltimore and London, 1988).

CHAPTER 5: *Playing by the Rules*

G. Ackerman, "Lomazzo's Treatise on Painting," *Art Bulletin* 49 (Dec. 1967), p. 312ff.

G. Armenini, *De Veri Precetti della Pittura*, ed. M. Gorreri (Turin, 1988).

G. Bellori, *Le Vite de' Pittori, Scultori, et Architetti moderni* (Rome, 1672).

A. Boscholoo, ed., *Academies of Art Between Renaissance and Romanticism* ('s-Gravenhage, 1989).

A. Bosse, *Sentiments de la distinction des diverse manières de peintre, dessein et graveure et des originaux d'avec leur copies* (Paris, 1649).

———, *Traité des practiques geometrales et perspectives enseignées dans l'Academie Royale de la Peinture et Sculpture* (Paris, 1665), Chap. VIII.

F. Caroli, *Leonardo: Studi di fisiognomica* (Milan, 1991).

R. Chambray, *Idée de la perfection de la peinture demonstrée par les principes . . .* (Paris, 1662).

Charactures by Leonardo da Vinci from Drawings by Wenceslaus Hollar out of the Portland Museum (London, 1786).

R. Descartes, *Oeuvres et lettres*, ed. A. Bridoux (Paris, 1953).

A. Dezallier d'Argenville, *Abrégé de la vie des plus fameux peintres*, 3 vols. (Paris, 1745).

C. Du Fresnoy, *The Art of Painting by C. A. Du Fresnoy with Remarks. Translated into English, with an Original Preface, containing a Parallel between Painting and Poetry by Mr. Dryden* (London, 1750).

A. Félibien, *Entretiens sur les vies des plus excellens peintres anciens et moderns*, 2 vols. (Paris, 1685; 2nd ed.).

A. Fontaine, *Les Doctrines d'Art en France* (Paris, 1909).

C. Goldstein, *Visual Fact Over Verbal Fiction: A Study of the Carracci and the Criticism, Theory, and Practice of Art in Renaissance Italy* (Cambridge, Eng., 1988).

C. Le Brun, *Conference de Monsieur Le Brun Premier Peintre du Roy de France, Chancelier et Directeur de l'Académie de Peinture et Sculpture sur l'Expression générale et particulaire, enrichie de figures gravées par B. Picart* (Paris, 1698).

———, *Heads Representing the Various Passions of the Soul as they are Expressed in the Human Countenance by the Great Master Mons. Le Brun and finely Engraved on Twenty Folio Plates Nearly the Size of Life* (London, 1813).

G. Lomazzo, *Scritti sulle arti*, intro. and comm. R. Ciardi, 2 vols. (Florence, 1973).

J. Mariette, *Recueil de Testes de caractère et de charges dessinés par Léonard de Vinci Florentin et gravés par M.C. de C.* (Paris, 1730).

E. Panofsky, *The Codex Huygens and Leonardo da Vinci's Art Theory* (London, 1940).

C. Pedretti, *Leonardo da Vinci: Fragments at Windsor Castle from the Codex Atlanticus* (London, 1957). On the removal of the grotesque heads from their original context.

R. Pennington, *A descriptive catalogue of the etched work of Wenceslaus Hollar 1606–77* (Cambridge, Eng., 1982).

N. Pevsner, *Academies of Art Past and Present* (New York, 1970). Originally published in 1940, this remains a good overview, though dated in some particulars.

R. de Piles, *Abrégé de la Vie des peintres avec des réflexions sur leur ouvrages* (Paris, 1699).

———, *Cours de peinture par principes* (Paris, 1708).

J. Reynolds, *Discourses on Art,* ed. R. Wark (New Haven and London, 1975).

J. Richardson, Jr., *An Account of the Statues, Bas-Reliefs, Drawings, and Pictures in Italy, France, etc. with Remarks,* 2nd ed. (London, 1754; originally published 1722).

F. Scanelli, *Microcosmo della Pittura . . .* (Cesena, 1657).

A. Scott-Elliot, "Caricature Heads After Leonardo da Vinci in the Spencer Collection," *Bulletin of the New York Public Library,* Vol. 62 (June 1958), p. 279ff.

F. Solinas, ed., *Cassiano del Pozzo* (Rome, 1989).

K. Steinitz, "Poussin, Illustrator of Leonardo da Vinci and the Problem of Replicas in Poussin's Studio," *Art Quarterly* (Spring 1953), p. 40ff.

CHAPTER 6: *Leonardo Goes Public*

C. Amoretti, *Memorie storiche su la vita gli studi et le opere di Leonardo da Vinci* (Milan, 1804).

P. Arbelet, *L'histoire de la peinture en Italie et les plageats de Stendhal* (Paris, 1914). Interesting account of Stendhal's unacknowledged borrowings in his writings on art.

G. Bossi, *Del cenacolo di Leonardo da Vinci, Libri quattro* (Milan, 1810).

———, *Scritti sulle Arti,* ed. R. P. Ciardi (Florence, 1982). Writings other than the book on *The Last Supper.*

C. Botta, *History of Italy During the Consulate and Empire of Napoleon Bonaparte,* 2 vols. (Boston, 1928).

D. Brown, *Leonardo's Last Supper: The Restoration* (New Haven, 1983).

G. Cambon, *Ugo Foscolo, Poet of Exile* (Princeton, 1980).

S. Canzio, *La prima Republica Cisalpina e il sentimento nazionale italiano* (Modena, 1944).

T. Celona, and E. and L. Travi, *Scrittori e architetti nella Milano napoleonica* (Milan, 1983).

J. Chamberlaine, *Original Designs of the Most Celebrated Masters of the Bolognese, Roman, Florentine and Venetian Schools . . .* (London, 1812).

G. De Toni, *Giambattista Venturi e la sua opera vinciana. Scritti inediti e l'Essai* (Rome, 1924). Includes Venturi's 1797 essay.

U. Foscolo, *Opere di Foscolo,* ed. M. Puppo (Milan, 1966).

G. Galbiati, *Il cenacolo di Leonardo da Vinci del pittore Giuseppe Bossi nel giudizio d'illustri contemporanei* (Milan and Rome, 1920).

P. Gault de Saint-Germain, *Vie de Léonard de Vinci suivie du catalogue de ses ouvrages dans les Beaux-Arts* (Paris, 1803).

C. Gerli, *Disegni di Leonardo da Vinci incisi e pubblicati da Carlo Giuseppe Gerli milanesi, con prefaxione dell'Amoretti* (Milan, 1784).

W. Goethe, *Goethe on Art,* trans. J. Gage (Berkeley and Los Angeles, 1980). I have quoted from this translation.

Goethe in Italia (Milan, 1986).

Goethe e l'Italia (Milan, 1989).

L. Heydenreich, *Leonardo: The Last Supper* (New York, 1974). The Goethe essay is abridged in this publication.

H. Honour, *Neo-Classicism* (Harmondsworth, Eng., 1968).

L. Lanzi, *Storia pittorica della Italia del risorgimento delle Belle Arti* . . . , 3rd ed. (Bassano, 1809).

L. Mazzucchetti, *Goethe e il Cenacolo di Leonardo* (Milan, 1939). Contains the Goethe essay in German, and the original French and English translations.

E. Möller, *Das Abendmahl des Lionardo da Vinci* (Baden-Baden, 1952).

G. Nicodemi, *La Pittura Milanese dell'Età Neoclassica* (Milan, 1915).

G. Orloff, *Essai sur l'histoire de la peinture en Italie depuis les temps plus anciens jusqu'à nos jours,* 2 vols. (Paris, 1823).

H. Ost, *Das Leonardo-Porträt in der Klg. Bibliothek Turin und andere Fälschungen des Giuseppe Bossi* (Berlin, 1980). (See review in *Kunstchronik,* Jan. 1982, p. 34ff.) An ingenious argument made mainly on historical grounds that the famous so-called self-portrait is a forgery by Bossi. This seems refutable on stylistic grounds, and the argument has found little acceptance.

A. Ottino della Chiesa, *Neoclassicismo nella Pittura Italiana* (Milan, 1967).

J. Pelikan, *Jesus Through the Centuries: His Place in the History of Culture* (New Haven and London, 1985).

D. Pino, *Storia genuina del cenacolo di Leonardo da Vinci nel refettorio de'padri dominicani di Santa Maria delle Grazie di Milano* (Milan, 1796). An example of pre-Bossi writing on *The Last Supper,* stressing theological rather than aesthetic issues.

E. Renan, *Vie de Jésus,* ed. J. Gaulmier (Paris, 1974).

R. Rosenblum, *Transformations in Late Eighteenth Century Art* (Princeton, 1967).

J. Seroux d'Agincourt, *Histoire de l'art* . . . , 6 vols. (Paris, 1823).

Stendhal, *Histoire de la Peinture en Italie,* ed. P. Arbelet, 2 vols. (Paris, 1924).

———, *Stendhal and the Arts,* ed. D. Wakefield (London, 1973). An anthology in translation, from which I have quoted.

G. Venturi, *Essai sur les ouvrages physico-mathématiques de Leonard de Vinci* (Milan, 1797). See De Toni for modern reprint.

C. Zaghi, *L'Italia di Napoleone* (Turin, 1989). I have taken the Napoleon quotation, and those of contemporaries' reactions to the city of Milan, from this book.

CHAPTER 7: *Leonardo the Harbinger of Modernity*

M. Abrams, *The Mirror and the Lamp* (Oxford, 1953). Still a fine introduction to earlier nineteenth-century literature.

M. Arnold, *Selected Essays,* intro. N. Annon (London, 1964).

S. Bann, *The Clothing of Clio: A Study of the Representation of History in Nineteenth Century Britain and France* (Cambridge, Eng., 1984).

P. Barolsky, *Walter Pater's Renaissance* (University Park, Penn., 1987).

———, *Why Mona Lisa Smiles and Other Tales by Vasari* (University Park, Penn., 1991).

C. Baudelaire, *Oeuvres complètes* (Paris, 1961).

H. Belting, *The End of the History of Art?,* trans. C. Wood (Chicago and London, 1987). Among other things, about the separation of art history and art criticism in the early nineteenth century.

G. Boas, "The Mona Lisa in the History of Taste," *Journal of the History of Ideas* I, no. 2 (April 1940), p. 207ff.

A. Brookner, *The Genius of the Future* (London, 1971). Introductory essays to nineteenth-century French critics.

J. Brown, *The Life of Leonardo da Vinci with a Critical Account of his Works* (London, 1828).

B. Bullen, "Walter Pater's 'Renaissance' and Leonardo da Vinci's Reputation in the Nineteenth Century," *The Modern Language Review* 24 (April 1979), p. 268ff.

P. Burke, ed., *A New Kind of History: From the Writings of Febvre* (London, 1973), p. 258ff. On Michelet and his invention of the Renaissance.

C. Clément, *Michel-Ange, Léonard de Vinci, Raphael* (Paris, 1861).

P. Clements, *Baudelaire and the English Tradition* (Princeton, 1985).

J. Coulon, *Walter Pater and the French Tradition* (Lewisburg, Penn., 1982).

C. Crossley, *Edgar Quinet (1803–75): A Study in Romantic Thought* (Lexington, 1983).

A. Culler, *The Victorian Mirror of History* (New Haven, 1985).

P. Dale, *The Victorian Critic and the Idea of History: Carlyle, Arnold, and Pater* (Cambridge, Mass., 1977).

E. Delécluze, *Saggio intorno a Leonardo da Vinci* (Siena, 1844), trans. into Italian from French. Not discussed in my text, this is a good example of pre-Michelet-Quinet criticism of Leonardo.

R. Dellamora, "Pater's Modernism: The Leonardo Essay," *University of Toronto Quarterly* (Winter 1977–78), p. 136ff.

P. Dodd, ed., *Walter Pater: An Imaginative Sense of Fact* (Totowa, N.J., 1981).

A. Dumesnil, *L'Art Italien* (Paris, 1854).

T. Gautier, *Guide de l'Amateur au Musée de Louvre* (Paris, 1882).

———, *Journeys in Italy,* trans. P. Vermiyle (New York, 1902). I have used this translation.

———, *Oeuvres complètes,* Vol. I (Geneva, 1928).

T. Gautier, A. Houssaye, and P. de Saint-Victor, *Les Dieux et les Semi-dieux de la peinture* (Paris, 1864).

D. Gordon, "Leonardo's Legend," *English Literary History* 51 (1982), p. 300ff.

L. Gossman, "The Go-Between: Jules Michelet 1798–1871," *Modern Language Notes* 89 (May 1970), p. 503ff.

A. Gruyer, "Léonard de Vinci au Musée du Louvre," *Gazette des Beaux-Arts* 35 (1887), p. 449ff.; and 36 (1888), p. 89ff.

I. Guerrins, *Quinet et Italia* (Geneva and Paris, 1981).

O. Haac, *Jules Michelet* (Boston, 1982).

H. Honour, *Romanticism* (New York, 1979).

G. Hough, *The Last Romantics* (London, 1947).

A. Houssaye, *Histoire de Léonard de Vinci* (Paris, 1869).

B. Inman, "Pater's Conception of the Renaissance: From Sources to Personal Ideal," *The Victorian Newsletter* 47 (Spring 1971), p. 19ff.

———, *Walter Pater's Reading: A Bibliography of His Library Borrowings and Literary References* (New York, 1981).

W. Iser, *Walter Pater: The Aesthetic Moment,* trans. D. Wilson (Cambridge, Eng., 1987). Original in German (1960).

A. Jameson, *Memories of the Early Italian Painters and the Progress of Painting* (London, 1868).

S. Kippur, *Jules Michelet: A Study of Mind and Sensibility* (Albany, 1981).

A. Kugler, *A Handbook of Painting from the Age of Constantine the Great to the Present Time* (London, 1892).

L. Lanzi, *La Real Galleria di Firenze* (Florence, 1782).

M. Levey, *The Case of Walter Pater* (London, 1978).

J. Longenbach, *Modernist Poetics of History* (Princeton, 1987).

R. McMullen, *Mona Lisa: The Picture and the Myth* (Boston, 1975).

J. Michelet, *Histoire de France,* Vol. 13: *La Renaissance* (Paris, 1855).

———, *Journal,* Vol. 2 (1849–60), ed. P. Villaneix (Paris, 1962). The pre-1855 quotations from Michelet on Leonardo are translated from this volume.

———, *Mother Death: The Journal of Jules Michelet 1815–1850,* trans. E. Kaplan (Amherst, 1984).

A. Mitzman, *Michelet, Historian: Rebirth and Romanticism in Nineteenth-Century France* (New Haven and London, 1990).

G. Monod, *La vie et la pensée de Jules Michelet 1798–1852,* 2 vols. (Paris, 1923).

G. Monsman, *Walter Pater* (Boston, 1977).

D. O'Hara, *The Romance of Interpretation: Visionary Criticism from Pater to de Man* (New York, 1985).

W. Pater, *Collected Works,* 10 vols. (Boston, 1910).

———, *The Renaissance: Studies in Art and Poetry,* ed. and intro. A. Phillips (New York, 1986). Standard critical edition.

D. Pinkney, *Decisive Years in France 1840–1847* (Princeton, 1986).

G. Planche, *Portraites d'artiste: Peintres et sculpteurs,* 2 vols. (Paris, 1853).

R. Powers, *Edgar Quinet: A Study in French Patriotism* (Dallas, 1957).

M. Praz, *The Romantic Agony* (London, 1977). A classic from 1933.

E. Quinet, *Les révolutions d'Italie,* 5th ed., 2 vols. (Paris, n.d.).

Reale Galleria di Firenze Illustrata, Serie I, Quadri di storia, Vol. VIII (Florence, 1828). Full-page engraving of the *Medusa,* which helped popularize the erroneous attribution more than any written description.

L. Rigolot, *Catalogue de l'oeuvre de Léonard de Vinci* (Paris, 1849). The confused state of knowledge of Leonardo's work at mid-century.

A. Rio, *De la poésie chrétienne dans son principe, dans sa matière, et dans ses formes* (Paris, 1836).

———, *Léonard de Vinci et son école* (Paris, 1855).

———, *L'Art chrétienne* (Paris, 1861). The *Medusa* is still accepted as an authentic Leonardo at this late date.

D. Rossetti, *Poems and Translations 1850–70* (London, 1913).

G. von Rumohr, *Italienische Forschungen*, 3 vols. (Berlin, 1827). Denies Leonardo is painter of the *Medusa*.

J. Ruskin, *The Queen of the Air: Being a Study of the Greek Myths of Cloud and Storm* (New York, n.d.; first pub., 1869).

———, *The Stones of Venice*, 4 vols. (London, 1885), p. 56. Deprecatory views of the Renaissance.

H. Schenk, *The Mind of the European Romantics* (New York, 1966).

R. Seiler, *Walter Pater: The Critical Heritage* (London, 1969).

M. Spencer, *The Art Criticism of Théophile Gautier* (Geneva, 1969).

R. Stein, *The Ritual of Interpretation: The Fine Arts as Literature in Ruskin, Rossetti, and Pater* (Cambridge, Mass., 1975).

A. Swinburne, *The Complete Works of Algernon Charles Swinburne*, ed. E. Gosse and T. Wise, Prose Works volume 2 (New York, 1926), pp. 156–7.

H. Taine, *Voyage en Italie*, 2 vols. (Paris, 1864).

———, *Nouveaux essais de critique et d'histoire*, 8th ed. (Paris, 1905).

G. Waagen, *Kunstwerke und Kunstler in Paris* (Berlin, 1839).

R. Wornum, ed., *Lectures on Painting by the Royal Academicians Barry, Opie, and Fuseli* (London, 1848).

H. White, *Metahistory: The Historical Imagination in Nineteenth Century Europe* (Baltimore, 1973).

O. Wilde, *The Critic as Artist*, ed. R. Ellmann (New York, 1968).

R. Wollheim, *On Art and the Mind* (London, 1973), p. 155ff., on Pater.

F. Zacchiroli, *Description de la galerie royale de Florence* (Florence, 1783).

CHAPTER 8: *The Mind of the Maker*

A. Arnold, *Paul Valéry and the Critics: A Bibliography* (Charlottesville, Va., 1970).

S. Bassett, "Pater and Freud on Leonardo da Vinci: The Views of the Hero of Art," *Literature and Psychology* 23 (1973), p. 21ff.

C. Beckford, *The Seeker: D. S. Merezhovsky* (Wichita, 1975).

M. Bémol, *Paul Valéry* (Paris, 1949).

———, *La méthode critique de Paul Valéry* (Paris, 1950).

B. Berenson, *The Florentine Painters of the Renaissance* (New York, 1896).

———, *The Drawings of the Florentine Painters . . .* , 2 vols. (New York, 1903).

———, *The Study and Criticism of Italian Art*, Third Series (London, 1916).

S. Bloch, "Marcel Duchamp's Green Box," *Art Journal* 34, no. 1 (Fall 1977), p. 25ff.

P. Cabanne, *Dialogues with Marcel Duchamp* (London, 1977).

Conferenze Fiorentine (Florence, 1910). Lectures given in 1906 which in juxtaposition give the panorama on thinking on Leonardo just after the turn of the century.

C. Crow, *Paul Valéry: Consciousness and Nature* (London, 1972).

———, *Paul Valéry and Maxwell's Demon: Natural Order and Human Possibility* (Hull, 1972).

P. Duhem, *Études sur Léonard de Vinci: Ceux qu'il a lus et ceux qui l'ont lu* (Paris, 1955). Turn-of-the-century writings by the first scholar to suggest Leonardo's considerable debt to late medieval thought.

K. Eissler, *Leonardo da Vinci: Psychoanalytic Notes on the Enigma* (New York, 1961). Gives an idea of how Freud's ideas on Leonardo have played out over the decades.

B. Farrell, "On Freud's Study of Leonardo," in *Leonardo da Vinci: Aspects of the Renaissance Genius,* ed. M. Philipson (New York, 1966).

L. Ferri, "Leonardo da Vinci: Scienziato e filosofo," *Nuova antologia* 22 (1873), p. 294ff.

S. Freud, *Eine Kindheitserinnerung des Leonardo da Vinci* (Vienna, 1910).

———, *Leonardo da Vinci and a Memory of His Childhood,* trans. A. Tyson (New York, 1964).

P. Gay, *Freud for Historians* (New York, 1985).

———, *Freud: A Life for Our Time* (New York and London, 1988).

E. Gombrich, "Verbal Wit as a Paradigm of Art: The Aesthetic Theories of Sigmund Freud (1856–1939)," in *Tributes* (Ithaca, 1984).

C. Gottlieb, "Something Else: Duchamp's Bride and Leonardo," *Konsthistorik tidsskrift* 45 (1976), p. 52ff.

H. Grothe, *Leonardo da Vinci als Ingenieur und Philosoph: Ein Beitrag zur Geschichte der Technik und der Induction Wissenschaft* (Berlin, 1874).

C. Hackett, "Teste and La Soirée avec Monsieur Teste," *French Studies* XXI (1967), p. 111ff.

A. Hauser, *The Philosophy of Art History* (New York, 1959).

A. von Humboldt, *Kosmos: Entwurf einer physischen Weltbeschreibung,* 5 vols. (Stuttgart, 1845–62).

R. Jones, "Poincaré and Valéry: A Note on the 'Symbol' in Art and Science," *The Modern Language Review* 42 (Oct. 1944), p. 485ff.

R. Kuenzli and F. Naumann, eds., *Marcel Duchamp: Artist of the Century* (Cambridge, Mass., and London, 1989).

G. Libri, *Histoire des sciences mathematiques en Italie . . . ,* 3 vols. (Paris, 1840).

S. Mallarmé, *Poésies* (Paris, 1943).

K. Marx, "Uber Marc Antonio della Torre und Leonardo da Vinci die Begrunder des bildische Anatomie," *Abhandungen des Königlischen Gesellschaft,* Vol. 2 (Göttingen, 1849).

D. Merejekowski, *The Romance of Leonardo da Vinci* (New York, 1931).

E. Müntz, *Léonard de Vinci: l'artiste, le penseur, le savant* (Paris, 1899).

J. Péladan, *La dernière lécon de Léonard de Vinci* (Paris, 1904). The extreme swan song of romantic writing on Leonardo, in which this strange Rosicrucian suggests that the androgynous *Saint John* is the greatest painting in the world.

J. Pierrot, *The Decadent Imagination 1880–1900* (Chicago, 1981).

E. Poe, "Eureka, a Prose Poem," in *Poetry and Tales* (New York, 1984), p. 1257ff.

F. Raab, *Leonardo da Vinci als Natur-Forscher: Ein Beitrag zur Geschichte der Naturwissen-schaft in Zeitalter der Renaissance* (Berlin, 1880).

C. Ravaisson-Mollien, "Les écrits de Léonard de Vinci," *Gazette des Beaux-Arts* 23 (1881), pp. 225ff., 331ff., 514ff.

T. Reff, "Duchamp and Leonardo: L.H.O.O.Q.-Alikes," *Art in America* (Jan.-Feb. 1977), p. 83ff.

J. Robinson, *L'Analyse de l'esprit dans les cahiers de Valéry* (Paris, 1963).

——, "Valéry's conception of the training of the mind," *French Studies* XVIII (1964), p. 227ff.

W. Rubin, "Reflexions on Marcel Duchamp," *Art International* 4, no. 9 (Dec. 1960), p. 49ff.

F. Scarfe, *The Art of Paul Valéry* (London, 1954).

M. Schapiro, "Leonardo and Freud: An Art Historical Study," *Journal of the History of Ideas* 17 (April 1956). The classic dismantling of Freud's argument from the point of view of the art historian.

A. Schwartz, *The Complete Works of Marcel Duchamp* (New York, 1969). Appendix on Duchamp and Leonardo.

G. Séailles, *Léonard de Vinci: L'Artiste et Savant. Essai de Biographie psychologique* (Paris, 1892).

R. Shattuck, "The Tortoise and the Hare: A Study of Valéry, Freud, and Leonardo da Vinci," in *Leonardo da Vinci: Aspects of the Renaissance Genius,* ed. M. Philipson (New York, 1966).

J. Spector, *The Aesthetics of Freud: A Study in Psychoanalysis and Art* (New York, 1973).

N. Suckling, *Paul Valéry and the Civilized Mind* (London and New York, 1959).

F. Sutcliffe, *La Pensée de Paul Valéry* (Paris, 1955).

P. Valéry, *Collected Works of Paul Valéry,* ed. J. Matthews, various trans., 15 vols. (Princeton, 1956–   ). In particular:

——, *Leonardo Poe Mallarmé,* trans. M. Cowley, J. Lawler (Princeton, 1972).

——, *Monsieur Teste,* trans. J. Matthews (Princeton, 1973). I have used translations from this and the above volume.

——, *Oeuvres,* ed. J. Hytier, 2 vols. (Paris, 1957).

——, *Cahiers 1894–1914,* ed. N. Celeyrette-Pietri and J. Robinson-Valéry (Paris, 1987).

W. Whewell, *History of the Inductive Sciences from the Earliest to Present Time* (London, 1847).

——, *On the Philosophy of Discovery, Chapters Historical and Critical* (London, 1860).

C. Whiting, *Paul Valéry* (London, 1978).

E. Wilson, *Axel's Castle* (New York, 1931).

H. Wölfflin, *Classic Art* (London, 1952).

R. Wollheim, *Sigmund Freud* (New York, 1971). An excellent concise introduction.

PART III: *Leonardo Now*

CHAPTER 9: *The Triumph of the Eye/I*

L. Alberti, *Alberti on Painting and Sculpture,* comm. and trans. C. Grayson (London, 1972).

F. Ames-Lewis, *Drawing in Early Renaissance Italy* (New Haven, 1981).

E. Battisti, *Brunelleschi: The Complete Work* (New York, 1981).

B. Baxandall, *Painting and Experience in the Fifteenth Century* (Oxford, 1972). Brilliant account of how art was viewed through fifteenth-century eyes.

C. Cennini, *The Craftsman's Handbook: "Il Libro dell Arte" Cennino d'Andrea Cennini,* trans. D. Thompson, Jr. (New Haven, 1933). Invaluable account of circa 1400 studio practice in Tuscany.

B. Cole, *The Renaissance Artist at Work from Pisano to Titian* (New York, 1983).

S. Edgerton, *The Renaissance Rediscovery of Linear Perspective* (New York, 1975).

——, *The Heritage of Giotto's Geometry: Art and Science on the Eve of the Scientific Revolution* (Ithaca, N.Y., 1991).

P. Grendler, *Schooling in the Renaissance* (Baltimore and London, 1989). The fundamental work on this subject.

O. Hardison, Jr., *Disappearing through the Skylight: Culture and Technology in the Twentieth Century* (New York, 1989). A commentary on, among many other things, the fate of the book and the status of visual knowledge in our time.

M. Kemp, "Analogy and Observation in the Codex Hammer," *Studi Vinciani in memoria di Nando di Toni* (Brescia, Italy, 1986).

——, *The Science of Art: Optical Themes in Western Art from Brunelleschi to Seurat* (New Haven and London, 1990).

A. Manetti, *The Life of Brunelleschi,* intro. H. Saalman, trans. C. Engass (University Park, Penn., and London, 1970).

E. Panofsky, "Artist, Scientist, Genius: Notes on the 'Renaissance-Dämmerung,' " in *The Renaissance* (New York, 1953). A brilliant essay, stressing the role of the unassisted naked eye and drawing in advancing knowledge.

G. Passavant, *Verrocchio* (London, 1969).

F. Prager and G. Scaglia, *Brunelleschi: Studies of His Technology and Inventions* (Cambridge, Mass., 1970).

——, *Mariano Taccola and His Book De Ingeneis* (Cambridge, Mass., 1972). Important works for an understanding of the background of Leonardo's technology.

R. Root-Bernstein, *Discovering, Inventing, and Solving Problems at the Frontiers of Scientific Knowledge* (Cambridge, Mass., and London, 1989).

D. Summers, *The Judgement of Sense* (Cambridge, Eng., 1987).

C. de Tolnay, *History and Technique of Old Master Drawings* (New York, 1943).

K. Veltman, *Linear Perspective and the Visual Dimensions of Science and Art* (Munich, 1986). Recommended only to those with basic mastery of the subject.

J. White, *The Birth and Rebirth of Pictorial Space* (Boston, 1967).

CHAPTER 10: *Possessing the World*

J. Bialostocki, "The Renaissance Concept of Nature and Antiquity," in *The Renaissance and Mannerism, Acts of the 21th International Congress of the History of Art*, Vol. 2 (Princeton, 1963). The history of the concepts *natura naturata* and *natura naturans*.

M. Campbell, *The Witness and the Other World: Exotic European Travel Writing 400–1600* (Ithaca and London, 1988).

L. Conato, *Leonardo e il Paesaggio Lombardo* (Brescia, Italy, 1987). Suggestive juxtaposition of Leonardo's represented landscapes with the actual landscape of Lombardy.

O. Dunn and J. Kelley, Jr., *The Diario of Christopher Columbus's First Voyage 1492–93* (Norman, Okla., 1989).

A. Gerbi, *Nature in the New World from Christopher Columbus to Gonzalo Fernandez de Oviedo* (Pittsburgh, 1985).

C. Glacken, *Traces on the Rhodian Shore . . .* (Berkeley, Los Angeles, and London, 1967). Magisterial study of Western attitudes toward nature from antiquity to the eighteenth century.

Leonardo e le vie d'acqua (Florence, 1988). Important study of Leonardo's hydraulics.

J. Lovelock, *The Age of Gaia: A Biography of Our Living Earth* (New York and London, 1988).

W. Wheeler, quoted in C. Curtis and F. Greenslet, *The Practical Cogitator* (Boston, 1946).

J. Wilford, *The Mapmakers: The Story of the Great Pioneers from Antiquity to the Space Age* (New York, 1981).

CHAPTER 11: *The Body as Nature and Culture*

J. Benthall and T. Polhemus, *The Body as a Medium of Expression* (New York, 1975). Wide-ranging essays, stressing the notion of nonverbal communication.

M. Berman, "The Body in History," in *Ways of Knowing*, ed. J. Brockmans, (New York, 1991).

M. Johnson, *The Body in the Mind* (Chicago and London, 1987).

Leonardo (see relevant entries in Leonardo bibliography, particularly O'Malley and Saunders).

L. Lind, *Studies in Pre-Vesalian Anatomy* (Philadelphia, 1975).

M. Pouchelle, *The Body and Surgery in the Middle Ages,* trans. C. Morris (New Brunswick, N.J., 1990).

J. Schilder, *The Image and Appearance of the Human Body* (New York, 1950).

N. Sirasi, *Medieval and Early Renaissance Medicine: An Introduction to Science and Practice* (Chicago, 1990).

CHAPTER 12: *A Blessed Rage for Order*

G. Bataille, *Visions of Excess: Selected Writings 1927–1939* (Minneapolis, 1986).

F. Chabod, *Machiavelli and the Renaissance,* trans. D. Moore (Cambridge, Mass., 1958).

C. Cipolla, *Guns, Sails, and Empires* . . . (Manhattan, Kan., 1985).

C. von Clausewitz, *On War,* ed. and intro. A. Rapoport (London, 1968). The 1832 German classic on the nature and conduct of war.

P. Contamine, *War in the Middle Ages,* trans. M. Jones (London, 1984).

M. van Creveld, *Technology and War from 2000 B.C to the Present* (New York, 1989).

J. Gantner, *Leonardos Visionen von der Stintflut und vom Untergang der Welt* (Bern, 1958). The deluge drawings and related matters.

F. Gilbert, "Machiavelli: The Renaissance of the Art of War," in *Makers of Modern Strategy,* ed. E. Earle (Princeton, 1952).

J. Hale, "War and Public Opinion in Florence," *Italian Renaissance Studies,* ed. E. Jacob (London, 1960).

———, *War and Society in Renaissance Europe* (Baltimore, 1985).

———, *Artists and Warfare in the Renaissance* (New Haven and London, 1990).

R. Holmes, *On War and Morality* (Princeton, 1989).

J. Keegan, *The Illustrated Face of Battle* (New York, 1988).

N. Machiavelli, *Opere di Niccolò Machiavelli* (Milan, 1954).

———, *The Prince,* trans. and intro. G. Bull (Harmondsworth, Eng., 1961). My quotation from *The Prince* is from this translation.

———, *Machiavelli: The Chief Works and Others,* trans. A. Gilbert, 3 vols. (Durham, N.C., and London, 1989). The quotation from *The Ass* is from Gilbert's translation.

M. Mallett, *Mercenaries and Their Masters* (London, 1974).

———, "Preparations for war in Florence and Venice in the second half of the fifteenth century," in *Florence and Venice: Comparisons and Relations* (Florence, 1979).

P. Marani, *L'architettura fortificata negli studi di Leonardo da Vinci* (Florence, 1984).

W. McNeill, *The Pursuit of Power* (Chicago, 1982).

R. O'Connell, *Of Arms and Men* (New York and Oxford, 1989).

L. Reti, *The Unknown Leonardo* (London, 1974). Includes an essay on military matters.

Index

Italicized page numbers indicate illustrations.

PERMISSIONS ACKNOWLEDGMENTS

Grateful acknowledgment is made to the following for permission to reprint previously published material:

Dover Publications: Excerpt from *Vasari on Technique* by Giorgio Vasari, translated by Louisa Maclehose; and excerpt from *Leonardo da Vinci on the Human Body* by C. D. O'Malley and J. B. de C. M. Saunders. Reprinted by permission.

Harcourt Brace & Company and Faber and Faber Limited: Excerpt from "East Coker" from *Four Quartets* by T. S. Eliot, copyright © 1943 by T. S. Eliot and renewed 1971 by Esme Valerie Eliot; excerpt from "The Hollow Men" from *Collected Poems 1909–1962* by T. S. Eliot, copyright © 1936 by Harcourt Brace & Company, copyright © 1963, 1964 by T. S. Eliot. Rights outside the United States administered by Faber and Faber Limited, London. Reprinted by permission of the publishers.

Oxford University Press: Excerpt from "Introduction" by W. B. Yeats from *The Oxford Book of Modern Verse* (Oxford University Press, Oxford, England 1936). Reprinted by permission.

Penguin Books Ltd.: Excerpts from *Lives of the Artists, Vol. I* by Giorgio Vasari, translated by George Bull (Penguin Classics, 1987), copyright © 1965 by George Bull. Reprinted by permission.

Phaidon Press Limited: Excerpts from *Stendhal and the Arts,* edited by David Wakefield, copyright © 1973 by Phaidon Press, London; and excerpts from *The Literary Works of Leonardo da Vinci,* 3rd edition, edited by J. P. Richter, copyright © 1970 by Phaidon Press, London. Reprinted by permission.

Princeton University Press: Excerpts from "Introduction to the Method of Leonardo da Vinci" from *The Collected Works of Paul Valéry, Vol. 8: Leonardo, Poe, Mallarmé,* translated by Malcolm Cowley and James Lawler, copyright © 1972 by Princeton University Press. Reprinted by permission.

University of California Press: Excerpts from *Goethe on Art* by Johann Goethe, edited and translated by John Gage, copyright © 1980 by John Gage. Reprinted by permission.

A NOTE ABOUT THE AUTHOR

A. Richard Turner is Professor of Fine Arts at New York University. He is the author of *The Vision of Landscape in Renaissance Italy* and co-author of *The Art of Florence*. He lives in Cape May, New Jersey.

A NOTE ABOUT THE TYPE

This book has been set in an electronic version of the well-known Monotype face Bembo. This letter was cut for the celebrated Venetian printer Aldus Manutius by Francesco Griffo, and first used in Pietro Cardinal Bembo's *De Aetna* of 1495.

Composed by Creative Graphics,
Allentown, Pennsylvania.
Printed by Arcata Graphics Martinsburg,
Martinsburg, West Virginia
Designed by Peter A. Andersen